Close Relationship Loss

Terri L. Orbuch
Editor

Close Relationship Loss
Theoretical Approaches

Springer-Verlag
New York Berlin Heidelberg London Paris
Tokyo Hong Kong Barcelona Budapest

Terri L. Orbuch
Department of Sociology
University of Michigan
Ann Arbor, MI
USA

With four figures.

Library of Congress Cataloging-in-Publication Data
Close relationship loss: theoretical approaches/Terri L. Orbuch,
   editor.
      p. cm.
   Includes bibliographical references and index.
   ISBN 0-387-97727-9.—ISBN 3-540-97727-9
   1. Interpersonal relations. 2. Loss (Psychology)
   [DNLM: 1. Anxiety. Separation. 2. Divorce. 3. Grief.
   4. Interpersonal Relations. 5. Models, Psychological.
   BF 575.G7 C645]
   HM132.C5346 1992
   158'.2—dc20
   DNLM/DLC
   for Library of Congress   91-5182

Printed on acid-free paper.

Production managed by Hal Henglein; manufacturing supervised by Jacqui Ashri.
Typeset by Best-set Typesetter Ltd., Hong Kong.
Printed and bound by Edwards Brothers, Inc., Ann Arbor, MI.
Printed in the United States of America.

9 8 7 6 5 4 3 2 1

ISBN 0-387-97727-9 Springer-Verlag New York Berlin Heidelberg
ISBN 3-540-97727-9 Springer-Verlag Berlin Heidelberg New York

This book is dedicated to the quest for understanding the experience of close relationship loss; to those loved ones and friends, past and present, who have given me meaning in my life; and more specifically, to my parents.

Preface

Social scientists from various disciplines have been increasingly concerned with the nature, structure, and function of close relationships. Although most of the early work on the topic of close relationships drew attention to the development of close relationships, since the mid-1970s researchers have begun to investigate the many different aspects connected to the loss of close relationships.

Despite the change to a more comprehensive conceptual framework, close relationship research is often criticized for being atheoretical; the research is criticized for being purely descriptive in nature and thus lacking a more theoretical framework. Contrary to this belief, I wish to argue that researchers in the area of close relationship loss employ several critical and prominent theoretical perspectives to describe, explain, and understand the endings of relationships—thus, the fruition of this book. The major aim of this edited book is to present and illuminate, within one volume, some of these major theoretical perspectives.

The volume as a whole has several unique qualities. First, within each chapter, the authors provide a general overview of the theoretical perspective or approach within which they examine close relationship loss. Each author then relates these tenets, concepts, and general perspective to the study of close relationship loss. Second, a pervading theme is the interdisciplinary nature of the collection of chapters. The volume assembles a variety of chapters written by scholars in sociology, social psychology, communication, clinical psychology, and family studies. In doing so, we are able to examine the wide range of theoretical perspectives driven by different disciplines.

Theory and research focusing on relationship loss can be categorized into three overarching viewpoints, and this volume is organized according to these three theoretical general orientations. The first set of theoretical perspectives focuses on the determinants of the loss; the cause or causes of the relationship loss are the main focus of the theory and research. Three chapters examine close relationship loss from this perspective. In Chapter 3, Sprecher examines close relationship loss from a social exchange perspective. After carefully explaining social exchange theories and models, she presents a complete review of research that uses social exchange variables to predict continuation or dissolution of close relationships, the process of breaking up, and coping with the loss. Then, Sprecher introduces an original model that integrates several social exchange variables. She uses this model as a framework for a discussion of future research in the area of social exchange and close relationship loss.

In Chapter 4, Sweet and Bumpass use a social demographic perspective to examine the disruption of marital and cohabitation relationships. They begin the chapter by examining conceptual and methodological issues that have been evident within the study of marital disruption and recent developments in the area that have improved our understanding of these patterns. Sweet and Bumpass then review extensively some of the major findings from social demographic studies, focusing on the levels, trends, and differentials in marital disruption in the United States and on recent findings and statistics from their own 1987 to 1988 National Survey of Families and Households. Finally, because of the increase in cohabitation, Sweet and Bumpass pay careful attention to these unions in their chapter. They discuss the patterns, trends, and stability of these unions; their association to marital unions and marital disruption; and the implications these unions have for the social demographic perspective.

In Chapter 5, Hazan and Shaver investigate close relationship loss from the perspective of attachment theory. When an individual experiences the loss of a relationship, he or she experiences the loss of an attachment figure. Attachment theory, although explicitly a life-span theory, spent much of its early concentration and formulation at the childhood stage. Hazan and Shaver recognize this focus and examine responses to broken attachments in both childhood and adulthood. The responses to broken attachments are remarkably similar in both age groups. Within the adulthood phase, Hazan and Shaver differentiate between the loss of an attachment figure that is due to death and loss that is due to estrangement; examine individual differences in attachment responses; and point out the consequences of insecure attachment bonds.

The second set of theoretical perspectives in the book examines the process of relationship loss. The stages and phases that an individual or relationship passes through become the main focus within these perspectives. Three chapters examine close relationship loss from this perspective. In Chapter 6, Metts discusses the language of disengagement from a face-management perspective. Metts develops and presents an original face-work model of disengagement by integrating the theory of face and face work proposed originally by Goffman (1967) with previous work and theory on disengagement language and strategies.

In Chapter 7, Cupach uses a dialectical approach to examine the disengagement of interpersonal relationships. He examines these oppositional forces or tensions in relationships, delineates their role in stages of relationship change and disengagement, and provides insight into their relevance during close relationship loss. The final chapter in this section is by Blieszner and Mancini (Chapter 8). They approach relationship loss from a developmental perspective and draw attention to research and theory stemming from three important frameworks: critical life events approach, family development theory, and theory of social provisions. They argue that future research on relationship loss requires the incorporation of knowledge at the individual, family group, and social level.

The third general set of theoretical approaches concerns the consequences of the relationship loss for the individuals and groups involved. Here, attention is specifically given to the effects of the loss and the adjustment and/or coping responses that follow. In Chapter 9, Grych and Fincham espouse an attributional perspective to understanding postdivorce adjustment. They note that little research has examined the functions and consequences of attributions in an individual's postdivorce adjustment and present a typology based on the degree to which postdivorce attributions provide a sense of control and positive self-image. Grych and Fincham also examine attributions of marital disruption for adults, parents, and children and discuss the association of these attributions to family functioning as a whole after divorce.

In Chapter 10, Weber examines relationship loss from a phenomenological perspective. She presents rich, detailed, and naturalistic accounts of relationship loss to illustrate and posit that accounts, as presented, are the essential phenomena of interest in understanding relationship loss. Weber posits that an account may be a strategy for coping with relationship loss but that the account also is an end in itself, with meaning for the individual. She states that relationship researchers must pay careful attention to the account as a whole, as presented, rather than look for what the account symbolizes. Weber discusses poignantly the accounts and account-making literature, the phenomenological perspective, and the futility of using this perspective.

In Chapter 11, I address close relationship loss from a symbolic interactionist perspective. I conceptualize relationship loss as an "identity transformation" and draw on the principles and concepts in social structural symbolic interactionism to explore how social structure may impact on the meaning that individuals assign to their experiences of relationship loss. I postulate that this sociological social psychological perspective offers a new set of variables to consider when examining the experience and consequences of relationship loss. In addition, I illustrate how social institutions and groups differentially validate and support certain relationship losses.

The book also has two introductory chapters. The first is by Duck, who presents a comprehensive discussion regarding the role of theory in the examination of relationship loss. Duck takes a metatheoretical approach to theory on relationships and relationship loss to illuminate underlying complimentary foci in different theoretical perspectives. Further, Duck advocates a full process approach to the study of close relationship loss. He argues that we must not compartmentalize the study of relationship loss but, instead, must examine the topic within the context and theoretical richness of other relational processes such as relationship development and maintenance, as well as within the context of other forms of relating and human processes in general.

Although the book's major focus is on the importance of theory in the examination of relationship loss, in Chapter 2 Hendrick reminds us that theory is only one part of a larger process or "gestalt" of research. Hendrick discusses the integration of theory, research, and therapy within the context of examining close relationships and close relationship loss. Further, she argues provocatively that a researcher's own personal view on humankind and the world within which humans behave can in fact influence (or bias) both what theoretical approach one focuses on in the examination of relationships and relationship loss and the methodological approach in which one studies these relational processes.

Finally, the book concludes with two provocative commentaries that elucidate major questions and issues in the investigation of close relationship loss in general and, more specifically, that arise given the perspectives presented in the book. Spanier (Chapter 12) takes as his aim research and theory on marital relationship loss. First, using a social demographic approach, Spanier sets the stage for asserting that divorce has been and will continue to be a major social challenge for society and researchers in the social sciences. Although he states that the abundance of research on divorce in the 1970s and 1980s may have answered small questions regarding marital disruption, he is skeptical about whether this research has answered the larger questions surrounding divorce. Given the theoretical perspectives presented in this volume, he discusses their usefulness for both future research and these larger questions. Ultimately, Spanier challenges us, as social scientists, to look beyond the smaller questions and in doing so proposes several future directions of inquiry; questions and directions that may lead us to answer the larger questions at hand.

Levinger (Chapter 13) takes a comprehensive approach and discusses close relationship loss in general. He focuses on five concepts within the volume (which he creatively labels as inkblots) that need clarification and structure: close relationship, loss, determinants of relationship loss, processes of loss, and consequences of a loss. The contributors to this volume were given no requirements regarding the use and definition of the words *loss* and *close relationship*, nor were they given standards on how they construed a determinant, a process, or a consequence of a loss. Levinger astutely identifies that, given this lack of structure, authors in this volume have construed different meanings for these five concepts.

Levinger illuminates the differences and similarities between concepts in chapters and offers suggestions for future clarity and elaboration in the area.

Although these two commentaries tell a somewhat different story regarding plot and characters, the story endings are similar. I believe that the emphasis in both of these commentary chapters is on the pursuit of clarity or of answers to questions that will take us across discipline and theoretical lines. It is hoped that, as readers of this book, we will learn from each other.

Terri L. Orbuch

Reference

Goffman, E. (1967). On face work. In E. Goffman (Ed.), *Interaction ritual* (pp. 5–45). Garden City, NY: Anchor Books.

Acknowledgments

This is a project that has been in my mind for several years—a project initiated when I was in graduate school at the University of Wisconsin-Madison. I wish to express appreciation to several people who facilitated the work presented here. Foremost, I want to thank John H. Harvey, who believed in my work throughout my postdoctoral fellowship and who provided encouragement and advice when thoughts about the book finally turned into action. I wish to thank all the contributors to this book, without whose enthusiasm, commitment, and timely hard work, this volume would not have been possible. I am also grateful to the many students, clients, and friends who graciously shared their loss experiences with me.

Contents

Contributors

Rosemary Blieszner
Department of Family & Child
  Development and Center for
  Gerontology
Virginia Polytechnic Institute &
  State University
Blacksburg, VA 24061-0416 USA

Larry L. Bumpass
Department of Sociology
University of Wisconsin-Madison
Madison, WI 53706 USA

William R. Cupach
Department of Communication
Illinois State University
Normal, IL 61761 USA

Steve Duck
Department of Communication
  Studies
151 Communication Studies
  Building
University of Iowa
Iowa City, IA 52242 USA

Frank D. Fincham
Department of Psychology
University of Illinois
603 E. Daniel
Champaign, IL 61820 USA

John H. Grych
Department of Psychiatry
University of Wisconsin
600 Highland Avenue
Madison, WI 53792 USA

Cindy Hazan
Department of Human
  Development and Family Studies
Cornell University
Ithaca, NY 14853 USA

Susan S. Hendrick
Department of Psychology
Box 42051
Texas Tech University
Lubbock, TX 79409 USA

George Levinger
Department of Psychology
University of Massachusetts-
  Amherst
Amherst, MA 01003 USA

Jay A. Mancini
Department of Family and Child
  Development
Virginia Polytechnic Institute &
  State University
Blacksburg, VA 24061-0416 USA

Sandra Metts
Department of Communication
Illinois State University
Normal, IL 61761 USA

Terri L. Orbuch
Department of Sociology
University of Michigan
Ann Arbor, MI 48103 USA

Phillip R. Shaver
Department of Psychology
SUNY Buffalo
Buffalo, NY 14260 USA

Graham B. Spanier
Chancellor's Office
University of Nebraska-Lincoln
Lincoln, NE 68588 USA

Susan Sprecher
Department of Sociology,
  Anthropology, and Social Work
Illinois State University
Normal, IL 61761 USA

James A. Sweet
Department of Sociology
University of Wisconsin-Madison
Madison, WI 53706 USA

Ann L. Weber
Department of Psychology
University of North Carolina at
  Asheville
Asheville, NC 28804 USA

Part I
Introduction

1
The Role of Theory in the Examination of Relationship Loss

STEVE DUCK

Despite the momentous human tragedies played out in the loss of relationships throughout recorded (and probably unrecorded) time, scholarly work on the topic was limited until the decade of the 1980s opened up a more general interest (Baxter, 1984; Baxter & Philpott, 1980; Lee, 1984; Metts, Cupach, & Bejlovec, 1989). Earlier work invariably focused only on divorce, and the first scholarly book devoted entirely to the general topic of dissolving personal relationships was not published until 1982 (Duck, 1982).

The widening of interest is now quite diverse. It attaches to dating breakup (Lee, 1984); friendship loss (Baxter, 1984, 1985); children's attitudes to parental loss through divorce (see Chapter 9 in this volume); the influence of the style of developing relationships on their dissolution (Graziano & Mather Musser, 1982); communication strategies in relationship dissoution (Metts et al., 1989; Miller & Parks, 1982); rituals in dissolving relationships (La Gaipa, 1982); management of bond dissolution (McCall, 1982); and a variety of consequences of relationship loss through death and disease (Rosenblatt, 1983).

Some Basic Theoretical Points

Such a diversity immediately confronts us with three theoretical issues. A *first* question for any theorist is the issue of what is meant by *loss*. There are four responses, two obvious and two less obvious. First, one could mean the *occasion or event* of a loss of relationship, formalized (on analogy with the date of marriage), by the date of divorce, for example. One might then explore the events or partner characteristics leading up to it or those that follow from it. Alternatively, loss could be taken to mean the *processes leading to the severance or termination* of the relationship. Here one might be concerned with communicative or relational dynamics during the period when the loss occurred. Third, and less obvious, loss could be defined in terms of *decline of a given level of intimacy* in a relationship; for example, the case of two engaged partners deciding to break off the engagement but still remaining friends or of two married partners going through a rough period and becoming dissatisfied with their relationship. Here one might concern oneself with judgments that are characteristic of declining affection or with the negotiation of role or status decrements and disaffection (cf. Metts et al., 1989). Fouth, loss could be defined as the *complete reversal of a relationship* whereby two former friends become enemies. Here one may look at the relationship of "friendship" to "enemyship" (Wiseman, 1989) or the events that precipitate the spoiling of relational identity (McCall, 1982).

The *second* theoretical issue concerns manifest uneasiness in the field as to *whether theories about relationship breakups are really about divorce alone* or can be extended to other sorts of breakup. It seems that one set of theorists ("bottom-up theorists") has decided to limit itself to one particular area and make its contributions there, without judging the question of whether conclusions could be extended to the broader issue (e.g., Baxter, 1984, 1985; Lee, 1984; Metts et al., 1989). Others, by contrast ("top-down theorists"), employ large-scale theories of human behavior, such as exchange theory, and extract from those theories a subset of principles on the basis of which to predict or describe relationship loss, which, although based largely on evidence from divorce studies, can nevertheless be extended to loss of close relationships in general (see Chapter 3 in this volume). Both ways of dealing with this matter are evident in this volume.

A *third* theoretical issue concerns the *focus of research attention*, which is a matter not entirely independent of the first two. Should one look at the individuals experiencing relationship loss and learn how the loss affects their individual psychological processes and vice versa? Or should one focus on the issues of negotiation of relational change and the social management of bond dissolution? Or should one focus on the influence and impact of network issues? In 1981, I argued that a major overlooked area for research was the *social management* of relationship dissolution (Duck, 1981). I also argued that the time was ripe for research to "redress the balance" between cognitive and social processes and I hoped that "a view of the problems in ten or fifteen years will be able to tell us how social and cognitive processes interweave" (Duck, 1981, p. 27). Regrettably, that prediction was sadly off base, because our present knowledge increase is still largely confined to the social cognitive processes associated with relationship loss and its aftermath (Weber, Harvey, & Stanley, 1987). The research on social processes lags sadly behind, presumably because it is much harder to study—and researchers are essentially comfort-loving people, like everyone else.

Given these issues, an underlying theme in this chapter is presentation of a general perspective on the issues of theory making in the field of relationships loss. Of course, the conclusion will be that more research needs to be done—but we all knew that.

The task is not an easy one, because "theory" can mean many things, ranging from "conceptual analysis" to "approaches to human ontology." It also has many roles in academic study, comes in many guises, and applies at many levels of explanation. Throughout the chapter, I will attempt to unpick or illuminate those levels and their interaction with one another. Further, the range of theoretical issues is in part a reflection of the fact that, by their very nature, different disciplines focus on different key aspects of the phenomenon. I will try to give this old point a new edge.

In fact, although there appear to be opposing views of the role of theory (bottom-up or top-down), in practice they differ little in this field, because an unspoken axiom of all theory is that the phenomena must first be conceptualized in some form, whether implicitly through research methods (and hence through choices of what will count as data in need of explanation) or explicitly through ways in which phenomena are represented for the theory to explain. Thus, while theory guides our work, in every big theory there are other unspoken "theorettes," or little unspoken assumptions, about the shape of the phenomena before they are formally explained within the theory itself. In this chapter I will offer a "theorette" that proposes a process orientation to relationship loss and urges workers to proceed to differentiate between sorts of relationship loss according to theoretical principles that can be drawn from large-scale theories such as exchange, symbolic interaction, or systems theory.

Some of what I shall argue is based on the notion that relationships are themselves complex cognitive, social, and communicative phenomena that come apart in complex cognitive, social, and communicative ways. This claim involves the explicit belief that processes of relationship loss are firmly embedded in the general social, cognitive, communicative, and psychological processes of normal relating—that is, the processes that obtain when things are going well (Duck, 1981; 1982). I firmly believe that part of the theorist's job is to explain relationship loss in the context of, and against the background of, our increasing knowledge of the processes of relationship development and maintenance rather than to explain loss as a separate and encapsulated process of its own.

A Model About Models: Theory in Relation to Data and Methods

Theory is essentially a map of terrain that is distinct from the terrain itself but still useful in regard to it. Such maps are not arbitrary inventions and are modified as knowledge grows. The scientist's eternal goal is to refine theory, using as few concepts as possible, yet still to provide a good guide to the terrain of reality. The relation of theory to reality is thus a key issue, but theory relates to reality in many different ways. In following up on the previous points, it is helpful to explore those levels and look at the various roles of theory in academic work—two related issues.

As Clore and Byrne (1974) noted in a parable that, as they expected, was largely ignored, there are several ways to carry out research in a field and several levels at which empirical data relate to theory. One way of doing research is to try to tear down the work of scholars who use a different paradigm and to invite others to do as one does oneself. Another is to join a predominant paradigm, or a less visible one, and attempt to improve it or embellish is merits. A third is to set up one's own paradigm. My own approach, by contrast, will be to try to show that most of us have similar goals or objectives and that different approaches can complement one another in helpful ways, once the strengths of each are recognized and their differences of focus are distinguished.

Clore and Byrne (1974) also identified six levels at which to relate "empirical work" to "theory." Empirical data can, at the lowest level, serve to demonstrate patterns in a given human activity that show that X has an effect on Y. For example, loss of trust consistently results in lower commitment to a relationship (Johnson, 1982). By replication and consolidation of the empirical relationship, researchers begin to show an empirical consistency that invites explanation. At level 2 low-level empirical laws are generated and formed from the data rather than from larger theoretical principles. Such laws may represent the empirical findings mathematically, for example, and the problem of relationship loss could be expressed in terms of the degree of trust lost. At level 3, these empirical laws are linked to broader theoretical propositions and placed in a theoretical framework not limited to those situations in which data have been previously gathered. The theoretical work at this level is driven by the data but begins to step outside of the known empirical world to the unknown world about which the theory can speculate. For instance, one might note that breach of trust is a common theme in accounts of relationship loss, and one might begin to hypothesize a *system* to reports of relationship breakup. One could interpret this system in terms of a minitheory of breakup, such as one saying that people seek to put themselves in a good light and their former partner in a relatively bad light in accounts of breakup and that accounts based on breach of trust are a socially safe way to begin (La Gaipa, 1982). From such a proposition, one could go on to look for presently unrecorded instances of such face work and face management that could be found deeper in the data.

At level 4, more general hypotheses, not derived from the data directly, are created to extend the scope of the theoretical propositions to putative processes that would be found if the work were extended to other areas not previously studied. For example, one may hypothesize that processes of account making in breakup are linked to other processes of people telling stories or making up narratives and would follow the same principles as other sorts of justifications and excuses (cf. Antaki, 1987). This can lead to level 5, theorizing, where a general model (e.g., exchange theory) is offered, or where models of the processes of breakup are hypothesized to be the same as in the whole area of relationship development, maintenance, and growth (cf. Duck, 1981, 1982) and involve those processes of attribution, decision, intimacy management, accounting, and "provision fulfillment" located by research in those areas also. Finally, level 6 relates previous theorizing to general models of human behavior or metatheoretical structures representing a theorist's underlying values and the sorts of explanations that the theorist believes are acceptable. For instance, a theorist may depict people as basically profit maximizers in *all* their behaviors (including, but not limited to, those social behaviors represented in the versions of exchange theory that, at level 5, explain only social behavior) or the view that people are essentially free agents in the moral world. At this level, choices between theories are essentially ideological and are essentially based on claims or feelings that are, in the strict logical sense, irrefutable.

Clore and Byrne's (1974) distinctions are important when we turn our attention to the sorts of "theory" that exist in the relationship field; however, the distinctions are incomplete. There is a further key point that ties "theory" to "method"—a point not made by Clore and Byrne but equally important. The point is simply this: The links between theory and method or between theory and choice of datum are often implicit but nonetheless important "theoretical" statements. I use quotation marks here because researchers are often unaware, or unwilling to accept, that their choice of datum or of measures (whether empirical methods or statistical methods) does reflect a *theoretical* stance on the issues (Duck, 1990) and does so at several levels.

The Language and Consequences of Practical Choices

At the higher level of abstraction, some rhetoricians and philosophers of science have paid interesting and extensive attention to the "language of theory" as a rhetoric for accrediting the work that scientists claim to do (McGee & Lyne, 1987). An adoption of a "rhetoric or science" essentially, implicitly, and ineluctably commits one to particular ways of looking at "data." For instance, such a rhetoric makes certain sorts of methodologies (e.g., qualitative methods) appear to be fringe methods that do not match up to the demands of pure science; the form required for reporting the research implicitly undercuts or is inappropriate for the methods used. For instance, the requirements for writing up reports (e.g., the style manual of the American Psychological Association) happen to make it almost impossible to describe qualitative work in a manner suited to its assumptions (Bazerman, 1987).

Not only does choice of such position (or training) predicate certain *styles* of work, but the choice of datum—the choice of where to cut the problem—to some extent also dictates a style of research. Thus, if I choose to study the decision to leave a lover rather than disengagement processes, then I am essentially and ineluctably committed to an individualistic level of explanation. I would embark on research that identifies the characteristics of individual judgment, the ways in which individual characteristics lead to impressions, or the factors that individuals name as essentially unattractive. By contrast, the study of the social management of disengaging relationships would inevitably be a dyadic enterprise, focused on the ways in which people *inter*act, rather than on the singular impressions that they create in other individuals' minds. Equally, if I choose to study what it is that gets relationships off on the wrong foot (e.g., does dissimilarity of physical attractiveness lead to greater dissatisfaction in relationships?), then I am essentially negating any proposals that relationship *dynamics* matter. What I am essentially propounding (as are the dating agencies in their positive version of this claim) is the notion that two persons' individual characteristics alone determine the success or failure of the relationship. I am thereby implicitly denying or diminishing the role of social management or communication in relationships.

The choice to gather subjective accounts, for another example, amounts to a theoretical view of human behavior that assumes a key place for such accounts in relationship work (rather than assuming that relationship success or failure is all done by disembodied personality characteristics clashing together or by "communication patterns"). It credits accounts with a role in coping but also implies that memories or accounting influence persons during the process of disengaging, because people in troubled relationships not only argue over the account that is to be agreed to or accepted as truth but are also concerned about the way in which they will account "publicly" for the deterioration of their relationships (Burnett, 1987; La Gaipa, 1982).

One also can, by choice of methods, adopt a particular scientific stance. Study of accounts is one method that credits subjects with introspective awareness of the relevant phenomena; whereas, for instance, the choice to rely on "objective methods" credits the scientist with privileged access to the nature of human experience. The latter suggests, albeit implicitly, that subjects may be untrustworthy, unreliable, or biased if their reports happen to conflict with the scientists' objectively gathered data.

Table 1.1 presents a summary of these matters by means of a list of the different levels at which theory can be relevant in this area, based on, but extending, Clore and Byrne (1974). Part of the problem that both this representation of levels and the preceding discussion of such points in relation to social science reify is the simple one: the failure to reintegrate.

TABLE 1.1. Levels at which "theory" relates to data, methods, and conceptualization of phenomena.

1. Characterization of the phenomenon (beliefs about the nature of loss and the areas where it is profitable for research to focus its attention)
2. Choice of geography for phenomena (beliefs about which factors influence which variables)
3. Choice of method for study (beliefs that this or that method cuts deep to the true cause of relationship loss or uncovers its processes)
4. Discovery of empirical relationships (attempts to relate variable X to variable Y)
5. Discovery of empirical laws (attempts to present conceptual or mathematical relationship between variable X and variable Y)
6. Empirical laws turned into hypotheses (attempts to explain, rather than merely describe, the relationship between X and Y)
7. Extension of hypotheses to broader issues (attempts to show how the $X-Y$ relationship leads to a predictable but previously unobserved relationship between X and Z or between X and $Y2$)
8. Creation of a general model (attempts to specify $X-Y$ relationships as a special case of a larger group of related principles and concepts)
9. Relation to overall models of human nature and ontology (relates the $X-Y$ relationship to underlying philosophies about the nature of human existence, experience, or ontology)

In conducting research, it is very often conveniently necessary to focus on individual, dyadic, or social levels of analysis and to break down a complex phenomenon into manageable components. When the findings are not then reintegrated into the fuller context that was recognized at the outset, then errors of generalization become a problem and the essential picture does not get much clearer. The extrication of phenomena from relevant and important contexts (as distinct from the stripping away of trivial, irrelevant, or tangential situational factors) is one of the biggest shortcomings in the present work on relationship loss, as it is in social science at large.

Conceptualizing Relationship Loss

The foregoing points are not simply about theory but also relate to research practice in general, because they make us ask about our "theorette" of what relationship loss "looks like." Most high-level theories were in fact designed for general purposes other than accounting for relationship loss specifically; they therefore have no specific declared exposition of the way in which relationship loss is to be conceptualized before the theory can be applied to it. As far as many applications of theory are concerned, the nature of loss is self-evident, and the theorist's job is simply to explain it.

The crucial linkage between conceptualization of the phenomenon and theoretical explanation of it should not be minimized, however. The need to conceptualize or declare the hypothetical "shape" of the phenomenon is basic, and the fact that the nature of relationship loss is "obvious" should alert us immediately to the fact that we have a lot of unspoken assumptions (or "theorettes") about it.

To take one example, in many theories, the search is for explanation of outcomes and the goal is to lay the explanation at the feet of events or specific variables or individual decisions, each, by the subtle employment of methods that create the effect, discretely severed from the context in which in normally occurs. Such an approach implicitly credits individual judgments, outcomes, and events with major causal force, implicitly denies the force of social structure of dyadic management, and credits the individual with free will to make essentially unconstrained choices. Thus the approach is not an a priori neutral one.

Alternatively, and equally nonneutrally, we could believe that a relationship is multifaceted and involves not only cognitive activity in one partner but also negotiations between partners and interaction with the couple's respective families, networks, or associates. We are then covertly committed to the view that relationships are importantly influenced by partners' interaction with their society and their embedment within its various roles or subcultures, that individuals experience the dialectical tensions and forces as they face dilemmas created by the placing of their own individual needs and thoughts within such broad contexts. Then, a theory representing human relationships as simply based in individual free will, unfettered decisions or single outcomes or events, seems inherently incomplete.

Even if the individual provides the mind that processes a range of other stimuli, one needs to ensure that other influences on that mind, such as social structure or communicative process, are not forgotten at the theorette or data conceptualization stage, just as they are remembered at the theory or explanation stage. An important step, then, is to begin theoretical work by thoroughly analyzing, explicating, and depicting the phenomena that the specific researcher regards as "the problematic" to be explained. I regard all such researchers, however, whatever their disciplinary affiliation, as ultimately members of the same team with the same goals, and therefore I would rather find ways of integrating all styles of research than give greater priority or credit to any one style of work.

In the disciplinary context in which discussion of relationship loss occurs, we must begin to notice the varied implicit models of the phenomena that abound. This is best done in two phases.

The first phase is strictly anatomical: It depicts components of the whole. It is important not to consign such different foci to a status as local subphenomena, however: what we should ask is how they flow together. We should be not only anatomists but biologists and ecologists, looking at how the parts function as a whole in a living environment. Instead of seeing relationships or relationship loss as merely complex and multilayered, it makes more sense to see the phenomena as multilayered *by* something, or as flowing, moving, processes in which the different aspects reach the surface at some times and subside at others for some purpose or in relation to some function. In this case, my "theorette" of the complexity of relationships and relationship loss will thus include the notion of temporal development and change.

The second phase is thus to go beyond the mere identification of anatomical elements of relationship loss and to place them in conceptual and dynamic relationship to one another, and I shall do this in terms of the view that relationship loss is a process (Duck, 1990). This phase constitutes the conceptualization of relationship loss, not in terms of the ways in which it is studied by different researchers, but in terms of the way in which it may be experienced in living form by the relational partners themselves—a different perspective on the whole but an important one.

Some of the Anatomy of the Complex Beast We Study

The range of topics encompassed by the term *relationship loss* is now very large, as I indicated at the opening of this chapter. As the chapters in this book also make plain, relationship loss evidently involves social cognition (Chapter 9); emotion (Chapter 5); interactive behavior (Chapter 7); communication (Chapter 6); symbolic interaction (Chapter 11); life-span developmental concerns (as affecting, e.g., self-concept over time, position in the life cycle when the loss occurs) (Chapter 8); and other issues dealt with by colleagues in disciplines other than our own, whatever that discipline may be.

These different foci are not simply the identification of interesting issues but also have "theorettes" built into them. For instance, a sociologist who notices the role of gossip in relationship loss (La Gaipa, 1982) also espouses a systems-based understanding of relationsip loss or an approach based on face management. By contrast, a researcher who focuses on accounts (e.g., Burnett, 1987) is interested in individual cognitive factors in creation of accounts and thus buys into a different implicit world view. Although resolution of the two approaches is possible (e.g., if we view account making as based essentially on face work), but such resolution involves a gentle refocusing of the underlying "theorettes" such that both now attend to the self in social context rather than the self alone as an individual psychological entity.

For other examples, different researchers attend to the source or cause of the loss (Rusbult, 1991), focus on one partner rather than the other or on both together (Lloyd & Cate, 1985; Rose & Serafica, 1986), or indeed focus on the general processes of loss rather than the specifics of loss of a particular (sort of) relationship (Baxter, 1985). Again, writers sometimes, but do not always, write that the consequences of the loss depend to an

TABLE 1.2. Elements of relationship loss as seen from outside and exemplified by individual, dyadic, communicational, or social vantage points.

Elements of relationship loss	Issues that could be attended to by researchers
1. Identification of "causes" of breakdown rather than examination of decrements in the affective experience of it	I: Unattractive partner characteristic comes to light (Planalp, Rutherford & Honeycutt, 1985) I: Uncertainty is increased by some behavior or outcome (Berger & Bradac, 1982) D: Faulty process causes intimacy to falter or fail to develop (Noller & Venardos, 1986) D: Couple problems with NVC (Noller, 1984) S: Exterior events (relocation) S: Time point in relationship dictates "now or never" (Duck & Miell, 1986) S: Arrival of an alternative partner
2. Decline in intimacy versus desire to leave	I: Negative self-disclosure reduces intimacy level I: Bad mood causes decline in intimacy D: Arguments or conflict cause minor distress D: Mild marital distress S: DTM factor (Wright, 1985) increases S: One partner in a friendship gets involved in a courtship and withdraws from the network a little (Milardo, 1982)
3. Role of circumstantial and life-cycle forces	I: Perceived need to invest more time and energy in work-related identity or roles I: Personal difficulty handing long-distance relationship (Miller, 1990) D: Reassignment of job role spoils or changes relationship between the two individuals D: Romantic relationship at work "discovered" by others and has to be renegotiated S: Time point in relationship dictates "now or never" S: Changes in social attitudes to permissible relationship forms
4. Preexisting disabilities or lack of competence that predisposes to relationship difficulties	I: Shyness (Spitzberg & Cupach, 1985) I: Loneliness (Perlman & Peplau, 1981) D: Lack of interactive compatibility (Metts et al., 1989) D: Microstructure of interaction inadequate (Cappella, 1988) S: Poorly institutionalised education about relationships (Duck, 1991) S: Sex and/or gender differences (Helgeson Shaver & Dyer, 1987)
5. Problems of process loss rather than affect decline	I: Types of attribution about conflict affect its outcome (Fincham & Bradbury, 1989) I: Imperfect perception of partner messages creates mistrust (Noller & Venardos, 1986) D: Poor conflict management leads to frustration with relationship (Markman, 1987) D: Negotiation of sexual involvement leads to stress (Christopher & Frandsen, 1990) S: Comparison with social ideals for relationship type is unfavorable (McCall, 1982) S: "Relationship not going anywhere" (Duck & Miell, 1986)

TABLE 1.2. Cont.

Elements of relationship loss	Issues that could be attended to by researchers
6. Role of social forces and barriers	I: Commitment to religious ideals about relationship involvement (Altman, 1989) I: Individual decides to choose between clandestine relationship and another one D: Dyadically constructed culture influences relationship choice (L. A. Baxter, 1991, in preparation) D: Homosexual couple cannot create a socially accepted relationship form satisfactorily S: External (e.g., family pressure) discourages the relationship (Parks & Adelman, 1983) S: Influence of networks
7. Nature of relationship can define it as unstable	I: Neurosis I: Inability to tolerate intimacy D: Prolonged courtship style (Huston et al., 1981) D: Battered spouses S: One-night stand relationship S: It is a relationship form that implies test (e.g., engagement)
8. Different relationships might decline in different ways	I: Individual variation in awareness and/or experience of styles of relationship I: Premarital anxieties (Zimmer, 1986) D: Conflict friendship and loving relationships has different consequences for continuance D: Needs to negotiate liking versus loving (Metts et al., 1989) S: Norms surrounding loss of marital or nonmarital relationships S: Legal sanctions affect some relationship loss and not others

D, dyadic; DTM, difficult to maintain; I, individual; NVC, non-verbal communication; S, social.

extent on the degree to which the loss is voluntary in some sense (e.g., not brought about by death of a partner) and on the degree to which the studied person is the creator of the relationship's ending or is the victim (Hill, Rubin, & Peplau, 1976). Some scholars focus on the ways in which different people cope with loss by constructing accounts (see Chapter 10); some draw our attention to the strategies of disengagement (Miller & Parks, 1982) or to factors precedent on relationship redefinition (Metts et al., 1989).

Because I have already (Duck, 1981, 1982, 1988) laid out the various general classes of elements of relationship loss that can be extracted from the literature, I will not repeat the arguments here. Readers who wish to see the original detail, which I believe still holds good, can consult those sources, and all readers can look at the following outline of those components. I see essentially eight separate features that all feed into one general process that researchers are, in their own ways, investigating under the same general heading (Table 1.2). These are particular classes of research issues viewed *from the point of view of scholars*, researchers, and analytical thinkers. I have given special attention to the placement of the ideas discussed in the chapters in this volume when constructing this table. I have tried to illustrate rather than be exhaustive, but my point is a simple one: I want to show not only that there is a wealth of specific and uncoordinated work but also that the uncoordination is illusory and can be reconciled by the simple expedient of looking at relationship loss not from the privileged vantage point of the objective researcher but instead from the phenomenal, experiential viewpoint of the individuals in the relationship and the jobs that they do there as humans beings coping with life.

All of these aspects of relationship loss are clearly worthy of research attention, but we should note that implicit in them all is a way of viewing human nature, usually one that implies individual free will if the writer is a psychologist ("individual level" in Table 1.2); that implies mind-ful planning and control over events if the writer is a communication researcher ("dyadic level" in Table 1.2); and that explores influences of broader social forces if one is a sociologist ("social level" in Table 1.2). All of them have been analyzed so far from the outside—from the perspective, in other words, of the researcher.

Let us try another approach, one that looks at the experience of the relationship loss from the inside and one that attempts to integrate research into a coherent whole that reflects the different elements in living relation to one another. We can see human social life as partly mysterious and as demanding coping from us—that is, we can see part of the human problem as being to cope with chaos or to construe order in events that are ceaselessly original. We need an idea of individual human social experience that is based clearly on the notion of *individual expectation* as well as on the *dyadic negotiation* that takes place between two persons. Such a view would be based only on nothing more contentious than the idea that life is continuously presenting us with both individual and dyadic dilemmas that require solution. Not that hard to imagine!

Let us also assume that in dealing with and preparing for the future, people rely on their understanding of the past (i.e., they extrapolate from what-they-see-to-be-patterns in the past, patterns that they themselves construe in order to comprehend experience). Let us say that the individual element in the process is to create templates, constructs, or whatever, that help persons to anticipate what is coming.

Let us then suppose that much of a person's individual cognitive activity in relationships as a whole and relationship loss in particular is devoted toward establishing or confirming those expectations or anticipations. A person might do this confirmation in a number of ways. For instance, he or she might construct accounts, justifications, or excuses that preserve social face for future interactions or relationships. As La Gaipa (1982) argues, much of the purpose of accounts for failed relationships is to manage the face of the account maker, for instance. Or a person might choose selective interaction with specific members of the network, such as those who agree with and support the person's views or are prepared to listen and sympathize. Some of the work of Albrecht and Adelman (1987) suggests precisely this function for the social interactions that persons seek out in times of stress of personal difficulty. Further, the person may develop hostile feelings toward the ex-partner and may spend a lot of time fuming, constructing a model of the other person as someone with nasty and negative habits and psychology, or seeking to convey to others by account telling that this was the character of the former partner. Hagestad and Smyer (1982) are among a long list of researchers who have specifically suggested this type of functioning in persons experiencing relationship loss that is "done unto them."

Those who see relationships as deeply embedded in dyadic interaction or negotiation or the dialectics between the person and society might find these individualistic elements hard to swallow. If, by contrast, we take a view of relationship loss that implies that the relative importance of different factors changes as the process of relationship loss proceeds, then we not only place and credit the work of different researchers, but we also prevent a need for violation of the implicit "theorettes" of either. For instance, if one sees the possibility that individuals individually seek to expect and anticipate the future, then they would also show the same tendency when they are in dyads and we might also expect them to act individually first and dyadically second in this respect. We might expect them to spend considerable time (in both relationship development and relationship deterioration) working out agreed impressions, stories, or expectations. Indeed, we find that they do this in a variety of ways. Miell (1987), for instance, has shown how pairs remember the past as a way of constructing a context for future interaction. Furthermore, it is possible to reinterpret studies of commitment as dealing essentially with the future; that, indeed, is what *commitment* implies, a given and specifiable expectation about the future (see Johnson, 1982). Commitment is essentially and inherently a future-oriented concept. Conflict, another dyadic concept, is very often *about* the future form of the relationship as well as it is influential on it (cf. Lloyd & Cate, 1985).

These are a few examples, and I believe that readers could readily work out others, such as reconceptualizations of work on plans (Berger, 1988); uncertainty reduction (Berger & Bradac, 1982); trajectories of relationship (Surra, Arizzi, & Asmussen, 1988); work on relational anxieties, concerns over face management and how others will respond to relational changes, strategies, schemata, or symbolic interaction—all in their own ways future-oriented concepts. Thus, in other words, resolution of some of the implicit conflicts between work in different disciplines seems remarkably easy if one builds in that one perpetual element that is so often not built into our "theorettes" of relationship loss: namely, *time* and all the paraphernalia that time and its companion, *change*, bring with them, including constant issues to be resolved and several familiar routine ways of dealing with those that are recurrent. Also intriguing are the changes to perspectives on a relationship, its state, or its historical development that are wrought in time during relationship loss as a process. To this I shall return, because I believe that a phasic approach to relationship loss helps to resolve other dilemmas and disagreements between researchers.

What the Partners Actually Experience

In the preceding analysis, I emphasize individuals' experience of life and hence I stress one overlooked but important concern: the daily events and routines that make up relationships. Relationship loss obviously occurs in the context and against the backcloth of *existing* relationship processes about which we know regrettably little at present for reasons reviewed elsewhere (Duck, 1980). Indeed, I am sure that future generations of researchers will find it incomprehensible, not to say negligent, that those of our generation did not find out more abut people's actual daily lives before we began to theorize vigorously about them. Nonetheless, in thinking about relationship loss, it is important *not* to see it as a merely discrete occurrence somehow tacked into daily experience without the context provided by those constant previous experiences in the relationship. It is important to see it not only in terms of relationship processes but in terms of wider human processes of experience of time and change, dealing with the future, and rooted in the commonplace.

As Marcel Proust, William James, and Ludwig Wittgenstein each in his own way observed, humans are in a flow of experience—the continually unfinished business of life—but find it much more convenient to break that flow into manageable segments and to interpret or construe those. Some of these segments, like days and months, seem obvious and are agreed to among us for convenience because they clearly reflect a regularity that is evident to us all. The demarcations that we agree to as societies, dyads, or groups of individuals, however, are essentially creative ways to interpret nature in a manner that helps us to deal with it and which we all accept, usually without challenge.

Others, like relational events, are not defined by such social agreement, and dyads have a great deal more freedom to define relationship reality for themselves. Nevertheless, it is often the case that the ways in which relationship occurrences are initially broken up or segmented by the two parties may be different and a cause of argument ("You started it when you . . ." "No you started it by . . . and I responded"). Thus, it is not self-evident, either as a general rule or in specific cases, when arguments start, when a relationship begins to break down, or even when it ends. Partners are as likely to disagree about such things as they are about anything else, as Gottman (1979) has so interestingly shown in his work on marital conflict. For example, a friend of mine told his family and everyone else except his wife that he was leaving and filing for divorce on a certain date. He spent several months planning it all, living his marriage as if all were well, and then left exactly as planned. Whatever one thinks of the morality of this, the question is "When did the relationship end?" Perhaps "When and for whom did it end?" is a better question.

Considerable empirical evidence supports this rather obvious, but neglected, point. People by no means always agree on what occurs in any realm of life but particularly in relationship—the vast research on attribution providing ample evidence of this. Any theory of relationship loss must deal with this point conceptually, but, related to the foregoing points, this probably pre-requires that we deal with the issue as it lurks beneath the field and conceptualizations of all relationship processes: the neglected issue of "perspectival differences on relationships" (Duck, 1990; Duck & Sants, 1983) and why they matter. Olson (1977) observed that there are insider–outsider perspectives on relationship events, and although this has, trivially, often been seen as a purely methodological problem that necessitates cross-checking of insider and outsider perspectives, it is in reality a deep and significant theoretical problem (Duck, 1990; Duck & Sants, 1983). It cuts deep to the role of "objective observers" or "subjective perceptions" of the phenomena that social scientists seek to explain. It is precisely because such differences exist, whether or not researchers credit them adequately, that couples need to negotiate with each other in the real world, or present themselves carefully to outsiders, or parade the relationship blatantly or perhaps conceal it from others.

How do our theories account for these obvious and oft-reported differences in perspective that are usually (wrongly and shortsightedly) relegated to the status of irritating difficulties that experimenters must ingeniously circumscribe to get at "the truth" about a relationship? The truth is that we are dealing not with a metaphysical issue but with an epistemological one. Two people in the same relationship very often have different views of what is going on in it, and this is neither worrying nor particularly or exclusively true in the case of relationship breakdown and loss. If the flow of experience differs for the two partners in a relationship, then they may be expected to segment it according to their own judgments of importance. People construe many things in their own ways. The corollary of this is that people attempt to persuade others to adopt their preferred view and do this in both grand and seemingly trivial ways (Duck & Pond, 1989). This is a *crucial* version of this increasingly common point in understanding relationship loss. As Billig (1987) recognized in his brilliant book on thinking and arguing, all thinking, arguing, and experiencing are continuous unfinished business. To this I merely add that dyadic experience of relationships is likewise the continuous unfinished business of rhetorical persuasion.

Relationships Between Different Parts of the Loss Experience

The reason for introducing these points is only partly to show that in dealing with the subjective experience of breakup or the objective analysis of reports, our choice of methods is not merely a methodological choice but also relates implicitly to the view that we take of the phenomena (Duck, 1990). Those who study relationship loss by asking subjects to report on their recollections or by crediting accounts are taking a metatheoretical perspective that differs implicitly from those who seek to study the effects of loss that are often not perceived directly by the subjects (e.g., the changes in their physiology or in styles or patterns of communication). Such a point is key as we try to see patterns in not only the ways in which relationships are lost and the ways in which people adapt to the loss but also the arguments of contending theorists who seek to explain relationship loss, whether by applying "large-scale" (level-6) theories or "lower level" (level-3) theories. It is also key if we are to make progress in this field, because this can best be done if we recognize and credit the different "theorettes" that different researchers adopt and if we spend more time trying to place them in the jigsaw rather than proving which of us is more right than the others.

The other reason for making the point about the method–theory linkage is that I argued the relatively uncontentious point that relationship loss is a multistructured, multilayered process. This involves, of necessity, the conceptualization of many different findings and phenomena in relation to each other, different methods in relation to each other, and different theoretical perspectives in relation to each other.

Conceptualizing Relationship Loss As a Process

Are Relationship Losses Processes or Events?

It is easy to see why people might think of divorce, or try to analyze relationship loss, as an event. We are often encouraged to give specific dates for the breakup of a marriage or friendship and to identify "the cause" for relationship loss. For example, social organizations such as courthouses and tax offices require us to assign dates for the official ending of a marriage, so that certain "official" consequences follow (e.g., the right to remarry without committing bigamy; the right to file tax returns as a single rather than a married person). Early work took up this natural assumption and attempted to find the demographic or personal characteristics of partners who had divorced. For instance, Murstein and Glaudin (1968) showed that persons with gross psychiatric symptoms have low marital adjustment; Athanasiou and Sarkin (1974) showed that the risk of divorce is increased for couples who had a high number of sexual partners before marriage. Researchers often hoped that divorce could be predicted in this way by such factors as socioeconomic status of the marriage partners, number of sex partners before marriage, and so on.

In a theoretical climate that encourages us to think of divorce as an event, the predictors of the event are worth knowing about. On a social or group level, such predictors are important, but their "true importance" depends on the level or vantage point taken by the reviewer (See Table 1.2). In some sense, these demographic factors themselves do not help us to differentiate why this pair divorced when that demographically equivalent pair did not. In other words, the mere discovery of the demographic factors that are associated with divorce does not help us to learn why, in a given case, the divorce occurred. Nor does it help us to do much more than statistical bookkeeping, because it recommends no specific helping procedures that may help prevent divorce in the couples who are in high-risk categories. Finally, although a number of such factors were identified, there remained the mystery of the dynamics of such influences (Duck, 1985). How does socioeconomic status affect the daily life of subjects in a way that increases the likelihood of divorce? What do the number of previous sexual partners tell us about the individuals' ways of conducting daily life that could inform us about the dynamics of everyday marital interchanges?

A different vantage point, on the other hand, would encourage us to look inside the dynamics of the relationships that end and to discover, within the demographic groups so identified by previous research, what characteristics of individual or partner psychology or communication patterns or behavior tend to be associated with the ending of relationships. We would look to the communications inside the relationships of people grossly classed by psychological variables, such as "neurotic," or "having liberal attitudes," or "low in commitment." Such an approach is not a full process approach, however, because it again tends to adopt the view of divorce as an event to be predicted but in ways that add to what has been learned about demographic influences on divorce.

If we add in such dynamics but seek to go beyond them to a full process approach, then we must add time and change. Also, we must not attempt to compartmentalize relationship loss and explain it of itself but map it onto a more general theory about relationship functioning that explains, for example, relationship development and relationship decline by reference to general human processes evident from research in a wide range of issues. Conceptualization of relationship loss as a process entails the embedment of a theory of loss within the context of broader theory of other relationship processes—or else we commit ourselves to seeing relationship loss as unconnected, whether psychologically, sociologically, developmentally, ontologically, or philosophically, to other aspects of relating (Duck, 1981).

Attempts to represent breakdown as a process (Baxter, 1984; Duck, 1982; Hagestad & Smyer, 1982) tried to explain relationship loss as a lengthy chaining of parts with extensive ramifications in people's lives, ranging from health issues to issues of management of face. Some (Baxter, 1984) focused on the factors leading up to the *decision* to break up and thus implicitly credited the purely cognitive influences. Others (Hagestad & Smyer, 1982) focused on the management of role change and thus emphasized social processes. Some (Baxter, 1984; Duck, 1982; Lee, 1984) attempted to depict changes of focus in an extended process of disengagement. Duck (1982) specifically built in his model the notion that there could be nonlinear decision loops in the whole process that added to partners' uncertainties about "what was really going on." La Gaipa (1982) drew attention to the role of network membership on a person's thinking during the breakup of a relationship. McCall (1982) encouraged us to explore issues of face management that would affect individual choices (and would effectively constrain or shape those choices).

Not only were these views focused on a longer time span than the previous work, but they looked at faulty or disadvantageous processes of operating in a full social context, such as failure to negotiate satisfactory roles for the partners or to agree on the arrangement of chores and leisure time (cf. Huston, Surra, Fitzgerald, & Cate, 1981, on the reverse process of relationship creation) or to manage the public image that one had with other members of the network, whether these were strongly or loosely tied to the central figures of the drama.

If we choose to represent relationship loss as a process, then there are some connotations that basically come down to the centrally important issue of the implications of seeing the roles of daily routines, time, and change as psychological impactors. One exciting new development in work on personal relationships is the increasingly fashionable tendency to talk of relationships as processes (Duck, 1986; Duck & Sants, 1983; Reis & Shaver, 1988). By such developments, researchers encourage one another to focus on the temporal change that characterizes relationships. Relationships are not static or at best have to be made to keep running on the spot. If one assumes that change, movement, expectation, anticipation, and temporality characterize relationships, then one will focus as much on what keeps relationships together as on what tears them apart. However, one will also depict processes as essentially open ended and indefinite at the time that they occur. As Shotter (1987) has argued, much social interaction takes its meaning from joint negotiation of a completion; that is, partners work toward a definition of the experience that *subsequently* can affect their view of the way the definition was reached.

I also believe (Duck, 1990) that it is critical to credit the fact that, at the time their relationship is disintegrating, the persons in it do not know for sure what the final outcome will be nor the shape that such outcome will have. Disintegrating relationships, like "stable" ones, life as a whole, culture, history, and much else, are always "unfinished business." A crucial point to realize about human social life is precisely this: that we are all engaged continuously in carrying out this unfinished business and we are all ignorant, necessarily, of how things will finally turn out. Thus, couples who are trying to sort out their relationship may later be able to see it all as merely "a rough patch" that they survived; or it may turn out to have been the beginning of the end. A critically important influence on the individual psychology and wider social processes in which it all occurs is exactly that people do not know the end result but have hopes, fears, anxieties, or expectations about it. Daily routine communication with others is an important way for individuals to assess the accuracy and validity of those future orientations, and communication can itself influence the process as well as reflect on inner states.

In conceptualizing relationship loss, therefore, we need not only draw maps of extended interrelated operations that make up a whole process, but we should credit, and explore the role of, expectations, time, change, and unfinished business in the psychological, communicative, sociological morass that the process embodies. This suggestion calls on us to map our theories of relationship loss on theories of relationship processes—indeed, of human processes—in general.

If we now revisit the preceding discussion and impose the constraints of routines, timing, expectation, change concern over others' views, and uncertainties about the future, then we end up with a process model that develops some of the foregoing points. I first proposed the model in Figure 1.1 (Duck, 1982) from some of the same and some different arguments. The model proposes that individuals move outward in the process of loss, starting with internalized complaints and ending with public action to ratify the life course of the relationship. The analogy is to the tide coming in: Each wave takes the process a little further forward, on the average, but the process is not a strictly simple linear one. The model is not a crude stage model and was explicitly stated as a process whereby components continually flowed back into one another—an argument represented here as showing the unfinished business of relationship loss. It has five phases: During the breakdown phase, at least one partner senses a problem in the relationship, although the other may not. Noller's (1986) work indicates that some partners in a relationship not only are unaware of problems but actually may be quite confident that all is well when the other person is distracted all the same. During the second, intrapsychic, phase the distressed person begins both to evaluate the relationship as a whole, rather than to identify a particular problem, and also to complain to other people who will listen. A key point here is

BREAKDOWN: Dissatisfaction with relationship

↓

| Threshold: I can't stand this any more |

↓

INTRA-PSYCHIC PHASE
Personal focus on Partner's behaviour
Assess adequacy of Partner's role performance
Depict and evaluate negative aspects of being in the relationship
Consider costs of withdrawal
Assess positive aspects of alternative relationships
Face "express/repress dilemma"

↓

| Threshold: I'd be justified in withdrawing |

↓

DYADIC PHASE
Face "confrontation/avoidance dilemma"
Confront Partner
Negotiate in "Our Relationship Talks"
Attempt repair and reconciliation?
Assess joint costs of withdrawal or reduced intimacy

↓

| Threshold: I mean it |

↓

SOCIAL PHASE
Negotiate post-dissolution state with Partner
Initiate gossip/discussion in social network
Create publicly negotiable face-saving/blame-placing stories and accounts
Consider and face up to implied social network effects, if any
Call in intervention teams?

↓

| Threshold: It's now inevitable |

↓

GRAVE DRESSING PHASE
"Getting over" activity
Retrospection; reformulative postmortem attribution
Public distribution of own version of break-up story

A sketch of the main phases of dissolving personal relationships.

FIGURE 1.1. A process model of relationship loss. *Note.* From "A Topography of Relationship Disengagement and Dissolution" by S. W. Duck in *Personal Relationships 4: Dissolving Personal Relationships* (p. 16) edited by S. W. Duck, 1982, New York: Academic Press. Copyright 1982 by Academic Press. Reprinted by permission.

that such listeners are not expected to report the distress back to the partner; the essence of the matter is letting off steam. During the next phase, the dyadic phase, the person breaks the issue to the partner, and the couple begins negotiating, conflict management, and reformulation of the future form of the relationship. Such work may succeed in preserving the relationship, or it may not. If it does not, then the couple moves into the social phase, during which effort is devoted to winning alliances with other members of the network and gaining support for one's own view of the relationship and its difficulties. The network may be able to reconcile the partners at this point but is rather more likely to split into factions and hence sanction the breakup. One function that the network serves here is to begin the process of creating a socially negotiable "story" about the ending of the relationship, placing blame, and distributing credit. This is continued into the final phase, grave dressing, when the purpose is to put the relationship to rest and erect a headstone that tells of its beginning, life course, and ending. At this phase, some creative work is necessary to save the partners' face and to allow them to cope with the loss of the relationship.

In sum, the model conceptualizes breakdown of relationships as an extended process that impinges on and involves many different aspects of subjects' lives while still being based on the intrinsic human concerns and processes that characterize all other human perception of social experience.

Individual concerns over the future of the relationship are conceived to arise first at the affective, then at the cognitive, then at the behavioral level. The individual starts to become concerned about the future of the relationship in an intrapsychic, internal, cognitive way, and then conveys this to the partner. After some wrangling and negotiating within the dyad, reference is made to the wider social network. A continuous part of the whole is "accounting," and the final phase is solely concerned with it. However, there is no suggestion that an account is constructed here once and for all. As later work has shown (Burnett, 1987; see also Chapter 10 in this volume), account construction is also unfinished business. Indeed, one final thought is clearly in order. Just like research and theorizing, for which "more research needs to be done" relationships are often unfinished business, even when they seem to be over.

Conclusion

Theory has several roles in the work of scholars, and often many different unspoken assumptions ("theorettes") are built into methods and choices of datum but are not spelled out in the theory itself. By examining the different roles of theories and the different theorettes inherent in different styles of work, researchers can coordinate their different sorts of work by explicating a process approach to relationship loss that takes account of the everyday experience of individuals coping with the world and that attempts to explain relationship loss within that continuous context rather than as a separate and special sort of experience.

Acknowledgment. I am grateful to Russ Madden for his insightful and careful reading of an earlier version of this paper.

References

Albrecht, T. L., & Adelman, M. B. (and associates). (1987). *Communicating social support*. Newbury Park, CA: Sage.

Altman, I. (1989). Transactional contexts for relationships in a religious community. Paper presented to the second conference of the International Network on Personal Relationships, Iowa City, IA, May.

Antaki, C. (1987). Performed and unperformable: A guide to accounts of relationships. In R. Burnett, P. McGee, & D. Clarke (Eds.), *Accounting for relationships* (pp. 97–113). London: Methuen.

Athanasiou, R., & Sarkin, R. (1974). Premarital sexual behaviour and post-marital adjustment. *Archives of Sexual Behavior*, *3*, 207–225.

Baxter, L. A. (1984). Trajectories of relationship disengagement. *Journal of Social and Personal Relationships*, *1*, 29–48.

Baxter, L. A. (1985). Accomplishing relationship disengagement. In S. W. Duck & D. Perlman (Eds.), *Understanding personal relationships* (pp. 243–265). London: SAGE.

Baxter, L. A., & Philpott, J. (1980, November). *Relationship disengagement: A process view*. Paper presented at the meeting of the Speech Communication Assocation, New York.

Bazerman, C. (1987). Codifying the social scientific style: The APA *Publication Manual* as a behaviorist rhetoric. In J. S. Nelson, A Megill, & D. N. McCloskey (Eds.), *The rhetoric of the human sciences: Language and argument in scholarship and Public Affairs* (pp. 125–144). Madison: University of Wisconsin Press.

Berger, C. R. (1988). Uncertainty and information exchange in developing relationships. In S. W. Duck, D. F. Hay, S. E. Hobfoll, W. Ickes, & B. Montgomery (Eds.), *Handbook of personal relationships* (pp. 239–256). Chichester, England: Wiley.

Berger, C. R., & Bradac, J. (1982). *Language and social knowledge*. London: Arnold.

Billig, M. (1987). *Arguing and thinking: A rhetorical approach to social psychology*. Cambridge, England: Cambridge University Press.

Burnett, R. (1987). Reflection in personal relationships. In R. Burnett, P. McGee, & D. Clarke (Eds.), *Accounting for relationships* (pp. 74–93). London: Methuen.

Cappella, J. N. (1988). Personal relationships, social relationships and patterns of interaction. In S. W. Duck, D. F. Hay, S. E. Hobfoll, W. Ickes, & B. M. Montgmery (Eds.), *Handbook of Personal Relationships* (pp. 325–342) Chichester: Wiley.

Christopher, F. S., & Frandsen, M. (1990). Strategies of influence in sex and dating. *Journal of Social and Personal Relationships*, *7*, 89–106.

Clore, G. L., & Byrne, D. (1974). A reinforcement affect model of attraction. In T. L. Huston (Ed.), *Foundations of interpersonal attraction* (pp. 174–196). New York: Academic Press.

Duck, S. W. (1980). Personal relationships research in the 1980s: Towards an understanding of complex human sociality. *Western Journal of Speech Communication*, *44*, 114–119.

Duck, S. W. (1981). Toward a research map for the study of relationship breakdown. In S. W. Duck & R. Gilmour (Ed.), *Personal relationships 3: Personal relationships in disorder* (pp. 1–29). New York: Academic Press.

Duck, S. W. (1982). A topography of relationship disengagement and dissolution. In S. W. Duck (Ed.), *Personal relationships 4: Dissolving personal relationships* (pp. 1–30). London: Academic Press.

Duck, S. W. (1985). Social and personal relationships. In M. L. Knapp & G. R. Miller (Eds.), *Handbook of interpersonal communication* (pp. 655–686). Beverly Hills, CA: SAGE.

Duck, S. W. (1986). *Human relationships*. London: SAGE.

Duck, S. W. (1988). *Relating to others*. Monterey, CA: Dorsey/Brooks/Cole/ Wadsworth.

Duck, S. W. (1990). Relationships as unfinished business: Out of the frying pan and into the 1990s. *Journal of Social and Personal Relationships, 7*, 5–28.

Duck, S. W. (1991). *Friends, for life, revised second edition* Harvester-Wheatsheaf: Hemel Hempstead, UK [Published in USA as *Understanding Relationships*, New York: Guilford.].

Duck, S. W., & Miell, D. E. (1986). Charting the development of personal relationships. In R. Gilmour & S. W. Duck (Eds.), *Emerging field of personal relationships* (pp. 133–143). Hillsdale, NJ: LEA.

Duck, S. W., & Pond, K. (1989). Friends, Romans, countrymen: Lend me your retrospective data: Rhetoric and reality in personal relationships. In C. Hendrick (Ed.), *Review of social psychology and personality: Vol. 10. Close Relationships* (pp. 3–27). Newbury Park, CA: SAGE.

Duck, S. W., & Sants, H. K. A. (1983). On the origin of the specious: Are personal relationships really interpersonal states? *Journal of Social and Clinical Psychology, 1*, 27–41.

Fincham, F. D., & Bradbury, T. N. (1989). The impact of attributions in marriage: an individual difference analysis. *Journal of Social and Personal Relationships, 6*, 69–85.

Gottman J. M. (1979). *Marital interaction: Experimental investigations*. New York: Academic Press.

Graziano, W., & Matter Musser, L. (1982). The joining and the parting of the ways. In S. W. Duck (Ed.), *Personal relationships 4: Dissolving personal relationships* (pp. 75–106). London: Academic Press.

Hagestad, G. O., & Smyer, M. A. (1982). Dissolving long-term relationships: Patterns of divorcing in middle age. In S. W. Duck (Ed.), *Personal relationships 4: Dissolving personal relationships* (pp. 155–187). London: Academic Press.

Helgeson, V.S., Shaver, P. R., & Dyer, M. (1987). Prototypes of intimacy and distance in same-sex and opposite-sex relationships. *Journal of Social and Personal Relationships, 4*, 195–233.

Hill, C. T., Rubin, Z., & Peplau, L. A. (1976). Breakups before marriage: The end of 103 affairs. *Journal of Social Issues, 32*, 147–68.

Huston, T., Surra, C., Fitzgerald, N., & Cate, R. (1981). From courtship to marriage: Mate selection as an interpersonal process. In S. W. Duck & R. Gilmour (Eds.), *Personal relationships 2: Developing personal relationships* (pp. 53–88). New York: Academic Press.

Johnson, M. (1982). Social and cognitive features of dissolving commitment to relationships. In S. W. Duck (Ed.), *Personal relationships 4: Dissolving personal relationships* (pp. 51–74). New York: Academic Press.

La Gaipa, J. J. (1982). Rules and rituals in disengaging from relationships. In S. W. Duck (Ed.), *Personal relationships 4: Dissolving personal relationships* (pp. 189–209). Academic Press, London.

Lee, L. (1984). Sequences in separation: A framework for investigating the endings of personal (romantic) relationships. *Journal of Social and Personal Relationships*, *1*, 49–74.

Lloyd, S. A., & Cate, R. M. (1985). The developmental course of conflict in dissolution of premarital relationships. *Journal of Social and Personal Relationships*, *2*, 179–194.

Markman, H. J., Duncan, S. W., Storaasli, R. D., & Howes, P. W. (1987). The prediction and prevention of marital distress: A longitudinal investigation. In K. Hahlweg & M. J. Goldstein (Eds.), *Understanding major mental disorder: The contribution of family interaction research* (pp. 266–289) New York: Family Process Press.

McCall, G. (1982). Becoming unrelated: The management of bond dissolution. In S. W. Duck (Ed.), *Personal relationships 4: Dissolving personal relationships* (pp. 211–232). New York: Academic Press.

McGee, M. C., & Lyne, J. (1987). What are nice folks like you doing in a place like this? Some entailments of treating knowledge claims rhetorically. In J. S. Nelson, A. Megill, & D. N. McCloskey (Eds.), *The rhetoric of the human sciences: Language and argument in scholarship and public affairs* (pp. 381–406). Madison: University of Wisconsin Press.

Metts, S., Cupach, W., & Bejlovec, R. A. (1989). "I love you too much to ever start liking you": Redefining romantic relationships. *Journal of Social and Personal Relationships*, *6*, 259–274.

Miell, D. E. (1987). Remembering relationship development: Constructing a context for interaction. In R. Burnett, P. McGee, & D. Clarke (Eds.), *Accounting for relationships* (pp. 60–73). London: Methuen.

Milardo, R. M. (1982). Friendship networks in developing relationships: Converging and diverging social environments. *Social Psychology Quarterly*, *45*, 163–171.

Miller, G. L., & Parks, M. R. (1982). Communication in dissolving relationships. In S. W. Duck (Ed.), *Personal relationships 4: Dissolving personal relationships* (pp. 127–154). New York: Academic Press.

Miller, L. (1990). Metaphors in long distance relationships. Unpublished manuscript, University of Iowa.

Murstein, B. I., & Glaudin, V. (1968). The use of the MMPI in the determination of marital maladjustment. *Journal of Marriage and the Family*, *30*, 651–655.

Noller, P. (1984). *Nonverbal communcation and marital interaction*. New York: Pergamon.

Noller, P., & Venardos, C. (1986). Communication awareness in married couples. *Journal of Social and Personal Relationships*, *3*, 31–42.

Olson, D. H. (1977). Insiders' and outsiders' views of relationships: Research studies. In G. Levinger & H. Raush (Eds.), *Close relationships: Perspectives on the meaning of intimacy* (pp. 115–135). Amherst: University of Massachusetts Press.

Parks, M., & Adelman, M. (1983). Communication networks and the development of romantic relationships: An expansion of uncertainty reduction theory. *Human Communication Research, 10*, 55–79.

Perlman, D., & Peplau, L. A. (1981). Toward a social psychology of loneliness. In S. W. Duck & R. Gilmour (Eds.), *Personal Relationships 3: Personal Relationships in Disorder* (pp. 31–56). London & New York: Academic Press.

Planalp, S., Rutherford, D. K., & Honeycutt, J. M. (1988). Events that increase uncertainty in personal relationships II: Replication and extension. *Human Communication Research, 14*, 516–547.

Reis, H. T., & Shaver, P. R. (1988). Intimacy as an interpersonal process. In S. W. Duck, D. F. Hay, S. E. Hobfoll, W. Ickes, & B. M. Montgomery (Eds.), *Handbook of personal relationships: Theory, research and interventions* (pp. 367–389). New York: Wiley.

Rose, S., & Serafica, F. C. (1986). Keeping and ending casual, close, and best friendships. *Journal of Social and Personal Relationships, 3*, 275–288.

Rosenblatt, P. C. (1983). *Bitter, bitter tears: Nineteenth century diarists and twentieth century grief theories*. Minneapolis: University of Minnesota Press.

Rusbult, C. E. (1991). Exit, Voice, Loyalty, Neglect. Paper presented to the third conference of the International Network on Personal Relationships, Normal, IL, May.

Shotter, J. (1987). Accounting for relationship growth. In R. Burnett, P. McGhee, & D. Clarke (Eds.), *Accounting for relationships* (pp. 157–181). Methuen: London.

Spitzberg, B. H., & Cupach, W. (1985). *Interpersonal communication competence*. Newbury Park, CA: SAGE.

Surra, C. A., Arizzi, P., & Asmussen, L. (1988). The association between reasons for commitment and the development and outcome of marital relationships. *Journal of Social and Personal Relationships, 5*, 47–63.

Weber, A., Harvey, J. H., & Stanley, M. A. (1987). The nature and motivations of accounts for failed relationships. In R. Burnett, P. McGhee, & D. D. Clarke (Eds.), *Accounting for relationships* (pp. 114–133). London: Methuen.

Wiseman, J. P. (1989, May). *Friends and enemies: Are they opposites?* Paper presented at the Iowa Conference on Personal Relationships, Iowa City.

Wright, P. H. (1985). The Acquaintance Description Form. In S. W. Duck & D. Perlman (Eds.), *Understanding personal relationships* (pp. 39–62). London: SAGE.

Zimmer, T. A. (1986). Premarital anxieties. *Journal of Social and Personal Relationships, 3*, 149–160.

2
Integration of Methodology, Theory, and Therapy

Susan S. Hendrick

The Methods of Methodology

Overview

The task of this chapter is twofold. First, the chapter attempts to provide a methodological anchor for the volume by articulating some of the myriad ways in which reseachers approach the study of close relationships, particularly relationship loss. Some of the methods discussed in the chapter are presented in the topical research discussions in other chapters in the volume (e.g., Chapters 4, 8, 9, and 10). However, other approaches may not appear elsewhere in the book. Thus, the chapter overlaps only modestly with other contributions. The second purpose of this chapter is to acknowledge the utility—even the necessity—of letting methodology, theory, and therapy function in a gestalt, with ongoing feedback loops between. Just as in Chapter 1, where Duck describes relationship loss as a "process" rather than as an "event," so also is the integration of method, theory, and therapy an ongoing process rather than an arbitrary melding conducted at one point in time.

Although I pay attention to particular methodological approaches in current use, and sometimes to particular research programs that most clearly demonstrate such approaches, my intention overall is to highlight and illuminate rather than to exhaustively list. Such a choice reveals a bias of mine and segues into an issue that can be considered as a basis for all the issues to follow in this chapter: How may the researcher's own personal and professional theoretical perspective or world view (complete with biases) be taken into account in the choice of a methodological approach?

Methodology Is in the Eye of the Beholder

How does one see the world and the place of humankind within it? Such a question must, in its answer, take into account family background (including race, ethnicity, religion, socioeconomic status, birth order, health history, etc.); previous professional training as well as current professional position and commitments; and personal relationships. Such an analysis, however, only partially explains one's current world view. How one views the individual's relationship with his or her environment is also important when trying to explain one's world view or theoretical perspective. Does one see humans as naturally seeking growth and development, sometimes stymied by internal forces and sometimes by external ones, but always moving toward some positive end? Does one view humans largely as reactors, governed by early experiences and feelings, driven often to repeat previous mistakes in a search to reenact and rectify the past? Does one see humans as essentially blank and malleable, learning to embrace some behaviors and avoid others, largely a product of external shaping?

What seems to me most critical at this juncture is not that the reader embrace one or another world view but rather that she or he be aware of what theoretical perspectives or views he or she holds. For instance, a world view that articulates human movement as largely positive might employ a methodology consisting of self-report measures and mechanisms, believing that most individuals will respond to such measures with honesty and some amount of self-reflection. On the other hand, if humans are largely driven by early (often painful) emotions and experiences, one is less likely to trust individuals to veridically identify (much less report) their current thoughts, feelings, and behaviors. One might then be more likely to employ a laboratory-based methodology, observing a subject interacting with either a stranger or a significant other. Or better yet, physiological measurement may be used to infer other processes. If one views humans largely as a product of social learning, a laboratory approach might be favored but with less interest in observational work and more interest in experimental designs that would enable the researcher to more clearly get at issues of causality. There might still be interest in observing relationship partners, but only if their interaction sequences could be quantitatively analyzed.

Another aspect of one's world view regarding human development involves notions about the best source of "truth" and the legitimate source of power. If human beings are proactive, rather than reactive, creatures, then they are legitimate holders of both power and "truth." Therefore, research methods that actively engage the subject, often in real-world settings (e.g., field research), are likely to be employed. If, however, humans are viewed as largely determined, reactive creatures, then they are not as legitimately powerful. The researcher must take responsibility for embodying power and "truth" and must make methodological decisions accordingly (e.g., experimental designs with random assignment).

In conjunction with personal backgrounds and views of humankind, one's own particular "style" of scholarship may reflect a special affinity

TABLE 2.1. Four types of research methods.

	Type of data	
Reporter's frame of reference	Subjective	Objective
Insider	Self-report methods	Behavioral self-report methods
Outsider	Observer subjective reports	Behavioral methods

Note. Adapted from "Insiders' and Outsiders' Views of Relationships: Research Studies" by D. H. Olson in *Close Relationships: Perspectives on the Meaning of Intimacy* (p. 118) edited by G. Levinger and H. L. Raush, 1977, Amherst, MA: University of Massachusetts Press. Copyright 1977 by University of Massachusetts Press.

for quantitative or for qualitative approaches. One may, for instance, like to use "words" in research. Interviews, open-ended questions on self-report measures, or accounts given by subjects in their own words in their own journals are all of great interest to a word lover. A more quantitative approach might involve Likert scales, measures of reaction time, or length of eye gaze at a partner during a conflict resolution task. One's passionate interest may be in describing things as they are, in giving shape and color to ongoing human experience, just as it is. A fierce wish to know "why" things are as they are, and a search for causality may drive an individual's work. For some, the phenomenal experience of doing research is most satisfying when in one particular setting (e.g., field setting), using one particular methodological approach (e.g., interview). Just as one may enjoy certain aspects of the research more than other aspects (e.g., designing a study, analyzing data, integrating ideas in a discussion section), so also one or another research setting may be preferred. It is important to note, however, that approaches (and settings) are not mutually exclusive and that a researcher can be *both* qualitative and quantitative.

Thus, while a researcher's choice of methodological approach(es) is in some ways fortuitous, influenced by graduate training, the prevailing local research rules and myths (see Jones, 1989), realistic professional pressures (e.g., self-report studies are easier to do than are observational ones and may be more useful to a young scholar seeking tenure), it is also very likely that fortuitousness is not the only governing variable. The researcher's methodological approach is also influenced by her or his beliefs about the *subject* (i.e., humans) as well as the *topic* (i.e., relationship loss). Thus it behooves each of us to reflect at least briefly on the "why" of both "how" we study and "what" we study.

One little-known but to me elegantly parsimonious model of research methods used in close relationship research was developed by Olson (1977). The model is presented in Table 2.1. The "insider" perspective uses only self-report methods. Self-report measures can be divided into questionnaires or scale measures, and behavioral measures, eliciting what Olson views as subjective and objective data, respectively. Traditional paper and pencil instruments may require that the subject focus on the self, the partner, the relationship, or all three, in some interrelated fashion. Behavioral self-report, which Olson views as bridging the gap between self-report and observational data, typically focuses on micro-level behaviors or events and is "objective" to the extent that the behavior could ostensibly be observed and tallied by an outside observer. The "outsider" perspective may include measures similar to the insider ones, but the agent is someone outside the research subject or research dyad. Subjective reports in this perspective may be made with various measures or with global ratings of observed behavior, emotions, and attitudes, or may be more objective and may include tallying of verbal or nonverbal behaviors during a bracketed time sequence or measurement of blood pressure after an intense interaction between relationship partners. Although Olson's model is not exhaustive in its categories, it offers a succinct approach to conceptualizing and categorizing methodological approaches used in relationship research.

Although it is important to understand one's own motivations for employing particular methodological approaches, it is also important to consider the range of methodological options available to the relationship researcher. Expanding on, and sometimes departing from, Olson's model, some of those options are discussed in the following section.

Approaches to Studying Relationships and Their Loss

Self-Report

Measures and Scaling

Perhaps the single most popular data-gathering approach in close relationship research is self-report (which can refer either to a single measure or to a more general methodological approach). Self-report may include a subject's reported thoughts, feelings, or behaviors or may include the subject's perceptions of another person's (usually the partner's) thoughts, feelings, and behaviors. Reasons for employing self-report are summarized by Harvey, Christensen, and McClintock (1983):

This method has several unique advantages. First, participant verbalizations about subjective experiences are the only currently available means for investigators to tap directly such covert activities as perceptions, feelings, thoughts, expectations, and memories. Second, participants can describe events that, though overt, are usually private to the relationship, such as sexual behavior or conflict. Finally, participant reports are relatively easy to obtain and involve much less inconvenience and expense than observer reports. (p. 452)

Self-report techniques include questionnaires, behavioral records, interviews, and accounts. Questionnaires are particularly popular because of their flexibility and simplicity. What other research device can collect information about everything from a subject's personality traits to sexual experiences to relationship satisfaction, all within about $1\frac{1}{2}$ hours? Because my focus is on the "process" of using such measures rather than on the "content" of such measures, the reader is referred to Harvey, Hendrick, and Tucker (1988) for a more detailed discussion of various measures.

A wide array of scales is used in relationship research, though most are not specifically aimed at the process of relationship dissolution and loss. Scales measuring such topics as love and sexuality (e.g., S. S. Hendrick & Hendrick, 1987), intimacy (e.g., Lund, 1985), self-disclosure (e.g., Miller, Berg, & Archer, 1983), relationship satisfaction (e.g., S. S. Hendrick, 1988; Spanier, 1976), and romantic beliefs (e.g., Sprecher & Metts, 1989) are all currently in use. Measures may be used alone or in a type of questionnaire "battery" or with complementary techniques such as interviews (underlining the notion that different approaches are not mutually exclusive). The availability of close relationship measures has occurred largely within the last few years, and thus issues of scale development have become increasingly important to researchers in the area.

Development of a really valid and reliable measure requires extensive item development and refinement, generation of many more items than can be retained in the final scale version (largely because of item loss through statistical approaches such as factor analysis), computation of internal and test–retest reliabilities, comparison of the measure with similar measures or various relevant behavioral criteria (criterion validity), and demonstration of a measure's construct validity through known groups analyses or various other examples of convergent and divergent approaches. Systematic scale construction is a time-consuming enterprise, and its difficulty probably should lead many researchers to seek diligently for existing measures that may fit the researcher's needs rather than begin the long process of developing one's "own" scale. Fortunately, many such measures are now available.

When using scales to measure one or more relationship qualities, a researcher may focus on a particular construct such as love, exploring the utility of several measures, all of which purport to assess some aspect of the construct (e.g., C. Hendrick & Hendrick, 1989). Or one may seek correlates of a particular construct. Still others prefer looking at multiple constructs or variables. For example, Simpson (1987) used both single-item and multiple-item measures to assess satisfaction with the partner, relationship closeness, relationship duration, sexual aspects of the relationship, alternative relationship partners, relationship exclusivity, and self-monitoring.

There are numerous examples of self-report approaches to the specific topic of relationship loss. In research specifically focused on relationship disengagement, Banks, Altendorf, Greene, and Cody (1987) assessed a wide variety of variables in an exploration of breakup perceptions, strategies, and outcomes. These variables included relationship adjustment, trust, intimacy, partner desirability, network overlap, relational problems contributing to the breakup, disengagement strategies, and consequences of the breakup (e.g., depression, guilt, anger, feeling free, and whether the partners remained friends). Tschann, Johnston, and Wallerstein (1989) used questionnaire measures along with clinical ratings to examine resources, stressors, and attachments as predictors of post-divorce adjustment. Still other research has asked subjects to select from a provided list those statements that describe the predicted direction of the subjects' current intimate relationship (Kingsbury & Minda, 1988). Dindia and Baxter (1987) administered questionnaires, provided descriptive vignettes, and asked subjects to list strategies used for both relationship maintenance and repair, whereas Baxter (1984) asked subjects to list important relationship stages, periods, and turning points on index cards and to describe in a paragraph the particular event or period. All the foregoing approaches may be considered to fit within a self-report paper and pencil paradigm.

Although behavioral self-report is less commonly used, the Rochester Interaction Record (RIR; e.g., Nezlek, Wheeler, & Reis, 1983), which is a record of social interactions lasting for a fixed period (10 min or longer), has been successfully employed. The RIR is used by subjects on a daily basis for 1 or 2 weeks and provides measures of intimacy, disclosure, satisfaction, pleasantness, initiation, influence, number of interaction partners, frequency of contact, time spent socializing, length of each particular contact, and whether the contact partners were men or women. Subjects seem to be able to keep such records quite easily, and they perceive that their records are accurate. Various studies have successfully employed the RIR (e.g., Baxter & Wilmot, 1985; Duck & Miell, 1986).

Interviews

One fairly classic approach to collecting data is through interviews. A series of studies by Huston and his colleagues (e.g., Huston, Surra, Fitzgerald, & Cate, 1981; Lloyd & Cate, 1985) varied standard interview techniques in the assessment of courtship and subsequent marriage- or relationship-termination experiences. The researchers used the Retrospective Interview Technique (Fitzgerald & Surra, 1981), which requires separate interviews with each partner in a relationship. Subjects were asked to judge the likelihood of marriage (at various points in time) and to identify events influencing this likelihood. They were also asked to identify relationship "stages" of casual dating, serious dating, and commitment. This technique has been used to study courtship, progression toward marriage, and relationship termination. For those whose relationship terminated, two additional relationship stages were added: uncertainty and certainty.

Additional verification of the value of interview research was offered by Amato and Ochiltree (1987) in their comparison of three sources of data: (a) interviewers' ratings of children's behavior during an interview, (b) missing data across interview items, and (c) agreement between parents and children on several relatively objective family characteristics (p. 669). The authors concluded that although adolescents provided more accurate data than did primary school children, "the quality of data for primary school children is high in absolute terms" (p. 669). Still another interview study (Allen & Picket, 1987), with women from the 1910 birth cohort, reveals the flexibility and phenomenological richness of this approach. Although the topic of the study (pathways through which women either remained single or married and became mothers) is not particularly relevant to relationship loss, the methodology of successive, detailed interviews allowed the authors to develop conceptual insights into women's variable ways of enacting nurturant behavior that could probably have been obtained in no other way. Such research is actually not too far from that involving subjects' "accounts" of their relationships.

Accounts

Although people may use accounts and diaries to simply record life events and personal reactions to such events as they occur, relationship researchers are particularly interested in accounts "as people's story-like explanation for past actions and events which include characterizations of self and significant others" (Harvey, Agostinelli, & Weber, 1989, p. 40). Viewed within the framework of social psychology's attribution theory, accounts allow people to assign causality—sometimes to self, sometimes to others—and thus maintain some sense of control and order in their world.

Although accounts can refer to a range of behavioral events, they often serve as an explanation and a catharsis in the wake of negative life events, such as relationship dissolution or loss (Harvey, Orbuch, & Weber, 1990). Both quantitative and qualitative approaches may be taken when studying accounts. The former might involve coding of certain types of attributions or of positive versus negative adjectives describing a relationship partner, as these are embedded in the subject's account of the events leading up to a decision to divorce. A more qualitative approach might seek out overarching themes in an individual's account of some relationship phenomenon.

One of the most evocative, though not the most empirically defensible, uses for accounts is as sheer description. Some of the most moving passages in literature may be found in personal accounts of relationship dilemmas (see Chapter 10 in this volume for a fuller treatment of accounts).

A more structured use of accounts and diaries was made by Kirchler (1988), who had 21 couples fill out, at several points during a given day, diaries containing structured questions. Partners filled out these diaries for a 2-week pilot period and a 4-week study period, consulting with each other to code the diary entries that each had made separately. Partners also had regular contact with the investigator or with research assistants during the study period. Although several of the findings were quite interesting (e.g., happy spouses reported being in conflict much less of the time than did unhappy spouses; husbands' positive feelings were more dependent on the wives' presence than the reverse), the key finding is that a structured diary approach offers the possibility of rich, detailed, and naturalistic self-report data. The drawback to this approach, however, is that it is very labor intensive. Another descriptively rich but labor-intensive effort is that of "structural analysis" (sequential linguistic analysis of the data of communication), employed by Conville (1988) to analyze relational transitions.

Personal Constructs

Finally, a mode of inquiry that offers some promise in relationship research (including relationship loss) has evolved out of Kelly's (1955) theory of personal constructs and employs the Role Construct Repertory Test. Combining aspects of interviews, standardized paper and pencil assessments, and diary approaches, the Repertory Test focuses on how people construe their world (including their relationships). This approach has been used to examine the relationship between cognitive complexity and marital satisfaction (Neimeyer, 1984) and between various construct dimensions and love styles (Hall, Hendrick, & Hendrick, 1991) and can be either more or less labor intensive depending on whether basic constructs are elicited or provided.

Survey Approaches

Some survey approaches could appropriately be considered under self-report approaches; however, the very breadth of survey research merits special considerations. Some surveys are made up entirely of self-report measures given to large groups of subjects, yet other sociological studies use official records and/or statistics or international data sets. Still others analyze economic and/or structural variables at a macrosociological level.

Although most of the research approaches discussed in this chapter are appropriate for small groups of subjects—typically no more than a few hundred—survey research conducted by some relationship researchers (e.g., sociologists) can also answer valuable questions about relationship-relevant variables. (For example, see Chapter 4 in this volume.)

A research program conducted within the survey framework has examined the relationship between marital dissolution or divorce and suicide in Canada (e.g., Trovato, 1986, 1987, Trovato & Lauris, 1989) and in Norway (e.g., Stack, 1989). Using demographic data from all Canadian provinces, Trovato (1986) assessed the impact of divorce on suicide, while attempting to take into consideration several intervening variables: (a) educational level, (b) religious preference, (c) the migration rate between provinces, and (d) the provincial marriage rate. The author concluded that "Even after the influence of relevant controls, divorce has a strong effect on the rate of suicide" (Trovato, 1986, p. 345).

In a study assessing the link between divorce and suicide in Norway, Stack (1989) employed time-series analyses with World Health Organization data to assess the impact of divorce on suicide. Even when controlling for the rate of unemployment (very low in Norway), an increase in divorce was indeed related to a significant increase in suicide. These methodological approaches employing exceedingly large samples are informative at a content level (i.e., relationship loss can be a truly devastating personal event) as well as providing methodological alternatives to self-report, observational, and laboratory studies.

Other research of a similar nature was conducted by Maneker and Rankin (1985), who selected a random sample (10%) of all 1977 divorce cases in California and examined several demographic variables. Their goal was to explore relationships among marital duration, spouses' education, and spouses' age at time of marriage. Although the authors found that neither age at marriage nor educational level was related to marital duration, the authors did not preclude the possibility that lower age and education could contribute to a higher rate of divorce *eventually*. "It is entirely possible that youthful marriages may experience higher divorce rates than other kinds of marriages but still endure relatively longer" (Maneker & Rankin, p. 681). Questions about relationships among variables of interest may thus be usefully answered with large data sets and survey approaches.

Observational Approaches

Returning briefly to Olson's (1977) paradigm of insider–outsider and subjective–objective methodological approaches, most of the perspectives considered in this chapter are insider focused. Whether self-report measures or interviews or accounts, the focus is typically on the individual's perceptions of his or her personal reality. Another valid perspective is taken, however, by those who employ observational paradigms, usually within a laboratory setting.

In their discussion of a conceptual approach to marital satisfaction research that blends both sociological and behavioral elements, Bradbury and Fincham (1989) detail the "Talk Table studies." Using this procedure, partners sit at either end of a table and take turns speaking, usually focusing on a relationship problem. The speaker pauses and rates the "intent" of the communication, and the partner rates the experienced "impact" of the communication. Ratings are subsequently coded, and various partner similarities and descrepancies computed. Some findings emerging from this approach have been viewed as "classic" in marital interaction research (e.g., Gottman, 1979).

A direct comparison of insider–outsider data was obtained by Floyd and Markman (1983), who compared partners' perceptions of each other's interaction behaviors with observers' perceptions of these same behaviors. Although considerable discrepancies were found between insider and outsider perceptions (for a fuller explanation, see Bradbury & Fincham, 1989), what is noteworthy is Floyd and Markman's implementation of the joint insider–outsider approach.

Still other research has employed videotaped observations of couples along with partners' later reactions to those videotapes to assess the impact of "visual reorientation" on partners' attributions of self and other (e.g., Fichten, 1984). Such an effort can provide useful research information (e.g., attributions of divorcing partner both before and after viewing self and partner trying to resolve a conflict) as well as serve a therapeutic function in clarifying and improving partner communication. Some outstanding research (both observational and more standard assessment) in the partner interaction area has been conducted by Fitzpatrick (e.g., 1988) and Noller and Gallois (e.g., 1988). A more complete description of contemporary methodological approaches to couples' interaction research can be found in Noller and Fitzpatrick (1988).

A rather recently developed but clearly articulated method for dyadic interaction that is largely outsider focused has been developed by Ickes and his colleagues (e.g., Ickes & Barnes, 1978; Ickes, Bissonnette, Garcia, & Stinson, 1990) with the Dyadic Interaction Paradigm. This paradigm employs sophisticated equipment (e.g., extensive videotape and playback equipment) and analytic tools (e.g., software written especially for this paradigm) to assess (typically) stranger dyads in brief episodes of naturalistic social interaction. Subjects interact in an unconstrained fashion while being videotaped. The tapes are later extensively analyzed, and most recently, the subjects themselves are given an opportunity to review the videotapes and then recall and record the actual thoughts and feelings they remember having *at specific points* during the interaction. Although this paradigm is too complex to be presented in greater detail, an excellent description is available in Ickes et al. (1990).

Innovative Approaches

Although it can be argued that many of the approaches characterized in this chapter are "innovative," there is no mistaking the timeliness of Gottman and Levenson's research on physiological predictors of relationship variables (which falls into the outsider–objective cell of Olson's, 1977, model). Levenson and Gottman (1985) reported findings that a pattern of broadly based physiological arousal in partners at one point in time predicted decline in marriage satisfaction (measured 3 years later). More recently, Gottman and Levenson (1988) have proposed some interesting explanations for gender differences in physiological responsiveness to relationship conflict, as well as the implications of these differences for partner interaction during a conflictual situation. It appears very likely that while psychophysiological research does not offer the only pathway for innovative couple research, it does offer one exciting alternative.

Although the overview of research relevant to close relationship loss has been admittedly brief, several referenced articles, chapters, and books, as well as other chapters in the *current* volume, provide excellent methodological ideas (e.g., Chapter 8 highlights one of our least exercised and most needed methodological options—longitudinal research). There is no shortage of options for what we can do.

Up to this point, the chapter has been concerned almost solely with the methodology of relationship research, focusing on general research strategies rather than on specific applications of these strategies to relationship loss. In the following section, however, relationship loss is the central concern.

The Therapy–Method Interface in the Study of Loss

Cognitive–Behavioral Approaches

Cognitive–behavioral therapy (e.g., Meichenbaum, 1985) is an approach that seems to draw much of value from both cognitive and behavioral paradigms. Simply put, it places the locus of emotional problems and dysfunction in the individual's *cognitions* (e.g., self-defeating thoughts, catastrophizing), while at the same time it allocates power for improving these dysfunctions to changing the individual's *behaviors* (e.g., self-monitoring, cognitive restructuring, skills training). Such an approach avoids moralizing and accepts, but does not highlight, emotional catharsis. While acknowledging that the individual's history is "responsible" for the current dysfunction, the present and future are of much greater concern to the cognitive–behavioral therapist than is the past. Such a view of therapy lends itself to particular ways of both conceptualizing and studying relationship loss.

For instance, even though the "roots" of marital dysfunction may reside far back in partners' individual histories, a cognitive–behavioral researcher–therapist might view the process of divorce as primarily a response to increasingly negative partner interaction (e.g., greater conflict, lower rewards, and higher costs). In dealing with a couple during this process, the cognitive–behavioral therapist might use structured interviews to assess the couple's marital history (e.g., reasons for marrying). Perhaps a methodology similar to the courtship work of Huston et al. (1981) could be employed, this time to study the significant events and turning points in a relationship's dissolution. Such data would be qualitatively rich yet quantifiable. Interviews (perhaps with the individual partners and then with the couple as a unit) not only would illuminate the dissolution process for the researcher but also might be therapeutically useful for the partners as they were forced to "restructure" some of their personal cognitions about the relationship. Also valuable in this context would be paper and pencil measures, perhaps targeting depression, conflict strategies, and sequential retrospective evaluations of marital satisfaction at various points during the marriage. This straightforward self-report technique can be enriched through asking each partner to answer an instrument *as they believe their partner would answer it*. Responses can then be compared and discrepancies noted. These data, also, can be discussed by the partners (facilitated by the researcher–therapist).

If therapy is the primary interest, the methodologies outlined previously, implemented on a case-by-case basis, would be quite effective. If data collection is the primary concern, however (assuming one could get divorcing couples to agree to participate in the research in the first place), then the structured interviews could perhaps be implemented as questionnaires, along with the other paper and pencil measures. (For discussions of the inherent difficulties in using couple data, see Browning & Dutton, 1986; Fincham & Bradbury, 1989; Kenny, 1988.)

Although it is possible, and perhaps desirable, to integrate one's theoretical and methodological approaches to research and one's theoretical and methodological approaches to therapy, it is very difficult to do research and therapy at the same time. One classic way of handling this problem is the case-study method. Such an approach was taken by Masheter and Harris (1986) in their study of a postdivorce couple. The procedure involved individual interviews; dialogue construction (jointly the partners reconstructed three scenes from their former marriage, complete with dialogue); interpretations of intentions in the dialogue; and finally, interpretations of effectiveness of communicating a particular intention. Using this procedure, the authors were able to trace this couple's transitions from marriage to divorce to friendship and to point out that there are more than just two alternatives for an intimate relationship (e.g., a "plateau of intimacy" or relationship termination). Rather, partners are "capable of defining and redefining their relationship on a variety of dimensions of meaning" (Masheter & Harris, 1986, p. 187). And researchers also appear capable of exploring the redefinition process. This particular case study approach has much in common with accounts, both of which would seem appropriate for therapy and research on bereavement.

Accounts as Therapy

As noted by Harvey et al. (1988), diaries and accounts are time-honored ways of documenting the pervasive sadness that follows the loss of a loved one. A researcher–therapist who believes that the real source of "truth" is the research subject might choose to "collaborate with" persons who had recently lost a spouse through death. The research process might involve either written retrospectives of the deceased partner and the relationship or could employ audiotaped, open-ended interviews that are later transcribed. Either data source could be coded and analyzed for particular themes and emotions (see Chapter 10). A similar approach could be taken if one wished to investigate the loss of a child, rather than a spouse. Such an approach appears to combine aspects of the case-study method with some of the larger sample, self-report study approaches.

Although the cognitive–behavioral therapies have considerable flexibility for both clinical work and research, the more affectively oriented therapies also lend themselves to research in close relationships.

Affective Therapies

Although virtually all therapies have an affective component, the references here are to therapies such as humanistic (e.g., client-centered) or Gestalt, which are also useful with groups and with reasonably well-functioning individuals. If one wished to study aspects of relationship breakup in college-aged young people, one might organize a series of "breakup workshops" of approximately 20 people. These could be either same-sex or mixed-sex groups. Therapy and research would be intertwined. First, after taking some "pretest" measures, participants might fill out various self-report measures (e.g., demographics, relationship history, depression) including a free listing of all the adjectives applicable to the breakup partner. The Repertory Test (Kelly, 1955) might even be used in the group format, with some adaptations (e.g., providing the constructs). This initial process would provide massive amounts of data but could also be very cathartic for the individuals involved. The next phase might involve group discussion of breakups (with measures of mood taken before and after the discussion). Then subjects might take turns (in dyads) enacting through role plays certain common themes in relationship breakup (e.g., one partner has found someone else; one partner does not want commitment). These role plays could be videotaped (and later analyzed), and the themes could be rated by the participants for their relevance to relationship breakup.

The affective therapists could turn more eclectic and bring in some cognitive–behavioral strategies for dealing with relationship loss (see earlier discussion). Participants could even rate the strategies according to (a) which strategies had been tried already (had worked/had not worked), (b) which strategies the subjects were likely to implement, and (c) which strategies subjects were unlikely to implement. Finally, participants could retake the "pretest" measures and also evaluate the workshop. Mechanisms could even be set up for short-term follow-up. Although such a workshop would probably require a full day, research and therapy benefits would likely be substantial. The integration of research and therapy has a richness that disparate approaches cannot offer.

Conclusion

Such a process of integrating research and therapy appears laborious because real integration of theory, therapy, and methodology is far from simple. To do justice to the topic, one would need a book rather than a brief chapter, and even a very substantial volume could not present all the possible combinations and permutations of the three.

For instance, someone whose theoretical stance is based on a learning paradigm would be likely to employ cognitive–behavioral therapy techniques and to favor a laboratory-based interaction approach to relationship partners in conflict, using both self-report measures and time-series analyses of interaction. Someone else, whose guiding theory or world view is phenomenological, might use existential therapy approaches and might obtain data from interviews and open-ended personal accounts of relationship disintegration and loss. Although such combinations are potentially endless, these two examples are constructed with an almost idealistic consistency. Seldom is there the luxury of such consistency, as noted earlier. Constraints of efficiency or local academic mores frequently intrude on a researcher's elegant blueprint, and decisions are often based on pragmatic rather than theoretical mandates.

Whether or not we directly inform our methodology by our theoretical perspective or world view, this perspective always is a part of us. We must look within ourselves if we wish to more completely understand the work that we do. To the extent that "who we are" guides "what we do," our theory always influences our therapy and our methodology, at least to some extent. Awareness—and intentionality—regarding this influence are what the current chapter is all about.

References

Allen, K. R., & Pickett, R. S. (1987). Forgotten streams in the family life course: Utilization of qualitative retrospective interviews in the analysis of lifelong single women's family careers. *Journal of Marriage and the Family*, *49*, 517–526.

Amato, P. R., & Ochiltree, G. (1987). Interviewing children about their families: A note on data quality. *Journal of Marriage and the Family*, *49*, 669–675.

Banks, S. P., Altendorf, D. M., Greene, J. O., & Cody, M. J. (1987). An examination of relationship disengagement: Perceptions, breakup strategies and outcomes. *The Western Journal of Speech Communication*, *51*, 19–41.

Baxter, L. A. (1984). Trajectories of relationship disengagement. *Journal of Social and Personal Relationships*, *1*, 29–48.

Baxter, L. A., & Wilmot, W. W. (1985). Taboo topics in close relationships. *Journal of Social and Personal Relationships*, *2*, 253–269.

Bradbury, T. N., & Fincham, F. D. (1989). Behavior and satisfaction in marriage: Prospective mediating processes. In C. Hendrick (Ed.), *Close relationships* (pp. 119–143). Newbury Park, CA: Sage.

Browning, J., & Dutton, D. (1986). Assessment of wife assault with the Conflict Tactics Scale: Using couple data to quantify the differential reporting effect. *Journal of Marriage and the Family*, *48*, 375–379.

Conville, R. L. (1988). Relational transitions: An inquiry into their structure and function. *Journal of Social and Personal Relationships*, *5*, 423–437.

Dindia, K., & Baxter, L. A. (1987). Strategies for maintaining and repairing marital relationships. *Journal of Social and Personal Relationships*, *4*, 143–158.

Duck, S. W., & Miell, D. E. (1986). Strategies in developing friendships. In V. J. Derlega & B. A. Winstead (Eds.), *Friendship and social interaction* (pp. 129–143). New York: Springer-Verlag.

Fichten, C. S. (1984). See it from my point of view: Videotape and attributions in happy and distressed couples. *Journal of Social and Clinical Psychology*, *2*, 125–142.

Fincham, F. D., & Bradbury, T. N. (1989). Perceived responsibility for marital events: Egocentric or partner-centric bias? *Journal of Marriage and the Family*, *51*, 27–35.

Fitzgerald, N. M., & Surra, C. A. (1981). *Studying the development of dyadic relationships: Explorations into a retrospective interview techniques.* Paper presented at the National Council on Family Relations pre-conference workshop on theory and methodology, Milwaukee, WI.

Fitzpatrick, M. A. (1988). A typological approach to marital interaction. In P. Noller & M. A. Fitzpatrick (Eds.), *Perspectives on marital interaction* (pp. 98–122). Philadelphia: Multilingual Matters.

Floyd, F., & Markman, H. (1983). Observational biases in spouse interaction: Toward a cognitive/behavioral model of marriage. *Journal of Consulting and Clinical Psychology*, *51*, 450–457.

Gottman, J. M. (1979). *Marital interaction: Experimental investigations.* New York: Academic Press.

Gottman, J. M., & Levenson, R. W. (1988). The social psychophysiology of marriage. In P. Noller & M. A. Fitzpatrick (Eds.), *Perspectives on marital interaction* (pp. 182–200). Philadelphia: Multilingual Matters.

Hall, A. G., Hendrick, S. S., & Hendrick, C. (1991). Personal construct systems and love styles. *International Journal of Personal Construct Psychology*, *4*, 137–155.

Harvey, J. H., Agostinelli, G., & Weber, A. L. (1989). Account-making and the formation of expectations about close relationships. In C. Hendrick (Ed.), *Close relationships* (pp. 39–62). Newbury Park, CA: Sage.

Harvey, J. H., Christensen, A., & McClintock, E. (1983). Research methods. In H. H. Kelley, E. Berscheid, A. Christensen, J. H. Harvey, T. L. Huston, G. Levinger, E. McClintock, L. A. Peplau, & D. R. Peterson (Eds.), *Close relationships* (pp. 449–485). San Francisco: W. H. Freeman.

Harvey, J. H., Hendrick, S. S., & Tucker, K. L. (1988). Self-report methods in studying personal relationships. In S. Duck (Ed.), *Handbook of personal relationships: Theory, research and interventions* (pp. 99–113). New York: Wiley.

Harvey, J. H., Orbuch, T. L., & Weber, A. L. (1990). A social psychological model of account-making: In response to severe stress. *Journal of Language and Social Psychology, 9*, 191–207.

Hendrick, C., & Hendrick, S. S. (1989). Research on love: Does it measure up? *Journal of Personality and Social Psychology, 56*, 784–794.

Hendrick, S. S. (1988). A generic measure of relationship satisfaction. *Journal of Marriage and the Family, 50*, 93–98.

Hendrick, S. S., & Hendrick, C. (1987). Love and sex attitudes: A close relationship. In W. H. Jones & D. Perlman (Eds.), *Advances in personal relationships* (Vol. 1, pp. 141–169). Greenwich, CT: JAI Press.

Huston, T. L., Surra, C. A., Fitzgerald, N. M., & Cate, R. M. (1981). In S. Duck & R. Gilmour (Eds.), *Personal relationships 2: Developing personal relationships* (pp. 53–88). New York: Academic Press.

Ickes, W., & Barnes, R. D. (1978). Boys and girls together—and alienated: On enacting stereotyped sex roles in mixed-sex dyads. *Journal of Personality and Social Psychology, 36*, 669–683.

Ickes, W., Bissonnette, V., Garcia, S., & Stinson, L. (1990). Implementing and using the dyadic interaction paradigm. In C. Hendrick & M. S. Clark (Eds.), *Review of personality and social psychology: Research methods in personality and social psychology* (pp. 16–44). Newbury Park, CA: Sage.

Jones, R. A. (1989, Fall). Academic freedom, or constrained academics? *Dialogue.* (Available from the Society for Personality and Social Psychology.)

Kelly, G. A. (1955). *The psychology of personal constructs.* New York: Norton.

Kenny, D. A. (1988). The analysis of data from two-person relationships. In S. Duck (Ed.), *Handbook of personal relationships: Theory, research and interventions* (pp. 57–77). New York: Wiley.

Kingsbury, N. M., & Minda, R. B. (1988). An analysis of three expected intimate relationship states: Commitment, maintenance and termination. *Journal of Social and Personal Relationships, 5*, 405–422.

Kirchler, E. (1988). Marital happiness and interaction in everyday surroundings : A time-sample diary approach for couples. *Journal of Social and Personal Relationships, 5*, 375–382.

Levenson, R. W., & Gottman, J. M. (1985). Physiological and affective predictors of change in relationship satisfaction. *Journal of Personality and Social Psychology, 49*, 85–94.

Lloyd, S. A., & Cate, R. M. (1985). The developmental course of conflict in dissolution of premarital relationships. *Journal of Social and Personal Relationships, 2*, 179–194.

Lund, M. (1985). The development of investment and commitment scales for predicting continuity of personal relationships. *Journal of Social and Personal Relationships, 2*, 3–23.

Maneker, J. S., & Rankin, R. P. (1985). Education, age at marriage, and marital duration: Is there a relationship? *Journal of Marriage and the Family*, *47*, 675–683.

Masheter, C., & Harris, L. M. (1986). From divorce to friendship: A study of dialectic relationship development. *Journal of Social and Personal Relationships*, *3*, 177–189.

Meichenbaum, D. (1985). Cognitive-behavioral therapies. In S. J. Lynn & J. P. Garske (Eds.), *Contemporary psychotherapies: Models and methods* (pp. 261–286). Columbus, OH: Charles E. Merrill.

Miller, L. C., Berg, J. H., & Archer, R. L. (1983). Openers: Individuals who elicit intimate self-disclosure. *Journal of Personality and Social Psychology*, *44*, 1234–1244.

Neimeyer, G. J. (1984). Cognitive complexity and marital satisfaction. *Journal of Social and Clinical Psychology*, *2*, 258–263.

Nezlek, J., Wheeler, L., & Reis, H. T. (1983). Studies of social participation. In H. T. Reis (Ed.), *Naturalistic approaches to studying social interaction* (pp. 57–73). San Francisco: Jossey-Bass.

Noller, P., & Fitzpatrick, M. A. (Eds.). (1988). *Perspectives on marital interaction*. Philadelphia: Multilingual Matters.

Noller, P., & Gallois, C. (1988). Understanding and misunderstanding in marriage: Sex and marital adjustment differences in structured and free interaction. In P. Noller & M. A. Fitzpatrick (Eds.), *Perspectives on marital interaction* (pp. 53–77). Philadelphia: Multilingual Matters.

Olson, D. H. (1977). Insiders' and outsiders' views of relationships: Research studies. In G. Levinger & H. L. Raush (Eds.), *Close relationships: Perspectives on the meaning of intimacy* (pp. 115–135). Amherst: University of Massachusetts Press.

Simpson, J. A. (1987). The dissolution of romantic relationships: Factors involved in relationship stability and emotional distress. *Journal of Personality and Social Psychology*, *53*, 683–692.

Spanier, G. B. (1976). Measuring dyadic adjustment: New scales for assessing the quality of marriage and similar dyads. *Journal of Marriage and the Family*, *38*, 15–28.

Sprecher, S., & Metts, S. (1989). Development of the Romantic Beliefs Scale and examination of the effects of gender and gender-role orientation. *Journal of Social and Personal Relationships*, *6*, 387–411.

Stack, S. (1989). The impact of divorce on suicide in Norway, 1951–1980. *Journal of Marriage and the Family*, *51*, 229–238.

Trovato, F. (1986). The relation between marital dissolution and suicide: The Canadian case. *Journal of Marriage and the Family*, *48*, 341–348.

Trovato, F. (1987). A longitudinal analysis of divorce and suicide in Canada. *Journal of Marriage and the Family*, *49*, 193–203.

Trovato, F., & Lauris, G. (1989). Marital status and mortality in Canada: 1951–1981. *Journal of Marriage and the Family*, *51*, 907–922.

Tschann, J. M., Johnston, J. R., & Wallerstein, J. S. (1989). Resources, stressors, and attachment as predictors of adult adjustment after divorce: A longitudinal study. *Journal of Marriage and the Family*, *51*, 1033–1046.

Part II
Determinants of Relationship Loss

3
Social Exchange Perspectives on the Dissolution of Close Relationships

SUSAN SPRECHER

One important element of any close relationship is the exchange of resources. Relationship partners exchange a variety of resources, including love, sex, money, services, gifts, information, and intrinsic characteristics (e.g., physical attractiveness). The exchange in a relationship can be described as rewarding, more desirable than alternatives, and fair, or as the opposite of these. The purpose of this chapter is to review the theory and research indicating the role of social exchange in the continuation or dissolution of close relationships (e.g., romantic relationships). In the first section I review social exchange theories and models that have been applied to the study of close relationships. In the second section I describe the empirical studies that have examined how social exchange variables affect the continuation or dissolution of close relationships. In the third section, I consider how social exchange variables can also affect the process of breaking up and coping after. In the final section, I present a framework for future research in this area.

Theories of Social Exchange

Several social exchange variables are hypothesized to affect, directly or indirectly, the continuation or dissolution of close relationships. These variables are included in general social exchange theories and in explicit models of relationship dissolution.

General Social Exchange Theories

All social exchange theories assume that individuals are motivated to maximize their rewards and minimize their costs and thus to have an overall profit or positive outcome from their relationships. It is assumed that individuals enter relationships they believe will provide rewards at little cost and will exit from relationships that become unrewarding and/or costly. A simple reinforcement perspective (e.g., Byrne & Clore,

1970; Lott & Lott, 1974) argues that individuals are selfish and concerned primarily with what they receive.

Other exchange theories state that the participants' satisfaction with and commitment to the relationship are affected not by an absolute level of outcomes but by outcomes compared to a particular standard. Thibaut and Kelley (1959), for example, argue that participants compare their outcomes from a relationship with the outcomes they expect to receive (comparison level), which determines their satisfaction, and with the outcomes they think would be available to them in an alternative relationship (comparison level for alternatives), which affects whether they actually stay in or leave the relationship.

In yet other perspectives, input/outcome ratios are compared, usually between partners. Homans (1961, 1974) identified the "law of distributive justice" and argues that it operates to ensure fair exchange. Participants in relationships expect that they will receive rewards proportional to costs and profits proportional to investments. Building on Homan's concept of distributive justice, equity theory (Adams, 1965; Walster [Hatfield], Walster, & Berscheid, 1978) states that if individuals perceive their relationship to be inequitable in either the underbenefiting or overbenefiting direction (i.e., they perceive that the participants' relative gains or losses are unequal), they will become distressed and will try to restore equity. They can restore actual equity by altering their own or their partner's relative gains in appropriate ways or can restore psychological equity by changing their perceptions of the situation. If attempts at equity restoration fail, individuals may terminate their relationship. While equity theory assumes that individuals compare their input/outcome ratio to that of their partner, reference group or relative deprivation theories (e.g., Crosby, 1976; Crosby & Gonzalez-Intal, 1984) assume that individuals compare this ratio to that of individuals in their reference group (see Buunk & Van Yperen, in press).

Equity is not the only justice principle that may be relevant to close relationships. For example, another standard of fairness is equality (Deutsch, 1975; Sampson, 1975; Steil & Turetsky, 1987). According to this justice rule, relationships will be more satisfying and last longer if both partners receive the same level of outcomes regardless of their inputs.

Social Exchange Models of Relationship Continuation or Dissolution

Although the preceding theories and perspectives are general and can be used to explain behavior in both intimate and nonintimate settings, more specific social exchange models have been developed that focus on explaining the continuation or dissolution of close relationships. In this section, I summarize two models from the social psychological literature.

(See Lewis & Spanier, 1979, for a summary of other models, primarily from the sociological literature in marriage and family).

Levinger's Model of Relationship Cohesiveness

Levinger (1965, 1976, 1979) proposed that the stability of a close relationship is a function of its cohesiveness, which can be defined as "the total field of forces" that act on the pair to keep them in the relationship. According to his model, three categories of forces affect cohesiveness. The first factor is the *attractiveness of the relationship*, which is assumed to be determined by the profit (rewards minus costs) received from the relationship compared to one's general comparison level or expectation. The higher the partners' attraction to the relationship, the more cohesive the relationship, and the less likely the relationship is to dissolve. The second factor is the *attractiveness of the alternatives*, including no relationship at all. Partners in relationships compare the profits received from their current relationship with the profits perceived to be available from the best potential alternative. Desirable alternatives lower the cohesiveness and increase the chances of relationship dissolution. The final factor is *external barriers*, which are thought of as "psychological restraining forces" that keep a person in the relationship. They include economic, legal, religious, and social barriers, and barriers that are due to children. (These barriers apply particularly to marriages.)

Concepts of Levinger's (1976) model have been used in several studies (see Udry, 1981), although the whole model has generally not been tested.

Rusbult's Investment Model

Rusbult's (1980, 1983) investment model developed from social exchange theory, particularly from interdependence theory (Kelley & Thibaut, 1978; Thibaut & Kelley, 1959). According to the investment model, one stays in or leaves a relationship depending on the level of commitment to the relationship, which, in turn, is affected by several social exchange variables. More specifically, a person's commitment to a relationship is predicted to be greater the more satisfying the relationship (defined by rewards minus costs as compared to a generalized expectation), the fewer desirable alternatives, and the more investments in the relationship. Rusbult defines investments as resources put into a relationship that increase the costs of ending the relationship. Investments may be either extrinsic (e.g., a house) or intrinsic (e.g., self-disclosures). The propositions of investment model are expressed in the following ways:

1. Satisfaction = (rewards − costs) − comparison level
2. Commitment = satisfaction − comparison level for alternatives + investments
3. Stay/leave = commitment

Several studies have been conducted to test aspects of this model (e.g., Duffy & Rusbult, 1986; Rusbult, 1980, 1983; Rusbult, Johnson, & Morrow, 1986; Sprecher, 1988).

Review of the Literature: Effects of Social Exchange Variables on the Continuation or Dissolution of Close Relationships

Prospective, longitudinal research is required to directly test the effects of the social exchange variables from the preceding theories and models on the continuation or dissolution of close relationships. In the typical design, individuals involved in a relationship complete a survey at time 1 about their relationship and then are contacted weeks, months, or years later to see if their relationship is still intact. Social exchange variables measured at time 1 are used as predictors of relationship status measured at the end of the study.

The effects of rewards and several other social exchange variables on the continuation or dissolution of dating relationships were examined by Lloyd, Cate, and Henton (1984) in a longitudinal study of undergraduate students involved in a dating relationship. Reward level for self, reward level for partner, level of involvement, and chance of marriage were significant predictors of relationship stability, controlling for length of relationship, at both a 3-month follow-up and at a 7-month follow-up. However, satisfaction, own comparison level for alternatives, and partner's comparison level for alternatives were not significant predictors of relationship stability. Using the same data, Cate, Lloyd, and Henton (1985) examined the relative degree to which equity, equality, and reward level discriminated between relationships that ended and relationships that remained intact over the time period of the study. Only reward level discriminated between these two types of relationships.

Lund (1985) conducted a 4-month longitudinal study with graduating university students in part to examine whether a "positive pull model" (rewards and love) or a "barrier model" (investments and commitment) better predicts the continuation or dissolution of dating relationships. The results indicated that investments and commitment (the barrier model) better predicted continuation or dissolution of the relationship, although love and rewards were also significantly related to the continuation or dissolution of the relationship.

Berg and McQuinn (1986) had members of newly formed dating relationships complete a questionnaire at two points in time, separated by 4 months. If the couple had broken up by time 2, they were asked to complete the survey based on how they felt at the time of the breakup. Both general relationship variables (e.g., love) and social exchange variables (i.e., reward level, general comparison level, comparison level for alternatives, and inequity) were measured. Although general relationship variables were stronger predictors of the continuation or dissolution of the dating relationships than the social exchange variables, many of the social exchange variables were significant predictors. Of the social exchange variables measured at time 1, comparison level and comparison level for alternatives significantly predicted relationship stability. All of the social exchange variables measured at time 2, with the exception of equity or inequity, predicted relationship continuation or dissolution.

A few other longitudinal studies have included one or two social exchange variables with several other types of predictors of relationship continuation/dissolution. In their classic study of the breakups of premarital relationships, Hill, Rubin, and Peplau (1976) found that unequal involvement was one of the major predictors of the continuation or dissolution of the dating relationships. Simpson (1987) examined how 10 factors, including ease of finding an alternative partner, evaluation of best alternative partner, and evaluation of best imagined alternative partner, predicted premarital relationship stability over a 3-month period. Although 5 of the 10 variables were significantly associated with relationship stability when the effects of the other variables were controlled, the variables referring to comparison level for alternatives were not among these. Hendrick, Hendrick, and Adler (1988) found that dating couples who remained together over a 2-month period reported higher investments than couples who broke up, controlling for other factors. Felmlee, Sprecher, and Bassin (1990) examined the effects of several predictor variables on the rate at which dating relationships terminated (or the timing of the breakup) over a 3-month period. Comparison level for alternatives was one of the few variables that significantly affected how quickly the relationship broke up. Inequity and investments, the other social exchange variables examined in this study, however, were not significant predictors. Lujanksy and Mikula (1983) also found that inequity did not affect the stability of dating relationships.

In sum, the longitudinal studies that have been conducted provide evidence that social exchange variables do affect whether a relationship continues or dissolves over time. However, the relative effects of social exchange variables have been found to vary from study to study. For example, some studies (e.g., Udry, 1981) suggest that comparison level for alternatives may be the most important predictor, whereas other studies (e.g., Lloyd et al., 1984) suggest that alternatives are not that important. For a more representative sample of breakups, longitudinal studies need to be conducted with larger samples, following couples for a longer period.

Although the longitudinal studies previously described examined the effects of static scores of the social exchange variables (usually the vari-

ables measured at time 1) on whether or not the relationship was continuing at the end of the study, other studies have considered how
changes in social exchange variables over time differ as a function of
the final outcome of the relationship. In a 13-wave longitudinal study
designed to test the investment model, Rusbult (1983) examined how
changes over a 7-month period in the investment model variables differed
for those who remained in their dating relationship over time and those
who broke up. All of the investment model variables were found to
change in significantly different ways for the two groups. Those who
remained in the relationship experienced a greater increase in rewards,
satisfaction, investment size, and commitment, a smaller increase in costs,
and a greater decrease in evaluation of alternatives relative to those who
experienced a breakup over the time period.

All of the studies reviewed here were conducted with dating couples.
Although longitudinal studies have been conducted that focus on the role
of social exchange in marital couples (e.g., VanYperan & Buunk, 1990),
no couples or only a few couples break up during the course of the
studies, and thus analyses on the ability of social exchange variables to
predict the breakup of marriages are generally not possible. A longitudinal study would have to extend over several years to have enough
marital breakups to be analyzed. Although there are extant data bases
that contain extended longitudinal data from married individuals or
couples, including from some who separate or divorce, generally no direct
measures are included for social exchange variables (however, see South
& Spitze, 1986, for an example of a study that uses demographic variables
as proxy measures for social exchange variables).

In one exception, Udry (1981) analyzed longitudinal data collected
from approximately 400 married couples from 16 urban areas in the
United States. He examined how attractiveness of alternatives and marital satisfaction measured at time 1 predict marital dissolution within a
3-year period. He found that both the husband's alternatives and the
wife's alternatives explained a significant amount of variance in marital
dissolution. Satisfaction was also a significant predictor of the dissolution,
although it was not as important as alternatives. He concluded that his
results provide support for "Levinger's formulation that marital alternatives are indeed a significant and separate dimension determining marital
stability in contemporary American marriage" (Udry, 1981, p. 897).

Although longitudinal studies allow for the examination of whether
social exchange variables *predict* the likelihood of a relationship breaking up, the role of social exchange in relationship dissolution can be
examined indirectly by asking individuals who have already broken up
about their perceptions of the reasons for the breakup. In some studies,
the investigator provides a list of possible reasons for a relationship
breakup and asks the participants to indicate how important they perceive
each factor to be to the breakup. In other studies, the investigator

presents the participants with open-ended questions that ask them to write an account for the relationship breakup (see Chapter 10 in this volume, for a discussion of breakup accounts).

In general, this research on reasons for breakups suggest that one or both partners' comparison level for alternatives is believed to play a role in at least some of the breakups. For example, in their classic study of the breakups of premarital relationships, Hill et al. (1976) found that 40% of the women studied indicated that their own interest in someone else was a factor contributing to the breakup. Baxter (1986) had undergraduate students who initiated the breakup of a dating relationship within the past 12 months write an essay on "why we broke up" and found that issues of loyalty and fidelity were mentioned by 16.6% of the respondents. Research conducted with married individuals also indicates that 10% or more of participants believe that a potential alternative relationship or an actual extramarital affair was one of the factors that contributed to the breakup (e.g., Buunk, 1987; Cupach & Metts, 1986; Kitson & Sussman, 1982). Although direct references to "rewards" and "costs" have not been included in the investigator-provided lists and are generally not referred to in open-ended accounts written by research participants, many of the problems participants judge to be significant contributors to the breakup of their dating and marital relationships (e.g., physical separation, lack of attention) can be categorized as costs of the relationships or lack of rewards from the partner. Equity (or lack of fairness) has also not been included in the investigator-provided lists, but Baxter (1986) found that the absence of equity was mentioned in the breakup accounts of 12% of her subjects. In sum, these results suggest that individuals who experience a breakup perceive that aspects of the social exchange in the relationship contributed to some degree to their breakup.

Effects of Social Exchange Variables on the Process of Breaking Up and Coping After

Although most of the research applying social exchange variables to the study of the breakups has examined how social exchange affects the likelihood of a relationship ending (operationalized as an event), social exchange variables can also be studied as an aspect of the *process* of breaking up and as a determinant of what occurs *after* the breakup.

The Process

Duck (1982) wrote, "In my view the most important observation for research is that we must avoid the risk of seeing relationship dissolution as an event. On the contrary, it is a process, and an extended one with many facets" (p. 2). Duck presented a process model of the dissolution of relationships that contains four phases: intrapsychic phase (focusing on the negative aspects of the relationship and considering withdrawing); dyadic phase (confronting the partner and perhaps attempting reconciliation); social phase (providing accounts for the breakup to network members to get support); and grave-dressing phase (retrospection and getting over the breakup). The role of social exchange variables in each of these phases can be considered.

As suggested by theory and research previously reviewed, social exchange factors before the initiation of the breakdown process should affect whether an individual even enters into dissolution. Furthermore, social exchange should continue to play a role during each dissolution phase after it is entered. Duck (1982) suggested that the evaluation of equity and the exchange balance does not occur in earnest until the intrapsychic stage, when an individual reflects on the deficiencies of the relationship and the partner. A negative assessment of the exchange balance at this stage of the process can serve as a justification for withdrawing from the relationship and confronting the partner about termination plans.

Social exchange can also play a role in the dyadic phase, which is when the individual who desires the breakup confronts the partner. First, some research has suggested that the quality of the social exchange in the relationship while it was intact can affect how the partner is confronted at the time of the breakup. Individuals desiring to end their relationships have several disengagement strategies from which to select (see Chapter 6 in this volume). For example, Cody (1982) identified five disengagement strategies: behavioral de-escalation (e.g., avoiding contact); negative identity management (e.g., simply stating that they date other people); justification (e.g., explanation for one's desire to exit the relationship); de-escalation (e.g., cooling-off period); and positive tone (e.g., expressing regret and caring). With a sample of undergraduate students who had initiated a breakup, he found that those who had been underbenefited in their previous relationship were more likely to say that they had used justification strategies to end the relationship. On the other hand, individuals perceiving themselves as overbenefited in the relationship were more likely to report that they had used positive tone strategies.

Social exchange behavior, itself, can also be used as a strategy in the dyadic phase to de-escalate or end the relationship or get the partner to end the relationship. For example, an individual who wants the relationship to end but feels uncomfortable doing it directly may begin to treat the partner unfairly or lower the rewards contributed to the relationship as a strategy to get the partner to initiate the breakup. Baxter (1984) found evidence of this in a study in which she asked students to provide retrospective accounts of the stages and turning points of the breakup of a dating relationship. She found that some of the individuals who desired to end the relationship used strategies that she summarized as "cost escalation" as a way to indirectly communicate to the partner this desire.

Couples who reach the dyadic phase of the breakdown process do not always go on to break off the relationship. Sometimes individuals repair the relationship, and one way they might do this is by changing their social exchange behaviors. For example, an individual who has assessed that the relationship is inequitable may try to restore equity in the dyadic phase. He or she could communicate with the partner about the exchange in the relationship and offer to contribute more to the relationship (if overbenefited) or request that the partner contribute more (if underbenefited).

Social exchange may also play a role in the social and grave-dressing phases of Duck's (1982) model. In the social phase, an individual may gossip about the poor social exchange behavior of his or her partner as a strategy to seek support from the social network. In the grave-dressing phase, an individual may try to get over the relationship by remembering the relationship as unfair, unrewarding, and costly.

Coping After

After a relationship is formally terminated, the ex-partners, and particularly the ones who are left or who did not want the breakup, are likely to feel distress. The social exchange aspect of the relationship while it was intact may affect this degree of postbreakup distress. In one study that examined this issue, Simpson (1987) explored how 10 variables measured at time 1 while relationships were intact predicted the degree of emotional distress experienced by those whose relationship ended over the 3-month period of the study. Ease of finding a suitable partner, along with closeness and length of the relationship, which Simpson suggested are indirect measures of investments, were the only variables found to significantly predict emotional distress after the breakup. Those who were closer, who had dated longer, and who believed they would have a difficult time finding a new partner experienced more distress.

The quality of the exchange in a romantic relationship while it is intact might also affect whether or not the two partners remain friends after the breakup. This was one of the issues examined by Metts, Cupach, and Bejlovec (1989) in a study of how romantic relationships of undergraduate students are redefined after a breakup. Feelings at the time of the breakup, which included having taken advantage of partner and having been taken advantage of by partner, were one set of predictors of the current status of the terminated relationship. Of 12 predictors included in a model to explain the dependent variable, a measure of the degree to which former romantic partners are friends, feeling underbenefited (or taken advantage of) was one of only 3 significant predictors for the group of initators. Feeling underbenefited and using withdrawal

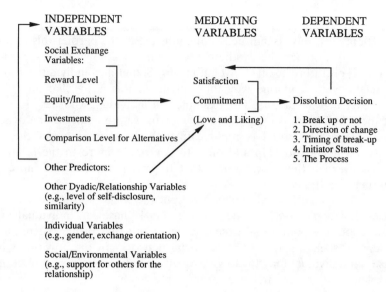

FIGURE 3.1. Framework for future research examining the role of social exchange in the dissolution of relationships.

strategies to disengage were negatively related to friendship behavior after the breakup, while being friends before the breakup was positively related. For the group that was "left," however, inequity measures were not significant predictors of current relationship status. When marriages and other long-term relationships dissolve, ex-partners must divide joint property and debts and make decisions about custody, visitation, and child support when there are children involved. (Dating couples may also have to divide up some joint possessions.) Issues of fairness can certainly arise at this stage (see Buehler, 1989). Ex-partners who believe that decisions were made in a fair way are likely to have more positive feelings about each other after the relationship dissolution than those who felt the decisions were made unfairly, although very little research has been done on this topic.

An Empirical Framework for Future Research

In this last section of the chapter, I present a framework, or model, for future research on the role of social exchange in the dissolution of close relationships. This is not an explicit social exchange model of relationship dissolution but is a summary of some of the issues that need further research. Figure 3.1 is a graphic display of the variables and their causal connections that will be discussed.

Social Exchange Predictors of Continuation or Dissolution

Presently, no social exchange model predicting relationship dissolution includes all of the social exchange variables discussed in this chapter. Although Rusbult's (1980, 1983) investment model is fairly comprehensive, it is missing equity or another justice norm. The four social exchange variables that I think are the most important to include in a social exchange model of relationship dissolution are reward or outcome level, equity–inequity, investments, and comparison level for alternatives. Previous research and/or theory suggest that these variables are related to the continuation or dissolution of the relationship, although the results of research, as reviewed here, have not been consistent.

Mediating Variables

Social exchange variables probably do not directly affect the decision to remain in or leave a relationship but do affect the dissolution decision indirectly through their effects on mediating or intervening variables, such as satisfaction and commitment in the relationship. Several cross-sectional studies and a few longitudinal studies have been conducted to examine the effects of social exchange variables on satisfaction (or distress–contentment) and commitment, although these variables have not been treated as intervening in the studies. Instead, the research has been conducted primarily to test certain propositions of social exchange theories that have commitment or satisfaction as the dependent variable. For example, proposition III of the Walster (Hatfield) et al. (1978) version of equity theory states: "When individuals find themselves participating in inequitable relationships, they will become distressed. The more inequitable the relationship, the more distress they will feel" (p. 6). Furthermore, investment theory predicts that satisfaction is affected by rewards minus costs as compared to a general expectation level and that commitment is affected by satisfaction, comparison level for alternatives, and investments. In general, this previous research has indicated that the quality of the social exchange is related to feelings of satisfaction and commitment in the relationship (Berg, 1984; Cate, Lloyd, Henton, & Larson, 1982; Cate, Lloyd, & Long, 1988; Lund, 1985; Martin, 1985; Michaels, Acock, & Edwards, 1986; Michaels, Edwards, & Acock, 1984; Rusbult, 1983; Rusbult et al., 1986; Sabatelli & Cecil-Pigo, 1985; Sprecher, 1986, 1988; VanYperen & Buunk, 1990). Certain social exchange variables, however, seem to have more predictive ability than others. For example, rewards have been found to be a stronger predictor of satisfaction than inequity or inequality.

Although the effect of social exchange variables on love and liking for the partner has typically not been examined (although see Berg, 1984;

Snell & Belk, 1985, for an examination of liking), love and liking for the partner may be other variables that mediate the effect of social exchange variables on the continuation or dissolution of the relationship. Thus, I have included these variables in parentheses in Figure 3.1 as two other possible mediating variables. Although satisfaction, commitment, love, and liking are all related constructs, they are not identical. Future research needs to examine which of these variables is most likely to mediate the effects of social exchange variables on dissolution or under what circumstances each acts as a mediating variable.

Furthermore, we need longitudinal research that tests the entire model, that is, examines the effects of social exchange variables on dissolution mediated by satisfaction, commitment, or another variable. Path analysis, which decomposes total effects into direct and indirect effects, is the appropriate statistical technique to use. Very few studies have attempted this type of analysis. In an unpublished paper, Sprecher (Fisher) (1980) measured equity and contentment–distress with 50 dating couples and found out which of these couples stayed together and which broke up over a 4-year period. Through path analysis, Sprecher found that inequities lead to breakups only when mediated by contentment–distress. Rusbult (1983) also included this type of analysis in her longitudinal study of dating couples. She tested whether the effect of the investment model predictor variables on the continuation–dissolution of the relationship was mediated by commitment. Although she performed several multiple-regression analyses rather than path analysis, she used the general logic of path analysis to interpret the results. She concluded from these analyses that "although rewards, costs, satisfaction, investments, and alternatives may exert some relatively small direct effect on stay/leave behaviors, their impact on stay/leave is largely indirect, mediated by changes over time in commitment" (Rusbult, 1983, p. 113). Clearly, more research is needed that examines the larger picture and considers both the direct and the indirect effects of social exchange variables on the continuation or dissolution of the close relationship. For example, we might consider under what conditions or for what people negative social exchange may automatically lead to a breakdown of the relationship without any mediating distress.

Other Predictors of the Continuation or Dissolution of the Relationship

The quality of the social exchange in the relationship is only one type of determinant of the continuation or dissolution of the close relationship. Several other factors are also likely to precipitate the breakup. For example, in the longitudinal studies previously cited, some of the other variables that were found to be significant predictors of the dissolution or continuation of the relationship (in addition to the social exchange variables and the mediating variables discussed previously) include self-disclosure, similarity–dissimilarity, maintenance behavior, closeness, reactions from friends and family, sexual intimacy, length of the relationship, exclusivity of the relationship, and orientation to a sexual relationship. The different types of variables that might affect the stability of the close relationship can be categorized into individual-level variables (e.g., personality variables); relationship–dyadic variables (e.g., similarity, self-disclosure); and social environmental variables (e.g., reactions from friends and family). In research that focuses on the effects of social exchange variables on relationship continuation or dissolution, these other variables can be examined in at least the three following ways.

Other Independent Predictors of Continuation or Dissolution

The main effects of other variables on continuation or dissolution of the relationship can be examined in conjunction with the main effects of the social exchange variables. Several variables of different types are likely to be included in an explanatory model when the purpose of the research is to explain a maximum amount of variance in the dependent variable, continuation or dissolution of the relationship. Furthermore, the effects of other variables can be compared with the effects of social exchange variables to see which types of variables explain the most variance in the breakup.

Predictors of Social Exchange Variables

Some of the other variables in the model, particularly individual variables, may affect the partners' actual exchange behavior and/or their perception of social exchange in the relationship. For example, several studies in the literature have found gender differences in equity and exchange. Women have been found to be more likely than men to report that they are underbenefited in the relationship (e.g., Davidson, 1984; VanYperen & Buunk, 1990) and to report that they give or invest more in the relationship (Berg & McQuinn, 1986; Duffy & Rusbult, 1986; Sprecher, 1988). Furthermore, structural and normative factors in society, such as position in the social structure, may limit an individual's access to alternatives and the opportunity to be a rewarding partner in an exchange relationship.

Variables That Interact With Social Exchange Predictors

Other variables in the model may interact with the social exchange variables to affect the dissolution of the relationship. For example, inequity may be more likely to lead to the dissolution of the relationship for individuals who are high rather than low in exchange orientation. Exchange orientation, as defined by Murstein, Cerreto, and MacDonald

(1977), refers to a concern that exchange in the relationship is equitable. As suggestive evidence of this, Bunnk and VanYperen (in press) found that a perception of inequity was related to dissatisfaction only for subjects high in exchange orientation.

Conceptualizing the Dependent Variable: Continuation or Dissolution

The independent and intervening variables in the model presented in Figure 3.1 are expected to affect the continuation or dissolution of the relationship, which is the final outcome variable in the model. This outcome variable can be conceptualized or operationalized in several ways: a dichotomy, a trichotomy, or a continuous variable.

Dichotomy

Most previous research on predictors of relationship continuation or dissolution has treated the dependent variable as dichotomous: The relationship either ends or continues over the time period examined. However, this tends to be a very highly skewed variable. The typical longitudinal study may last only a few months, and over this time, only a small proportion of the relationships will end.

Trichotomy: Direction of Change

The courtship continuum in the United States contains several premarital stages. For example, casually dating, seriously dating, living together, and engaged are some of the stages that couples may pass through on their way to marriage. In a few longitudinal studies conducted with premarital relationships (Leslie, Huston, & Johnson, 1986; Milardo, Johnson, & Huston, 1983), three groups have been compared: (a) those whose relationship declines in status or actually ends; (b) those whose relationship remains stable; and (c) those whose relationship advances in status. By conceptualizing the dependent variable in this way, we can examine whether the causal effects of social exchange variables in relationship development are the reverse of that in relationship dissolution.

Continuous Variable: The Timing of the Breakup

Although length of the relationship before the beginning of the study has been controlled for in some longitudinal studies (e.g., Lloyd et al., 1984; Simpson, 1987), duration of the relationship after the study begins has generally been ignored. Relationships, however, do not all break up at the same rate. Some relationships break up shortly after the initial data collection, while others may break up months or years later. A particular statistical technique called *hazard analysis* or *event history analysis* can be used if data are available on the dates the relationships ended. The dependent variable in this type of model is continuous and is referred to as the *hazard rate of relationship breakup*. This is generally defined as the probability of an event (a breakup) occurring during a specific period of time to an individual at risk for the event (e.g., Allison, 1984). See Felmlee et al. (1990) for an application of its use in premarital relationships.

The timing of the breakup has also been considered in more standard statistical techniques. For example, in a longitudinal study that examined the ability of the Relationship Closeness Inventory (RCI) to predict relationship breakup, Berscheid, Snyder, and Omoto (1989) compared differences on the RCI, via one-way analysis of variance, for three groups of respondents: (1) relationships that ended by a 3-month follow-up; (2) relationships that ended between 3 and 9 months; and (3) relationships that were still intact at the 9-month follow-up.

Another Trichotomy: The Leavers, the Lefts, and the Stayers

In most research examining the effects of social exchange variables on the dissolution of relationship, a distinction has not been made between those who initiate the breakup and those who are left. This would not be an important distinction to make if most breakups were mutual. Research suggests, however, that most breakups are initiated or desired more by one partner than by the other (e.g., Hill et al., 1976). Social exchange variables should be much stronger predictors of relationship dissolution for those who leave than for those who are left. Rusbult (1983) provides suggestive evidence that social exchange variables operate differently for these three groups. She found significant differences among "leavers," the "abandoned," and "stayers" in changes over time in the investment model variables. Compared to the leaver group, the abandoned group had a greater increase in rewards, satisfaction, investments, and commitment, a smaller increase in costs, and a decline in the quality of alternatives. The results suggest that the abandoned group was more similar to the stayers group than to the leavers group on many of the variables.

Another Continuous Variable: The Process of Breakup

Earlier, I summarized Duck's (1982) process model of relationship dissolution. Some individuals may go through early stages of the breakup process (the intrapsychic and dyadic phases) but then engage in repair and never experience a final separation and thus would never be included as part of a breakup group in a longitudinal study. However, we may want to examine the predictors of the likelihood of *beginning* the process of breakup as well as the likelihood of moving on to other phases of the breakup process. To investigate these issues, instruments need to be developed to measure when an individual enters the early phases of Duck's model. For example, Edwards, Johnson, and Booth (1987) developed a Marital Instability Index that measures cognitions and behaviors associated with seriously considering separation or divorce.

A Reconsideration of the Causal Processes Linking Social Exchange With Relationship Dissolution

Most of the research that has examined the relationship between social exchange variables and the dissolution of relationships has assumed unidirectional causality—that social exchange variables are precipitating factors in the breakup of relationships. However, if the breakup is conceptualized as a process that begins with ruminations about the negative aspects of the relationship, then we can also explore how the breakup process affects social exchange variables (either *actual* social exchange behaviors or *perceptions* of social exchange). Thus, the causal processes relating social exchange variables and the dissolution process are likely to work in both directions. To date, only a few researchers have tested causal directions between social exchange variables reverse from what is predicted from traditional social exchange theory. Johnson and Rusbult (1989) found evidence that levels of commitment to one's present relationship (i.e., desire to continue the relationship) affect how alternative relationships are valued. Individuals who are less committed evaluated a particular alternative as more attractive than did those who were more committed. Using cross-lagged panel correlation, VanYperen and Buunk (1990) found evidence that inequity is more likely to lead to dissatisfaction (as predicted by equity theory) than vice versa.

Conclusion

My overall purpose in the review and analysis presented in this chapter is *not* to argue that exchange and equity principles are the most important concepts to be used in understanding the dissolution of close relationships (one only needs to glance at the other chapters of this volume to see the array of concepts that are needed to understand the breakdown process). Social exchange, however, is one factor that contributes to the breakdown of at least some relationships and is also an aspect of the process of the breakdown of most relationships. More research is needed to fully understand the role of equity and exchange behaviors in the dissolution of relationships—as well as in their development and maintenance.

Acknowledgments. This paper benefited from the comments provided by Terri Orbuch, Sandra Metts, and Kathleen McKinney.

References

Adams, J. S. (1965). Inequity in social exchange. In L. Berkowitz (Ed.), *Advances in experimental social psychology* (Vol. 2, pp. 267–299). New York: Academic Press.

Allison, P. D. (1984). *Event history analysis: Regression for longitudinal event data.* Beverly Hills, CA: Sage.

Baxter, L. A. (1984). Trajectories of relationship disengagement. *Journal of Social and Personal Relationships, 1,* 29–48.

Baxter, L. A. (1986). Gender differences in the heterosexual relationship rules embedded in breakup accounts. Journal of Social and Personal Relationships, *3,* 289–306.

Berg, J. H. (1984). The development of friendship between roommates. *Journal of Personality and Social Psychology, 46,* 346–356.

Berg, J. H., & McQuinn, R. D. (1986). Attraction and exchange in continuing and noncontinuing dating relationships. *Journal of Personality and Social Psychology, 50,* 942–952.

Berscheid, E., Snyder, M., & Omoto, A. M. (1989). The relationship closeness inventory: Assessing the closeness of interpersonal relationships. *Journal of Personality and Social Psychology, 57,* 792–807.

Buehler, C. (1989). Influential factors and equity issues in divorce settlements. *Family Relations, 38,* 76–82.

Buunk, B. (1987). Conditions that promote breakups as a consequence of extradyadic involvements. *Journal of Social and Clinical Psychology, 5,* 271–284.

Buunk, B. P., & VanYperen, N. W. (in press). Referential comparisons, relational comparisons, and exchange orientation: Their relation to marital satisfaction. *Personality and Social Psychology Bulletin.*

Byrne, D., & Clore, G. L. (1970). A reinforcement model of evaluative responses. *Personality: An International Journal, 1,* 103–128.

Cate, R. M., Lloyd, S. A., & Henton, J. M. (1985). The effect of equity, equality, and reward level on the stability of students' premarital relationships. *The Journal of Social Psychology, 6,* 715–721.

Cate, R. M., Lloyd, S. A., Henton, J. M., & Larson, J. H. (1982). Fairness and reward level as predictors of relationship satisfaction. *Social Psychology Quarterly, 45,* 177–181.

Cate, R. M., Lloyd, S. A., & Long, E. (1988). The role of rewards and fairness in developing premarital relationships. *Journal of Marriage and the Family, 50,* 443–452.

Cody, M. J. (1982). A typology of disengagement strategies and an examination of the role intimacy, reactions to inequity and relational problems play in strategy selection. *Communication Monographs, 49,* 148–170.

Crosby, F. (1976). A model of egotistical relative deprivation. *Psychological Reports, 83,* 85–113.

Crosby, F., & Gonzalez-Intal, A. M. (1984). Relative deprivation and equity theories. In R. Folger (Ed.), *The sense of injustice* (pp. 141–166). New York: Plenum.

Cupach, W. R., & Metts, S. (1986). Accounts of relational dissolution: A comparison of marital and non-marital relationships. *Communication Monographs, 53,* 311–334.

Davidson, B. (1984). A test of equity theory for marital adjustment. *Social Psychology Quarterly*, *47*, 36–42.

Deutsch, M. (1975). Equity, equality and need: What determines which value will be used as the basis of distributive justice? *Journal of Social Issues*, *31*, 137–150.

Duck, S. (1982). A topography of relationship disengagement and dissolution. In S. W. Duck (Ed.), *Personal relationships 4: Dissolving personal relationships* (pp. 1–30). New York: Academic Press.

Duffy, S. M., & Rusbult, C. E. (1986). Satisfaction and commitment in homosexual and heterosexual relationships. *Journal of Homosexuality*, *12*, 1–23.

Edwards, J. N., Johnson, D. R., & Booth, A. (1987). Coming apart: A prognostic instrument of marital breakup. *Family Relations*, *36*, 168–170.

Felmlee, D., Sprecher, S., & Bassin, E. (1990). The dissolution of intimate relationships: A hazard model. *Social Psychology Quarterly*, *53*, 13–30.

Hendrick, S. S., Hendrick, C., & Adler, N. L. (1988). Romantic relationships: Love, satisfaction, and staying together. *Journal of Personality and Social Psychology*, *54*, 980–988.

Hill, C. T., Rubin, Z., & Peplau, L. A. (1976). Breakups before marriage: The end of 103 affairs. *Journal of Social Issues*, *32*, 147–168.

Homans, G. C. (1961). *Social behavior*. New York: Harcourt, Brace & World.

Homans, G. C. (1974). *Social behavior: Its elementary forms*. New York: Harcourt, Brace, Jovanovich.

Johnson, D. J., & Rusbult, C. E. (1989). Resisting temptation: Devaluation of alternative partners as a means of maintaining commitment in close relationships. *Journal of Personality and Social Psychology*, *57*, 967–980.

Kelley, H. H., & Thibaut, J. E. (1978). *Interpersonal relations: A theory of interdependence*. New York: Wiley.

Kitson, G. C., & Sussman, M. B. (1982). Marital complaints, demographic characteristics, and symptoms of mental distress in divorce. *Journal of Marriage and the Family*, *44*, 87–101.

Leslie, L. A., Huston, T. L., & Johnson, M. P. (1986). Parental reactions to dating relationships: Do they make a difference? *Journal of Marriage and the Family*, *48*, 57–66.

Levinger, G. (1965). Marital cohesiveness and dissolution: An integrative review. *Journal of Marriage and the Family*, *27*, 19–28.

Levinger, G. (1976). A social psychological perspective on marital dissolution. *Journal of Social Issues*, *32*, 21–47.

Levinger, G. (1979). A social psychological perspective on marital dissolution. In G. Levinger & O. C. Moles (Eds.), *Divorce and separation* (pp. 37–60). New York: Basic Books.

Lewis, R. A., & Spanier, G. B. (1979). Theorizing about the quality and stability of marriage. In W. R. Burr, R. Hill, F. I. Nye, & I. L. Reiss (Eds.), *Contemporary theories about the family* (Vol. 1, pp. 268–294). New York: The Free Press.

Lloyd, S. A., Cate, R. M., & Henton, J. M. (1984). Predicting premarital relationship stability: A methodological refinement. *Journal of Marriage and the Family*, *46*, 71–76.

Lott, A. J., & Lott, B. E. (1974). The role of reward in the formation of positive interpersonal attitudes. In T. Huston (Ed.), *Foundations of interpersonal attraction* (pp. 171–189). New York: Academic Press.

Lujansky, H., & Mikula, G. (1983). Can equity theory explain the quality and the stability of romantic relationships? *Journal of Social Psychology, 22,* 101–112.

Lund, M. (1985). The development of investment and commitment scales for predicting continuity of personal relationships. *Journal of Social and Personal Relationships, 2,* 3–23.

Martin, M. W. (1985). Satisfaction with intimate exchange: Gender-role differences and the impact of equity, and rewards. *Sex Roles, 13,* 597–605.

Metts, S., Cupach, W. R., & Bejlovec, R. A. (1989). I love you too much to ever start liking you: Redefining romantic relationships. *Journal of Social and Personal Relationships, 3,* 259–274.

Michaels, J. W., Acock, A.C., & Edwards, J. N. (1986). Social exchange and equity determinants of relationship commitment. *Journal of Social and Personal Relationships, 3,* 161–175.

Michaels, J. W., Edwards, J. N., & Acock, A. C. (1984). Satisfaction in intimate relationships as a function of inequality, inequity, and outcomes. *Social Psychology Quarterly, 47,* 347–357.

Milardo, R. M., Johnson, M. P., & Huston, T. L. (1983). Developing close relationships: Changing patterns of interaction between pair members and social networks. *Journal of Personality and Social Psychology, 44,* 964–976.

Murstein, B. I., Cerreto, M., & MacDonald, M. G. (1977). A theory and investigation of the effect of exchange-orientation on marriage and friendship. *Journal of Marriage and the Family, 39,* 543–548.

Rusbult, C. E. (1980). Commitment and satisfaction in romantic associations: A test of the investment model. *Journal of Experimental Social Psychology, 16,* 172–186.

Rusbult, C. E. (1983). A longitudinal test of the investment model: The development (and deterioration) of satisfaction and commitment in heterosexual involvements. *Journal of Personality and Social Psychology, 45,* 101–117.

Rusbult, C. E., Johnson, D. J., & Morrow, G. D. (1986). Predicting satisfaction and commitment in adult romantic involvements: An assessment of the generalizability of the investment model. *Social Psychology Quarterly, 49,* 81–89.

Sabatelli, R. M., & Cecil-Pigo, E. F. (1985). Relational interdependence and commitment in marriage. *Journal of Marriage and the Family, 47,* 931–937.

Sampson, E. (1975). On justice as equality. *Journal of Social Issues, 31,* 45–64.

Simpson, J. A. (1987). The dissolution of romantic relationships: Factors involved in relationship stability and emotional distress. *Journal of Personality and Social Psychology, 53,* 683–692.

Snell, W. E., Jr., & Belk, S. S. (1985). On assessing "equity" in intimate relationships. *Representative research in social psychology, 15,* 16–24.

South, S. J., & Spitze, G. (1986). Determinants of divorce over the marital life course. *American Sociological Review, 51,* 583–590.

Sprecher (Fisher), S. (1980). *Men, women, and intimate relationships: A study of dating couples.* Unpublished master's thesis, University of Wisconsin-Madison.

Sprecher, S. (1986). The relationship between inequity and emotions in close relationships. *Social Psychology Quarterly*, *49*, 309–321.

Sprecher, S. (1988). Investment model, equity, and social support determinants of relationship commitment. *Social Psychology Quarterly*, *51*, 318–328.

Steil, J. M., & Turetsky, B. A. (1987). Is equal better? In S. Oskamp (Ed.), *Family processes and problems: Social psychological aspects* (pp. 73–97). Newbury Park, CA: Sage.

Thibaut, J. W., & Kelley, H. H. (1959). *The social psychology of groups*. New York: Wiley.

Udry, J. R. (1981). Marital alternatives and marital disruption. *Journal of Marriage and the Family*, *43*, 889–897.

VanYperen, N. W., & Buunk, B. P. (1990). A longitudinal study of equity and satisfaction in intimate relationships. *European Journal of Social Psychology*, *20*, 287–309.

Walster (Hatfield), E., Walster, G. W., & Berscheid, E. (1978). *Equity: Theory and research*. Boston: Allyn & Bacon.

4
Disruption of Marital and Cohabitation Relationships: A Social Demographic Perspective

JAMES A. SWEET and LARRY L. BUMPASS

In social demography, there is a long tradition of research on marriage, marital disruption, and remarriage. (See Sweet, 1977, for a review of this tradition.) Research in this area has accelerated greatly since the early 1970s, resulting in an immense increase in our understanding of marriage behavior. A number of factors have contributed to this growth. The growth of social welfare programs and concern for the well-being of children, particularly those growing up in single-parent families, have made family processes increasingly relevant to social policy. Scientific interest in marital processes has grown with the diffusion of the life-course perspective in social science and with the realization that marital and family experience has a profound influence on experience in other life domains. At the same time, an expansion in the amount of available data, particularly retrospective and longitudinal data on family experience, has broadened the range of issues that can be addressed empirically. Developments in analytic methodology have improved our ability to use these new data to speak more directly to important scientific and policy questions.

In this chapter, we identify some of the characteristic features of a social demographic approach to the study of marital disruption. We then discuss some conceptual and measurement issues in the demographic study of marital disruption and review some of the major findings of research in this tradition, focusing primarily on our own recent work. Finally, because of the increase in cohabitation, and the complexity that it adds to the demographic analysis of the formation and termination of unions, we will discuss recent trends and differentials in the incidence and stability of cohabiting unions.

Features of a Social Demographic Perspective

There are several important characteristics of a social demographic approach to studying marital disruption.

1. The social demographer is concerned with what is going on in a clearly defined population, usually a spatially defined population. Social demographers work with samples that statistically represent populations.

2. The first and most fundamental task of a social demographer is to precisely describe what is. Precise and accurate description is central to the research process. This is not to say that social demographers are atheoretical but rather that the careful documentation of "the facts" is a necessary condition for explanation and for understanding the underlying social processes.

3. Social demographers are concerned with "rates" of marital disruption, relating the number of events of, for example, divorce to the population exposed to the "risk" of divorce. Identifying proper denominators is a critical aspect of a proper understanding of differential risk (a point that will be elaborated subsequently).

4. Decomposition of total population "risks" into rates for various structurally important subpopulations (e.g., education or ethnic groups) is an important tool for understanding social processes leading to marital disruption. Much of the theoretical development in social demography is inductive, drawing inferences about process from observed differential rates.

5. Similarly, the documentation of *change* in rates of marital disruption in the population at large, and among subpopulations, is a common theme in the attempt to understand both levels of marital instability and the relationship of these levels to other changes occurring in society. Two different, but complementary, approaches to change are often employed: the comparison of levels at different time periods and the comparison of the experience of successive cohorts.

6. In making comparisons across time, among cohorts, or among social groups, social demographers often decompose differences into compositional and rate components. For example, in the United States, the divorce rate declined in the early 1980s. Before deciding that there has been a resurgence of familism or some fundamental change in the nature of marriage, the social demographer would examine whether this decline resulted from a change in the composition of extant marriages by duration or other characteristics (e.g., education and age at marriage) associated with divorce or whether the characteristic-specific rates have declined. As it turns out, the recent decline was primarily compositional (see Castro Martin & Bumpass, 1989).

7. Social demographic work on marital disruption is increasingly taking a life-course perspective. The probability that a marriage will disrupt is affected by experience earlier in the life course, as well as by contemporary experience. One's early marital experience affects subsequent experience in many life domains. As we will note later, retrospective and longitudinal data are increasingly available, facilitating this sort of conceptualization and analysis.

Conceptual and Measurement Issues

Data on Marital Disruption

In the mid-1960s, there were only two sources of national data on marital disruption: the decennial census, which collects information on current marital status, and the vital registration system, which provides information on divorces granted. Data from the Current Population Survey (CPS) (U.S. Census Bureau, 1989) which in effect replicates the census in March of each year, were also available.[1]

With census data, it is possible to identify currently separated and divorced persons. However, the currently separated and divorced are only a small subset of the ever-separated or divorced, because most experiencing the dissolution of their first marriage marry again. In 1960, a question on the number of times each person had been married and the year of first marriage were added to the census, making it possible to compute the cumulative proportion of marriage cohorts whose first marriage had disrupted. However, because no information was included on when the marital disruption occurred, it was still not possible to calculate rates. Nonetheless, the large sample size makes the census and CPS extremely important sources for documenting cumulative disruption for marriage cohorts, for studying local area variation in marriage behavior, and for studying marriage behavior of relatively rare population groups, such as smaller racial and ethnic groups (see Sweet, 1978; Sweet & Bumpass, 1987). We have unfortunately lost this resource, because questions on date of first marriage and the number of times married were deleted from the 1990 census.

Marriage and divorce data derived from the vital registration system have also been used to monitor trends in marital dissolution, as well as documenting some differentials. This information is very important for the basic calibration of levels of divorce, though they are extremely limited for most analytical purposes.

The number of registered divorces (by duration of marriage at time of divorce) can be related to the number of marriages registered in earlier years to provide an estimate of disruption rates that is not subject to biases of coverage and nonresponse that occur in surveys. By comparing estimates of divorce for periods or birth cohorts from the vital statistics system to those calculated from survey data, we find that surveys consistently underestimate the level of divorce by approximately 20% (Castro Martin & Bumpass, 1989; Preston & McDonald, 1979; Sweet & Bumpass, 1987).

---

[1] Individual level data from the 1900, 1910 and 1940 through 1980 censuses, as well as all relevant CPSs, are available on computer tapes for research use.

Beyond this critical calibration function, however, vital statistics data are of rather limited analytical utility. This is so for several reasons:

1. A rate requires both a numerator and a denominator. Apart from aggregate rates of the sort described previously, it is very difficult to obtain appropriate denominators. Most of the published reports describe characteristics of divorcing persons, rather than differential risks of divorce. A limited number of statistics and occasional reports are produced based on assembling the proper denominators to calculate rates. Most important of these are the life tables of survival rates for marriage cohorts (Weed, 1980) (see also National Center for Health Statistics, 1973, 1978).

2. Although total figures are assembled for the nation as a whole, the divorce registration system currently covers only about 30 states. Further, only a limited number of characteristics are recorded on the divorce certificate, and not all reporting states include every characteristic (e.g., race was missing from over a quarter of the records from reporting states in 1980).

3. Most important, only divorces, the clearly defined legal event, are counted. What is of greater sociological interest is separation. This distinction is particularly important when making comparisons among subpopulations. The black–white difference in divorce rates is relatively small; the differential in rates of separation is very large. Many blacks who separate never go on to get divorced, and when they do divorce, they tend to spend a longer time in a separated state (Sweet & Bumpass, 1974).

Recent Improvements in Data on Marital Disruption

Three recent developments in data collection have greatly improved our ability to understand patterns of marriage and marital disruption: the routine collection of marriage histories in the CPS, the collection of marriage histories in other sample surveys, and longitudinal surveys that gather information on changes in marital status over time.

Marriage Histories in the Current Population Survey

The CPS is the monthly survey conducted by the U.S. Census Bureau to provide estimates of employment and unemployment. The sample is very large, about 60,000 interviews per month. Marriage histories were first collected in the 1967 Survey of Economic Opportunity (a survey, similar to the CPS, conducted by the Census Bureau). Beginning in 1971, marriage histories have been collected in the CPS about once every 5 years.

The importance of the CPS rests in its very large sample size. Despite the high lifetime prevalence of marital disruption, it is still a relatively rare event. Each year, only about 2% of extant marriages terminate by separation. The availability of the CPS marriage histories has resulted in a great deal of important new knowledge. Because the CPS is primarily a labor force survey, however, few relevant social, demographic, or economic characteristics are available, and no other retrospective information (apart from the birth histories, which are collected at the same time) is included. (Castro Martin & Bumpass, 1989, use the data from the 1985 CPS.)

Other Surveys Collecting Marriage Histories

Because of the importance of marriage to fertility patterns, fertility surveys usually include marital history questions. The 1970 National Fertility Survey made two very important innovations (Westoff & Ryder, 1977). In addition to collecting dates of divorce, women in the sample were asked their dates of separation. (This is now done in the marriage histories collected in the CPS and other surveys.) Respondents were also asked a series of retrospective questions concerning their (and their husband's) characteristics at the time of their first marriage. This permitted modeling the process of marital disruption with measures that have the proper temporal ordering. The inclusion of husband's characteristics at first marriage also made possible the study of effects of differences in spouse characteristics (see Bumpass & Sweet, 1972).

The 1987 to 1988 National Survey of Families and Households (NSFH) (Sweet, Bumpass, & Call, 1988), a comprehensive survey of American family life, continued all of these innovations, and in addition, collected nearly complete cohabitation histories, as well as more detailed information on the characteristics of the respondent and his or her spouse at the time of first marriage.

These surveys offer the opportunity to analyze marital disruption in the context of a much richer array of potential explanatory variables than is possible from official sources. The payoff has been great, though several concerns must be kept in mind:

1. Given that marital separation is a rare event, the sample size is usually quite limiting.
2. As already noted, marital disruption is underreported in all surveys. Measures of subgroup differences are biased to the extent that underreporting is greater for some groups than for others. Further, it appears that marriage histories are much less reliably reported by men than by women (see Castro Martin & Bumpass, 1989; Sweet & Bumpass, 1987; Cherlin & McCarthy, 1984).
3. Although it is feasible to retrospectively measure experiences such as educational enrollment and childbearing, other important variables such as attitudes or conflict are not likely to be accurately reconstructed for earlier periods. Hence, cross-sectional surveys are limited in the extent to which they can be used for the analysis of the marital disruption. Longitudinal surveys are essential for these purposes.

Longitudinal Surveys

Several longitudinal studies permitted the prospective investigation of marital transitions. Many of these studies followed a specific age group (or cohort) over time (see, e.g., Mott & Moore, 1979; Thornton, 1988). Two American studies that have followed a cross-section of the population are the Panel Study of Income Dynamics (Hoffman & Holmes, 1976; Lillard & Waite, 1989), which has been annually interviewing members of a panel of 5,000 households since 1968, and a telephone survey of 2,000 married respondents (under age 55) who were interviewed in 1980, 1983, and 1988 (see White & Booth, 1985).

The NSFH (Sweet et al., 1988) is also planned to be longitudinal, with a second interview in 1992 to 1993, 5 years after the initial interview. This will make it possible to examine the consequences for marital stability of a wide range of attitudes and characteristics of spouses (and cohabiting partners).

Developments in Analytic Methods

Important innovations in analytic methodology have improved our ability to analyze both retrospective and prospective marital history data, by extending in various ways the logic of life-table analysis. The key insight of a life-table approach to the analysis of family transitions from survey data is the recognition that rates must be based on all relevant exposure represented in the sample, including the years of risk experienced by those whose marriages have not (yet) disrupted. The proportion of marriages that have disrupted by the time of interview is obviously only a subset of those which will eventually disrupt. Life-table procedures calculate the risk of disruption at each duration of marriage and facilitate the description of these risks in terms of the cumulative experience of disruption by successive durations.

These procedures have been extended in two major directions. The first is the application of increment–decrement (multistate) life-table procedures, permitting estimation of the expected time the average person will spend in various marital states, assuming a given set of risks were to be experienced over a lifetime (Espenshade, 1985; Schoen, 1988; Schoen & Nelson, 1974; Schoen, Urton, Woodrow, & Baj, 1985). These techniques reveal, for example, that a decreasing proportion of adult life is being spent married and that blacks spend only half as many years married as whites.

The second elaboration of the life-table idea is the development of multivariate procedures referred to as "event history techniques" (Hoem, 1985; Menken, Trussell, Stempel, & Babakol, 1981; Teachman, 1982). This methodology is developing rapidly, with increasingly sophisticated applications, but the underlying idea is the estimation of differential

TABLE 4.1. Percentage of first-marriage cohorts experiencing marital separation by successive anniversaries.

Anniversary	Marriage cohort				
	1965–1967	1968–1970	1971–1973	1974–1976	1977–1979
2	5	8	8	9	9
5	14	17	20	21	
10	26	30			
15	35				

Note. The data are from the 1980 *Current Population Survey*, adapted in *American Families and Households* (p. 179) by J. A. Sweet and L. Bumpass, 1987, New York: Russell Sage Foundation. Copyright 1987 by Russell Sage Foundation. Used by permission.

risks based on observed duration-specific exposure, and duration-specific experience of marital disruption. Analyses may refer to overall "risk" with the assumption that variables have proportionately the same effect at each duration ("proportional hazard" models, Cox, 1972) or may use a variety of strategies for differentiating effects at specific durations (Hoem, 1985; Wu & Tuma, 1990). One key subclass of these procedures allows for the analysis of "time-varying covariates" so that effects can be estimated for variables that change over the course of marriage. An important example is Lillard and Waite's (1989) analysis of the effects of young children on the risk of divorce.

Next, we review some of what social demographers have learned about levels, trends, and differentials in marital disruption in the United States. Given limitations of space, we present only a very gross summary of some recent findings, and we focus largely on our own work. (For more detail see Bumpass, Castro Martin, & Sweet, 1991; Bumpass & Sweet, 1972; Castro Martin & Bumpass, 1990; Glenn & Supancic, 1984; Sweet & Bumpass, 1987.)

Levels and Trends in Marital Disruption

It is commonly reported in the popular press that approximately half of all marriages will end in divorce. This assertion is based on the use of life-table procedures to estimate the proportion of extant marriages that can be expected to eventually end in separation or divorce, given recent duration-specific rates.

We can track the experience of marriages begun in the mid-1960s using data from the 1980 CPS (see Table 4.1). The rows of this table show the increase in disruption by a given duration for successive marriage cohorts. The columns show the experience of a given cohort over the life course. More than one third of the marriages of the mid-1960s had ended in separation by the 15th anniversary. The increasing rate for later cohorts can be seen in the increase by the fifth anniversary (from 14% to 21%) between the 1965 to 1967 and 1974 to 1976 cohorts. The estimate of one half of marriages ending in separation is consistent with the fact that there will be further disruptions (beyond 35% at year 15) for the earliest cohort and subsequent increase in duration-specific proportions for more recent cohorts.[2]

Preston and McDonald (1979) provide historical estimates of the proportion of successive marriage cohorts experiencing divorce. The rise in divorce has been a slow, continuous process from at least the mid-19th century. About 7% of marriages in the 1860s ended in divorce; the fraction gradually increased to one sixth for marriages in the 1920s, and to about one half by the mid-1970s. (Other demographic studies of the trend in marital disruption include Castro Martin & Bumpass, 1989; Michael, 1978; Morgan & Rindfuss, 1985; Sweet & Bumpass, 1987; Thornton & Rodgers, 1987.)

Because many of the consequences of marital disruption are experienced by the children of separating couples, a series of studies has investigated the experience by children of parental marital disruption. Bumpass and Sweet (1989) show that 36% of children born between 1960 and 1969 did not live with both parents through age 16. Life-table estimates using the period rates of the 1970s and early 1980s suggest that about 44% of children will experience a parental marital separation (or were born to an unmarried mother) before they reach age 16. About half of these children (not living through their childhood with both parents) will live with a stepfather before they reach age 16. (See also Bumpass, 1984; for a description of remarriage patterns, see Bumpass, Sweet, & Castro Martin, 1990.)

Differentials in Marital Stability

Many studies have examined differentials in marital instability among population subgroups. Next we briefly review some recent findings on these differentials.

Marriage Duration

The risk of marital disruption is highest in the first few years of marriage and gradually decreases at longer durations. This is one of the reasons that it is so important to control duration when making comparisons of marital disruption in relation to other characteristics (Sweet & Bumpass, 1987).

---

[2] Based on adjustments for the underreporting of divorces in surveys noted earlier, Castro Martin and Bumpass (1989) suggest the proportion expected to disrupt may be even higher, perhaps reaching 60% (see also Bumpass, 1990).

Age at Marriage

According to the 1980 CPS estimates (cited in Sweet & Bumpass, 1987, p. 183), half of women who married in their teens experienced marital separation by their tenth anniversary. This compares with about one quarter of women marrying in their early 20s and one sixth of those marrying beyond age 30. (See Bacon, 1974; Booth & Edwards, 1985; Bumpass & Sweet, 1972; Kiernan, 1986; Morgan & Rindfuss, 1985; Teachman, 1983; for discussions of this pattern.)

Race and Ethnicity

Blacks have much higher rates of marital disruption than majority whites. The CPS data for recent experience show that about half of black women will experience marital disruption within 10 years of their first marriage (Castro Martin & Bumpass, 1989). This compares with a little over one quarter for majority whites. Mexican-Americans have a level that is very similar to that for whites. (For discussions of patterns of marital disruption in the black population see Cherlin, 1981; Espenshade, 1985; Sweet & Bumpass, 1987. For Mexican American patterns, see Frisbie, 1986; Sweet & Bumpass, 1987.)

Education

A long series of studies shows an inverse relationship between level of education and marital disruption (Bumpass & Sweet, 1972; Glick, 1984; Sweet & Bumpass, 1987). However, when other characteristics associated with educational level are included in a multivariate analysis, the educational difference is attenuated. Persons with a high level of education tend to marry at older ages and are also more likely to have grown up in an intact family. Education differences, however, seem to have increased in recent years (Castro Martin & Bumpass, 1989).

Religion/Religiosity

Marital disruption varies among religious groups, but the pattern is not what might be expected. Classifying persons by the religion in which they were raised, Sweet and Bumpass (1990a) found that persons with no religious preference, as well as Baptists and some fundamentalist groups have higher than average rates of marital disruption. Catholics and mainline Protestant groups tend to have similar levels that are near the average. Jews and some fundamentalist Christian groups (e.g., Pentecostals) have lower than average levels. (Because the number of sample cases in some of the religious groups is quite small, some of these estimates may not be statistically reliable.) Another analysis (Bumpass, Castro Martin, & Sweet, 1991) showed that when other characteristics are controlled, the Catholic–non-Catholic differential is increased, with Catholics having a marital disruption rate that is about 25% higher than average. The higher rate for Catholics, however, appears to be the result of a high rate of disruption in Catholic–non-Catholic marriages. This is discussed in the following section on homogamy. (For other discussions of religious variation in marital stability, see Bumpass & Sweet, 1972; Glenn & Supancic, 1984; Heaton, 1984; McCarthy, 1979; Thornton, 1978).

Other studies have shown that more "religious" individuals have a lower rate of marital disruption (Glenn & Supancic, 1984). This is likely true, but difficult to demonstrate empirically because it is difficult to retrospectively measure religiosity. We know of no prospective study that has documented this effect.

Family Background

A number of studies have found that persons whose parents experienced marital disruption have a higher rate of marital disruption themselves (Bumpass & Sweet, 1972; Castro Martin & Bumpass, 1989; Glenn & Kramer, 1987; McLanahan & Bumpass, 1988). For recent marriages in the NSFH (Sweet et al., 1988), women whose parents were not married when they were born or whose parents separated before they reached age 16 had a rate of separation that was about 25% higher than those whose parents remained married at least until they were age 16. This differential is net of a variety of other relevant characteristics.

Marriage order

There is some evidence that second and higher order marriages have a higher rate of dissolution than first marriages (McCarthy, 1978). However, the analysis of Castro Martin and Bumpass (1989) suggests that this differential is now quite small. The observed differential is associated with other characteristics. In a related analysis, they show that there is little difference in the stability of remarriages that bring children from a previous marriage into the household versus those that do not.

Early Marital Experience

Given that rates of marital disruption are very high early in marriage, it seems reasonable to look for early marital experiences that might be associated with marital disruption. In the NSFH, respondents were asked:

At any time during your first year of marriage were you:
a. attending school
b. in the armed forces
c. working full-time in a civilian job
d. working part-time
e. unemployed and looking for work

The same question was asked with respect to the respondent's first spouse.

Using this information, Bumpass, Castro Martin, and Sweet (1991) found that when the husband was in the armed forces during the 1st year of marriage, the rate of disruption was twice as high as when he was not. If the husband experienced unemployment, the rate of disruption was also much higher. Although the difference is not statistically significant, if the wife was employed full time and the husband was not, the rate of disruption was also higher. Enrollment in school does not seem to affect the level of disruption.

Heterogamy

There is a long tradition of speculation and research on the effects of marital heterogamy on marital instability. Bumpass and Sweet (1972) examined the effects of age, education, and religious heterogamy on marital disruption. Because similar questions were asked in the NSFH, this analysis has recently been updated (Bumpass, Castro Martin, & Sweet, 1991). Net of other characteristics, an age difference between spouses does not seem to have much of an effect on marital stability. Surprisingly, when the wife is 2 or more years older than her husband, the rate of separation is actually about 10% *lower* than when their ages are the same. Educational differences, however, do affect marital stability. Compared to couples in the same educational category, marital disruption rates are 31% lower if the husband is in a higher educational category and 43% higher if the wife is in a higher category than her husband. The rate of marital disruption in Catholic–Catholic marriages is identical to that in Protestant–Protestant marriages. However, Catholic–non-Catholic marriages have a disruption rate that is 37% higher than homogamous marriages. (For an interesting analysis and discussion of fundamentalist–nonfundamentalist intermarriage patterns, see Chi & Houseknecht, 1985.)

Cohabitation

By the late 1980s, over 5 million Americans were living with an opposite-sex partner to whom they were not married. In this final section, we will review some of what social demographers know about cohabitation patterns and trends. (For discussions of patterns of cohabitation in the United States and other countries, see Balakrishnan, Vaninadha Rao, Lapierre-Adamcyk, & Krotki, 1987; Burch, 1989; Carlson, 1986; Khoo, 1987; Schoen & Owens, 1990; Spanier, 1983; Tanfer, 1987; Thornton, 1988; Willis & Michael, 1988. For discussions of the "meaning" of contemporary cohabitation patterns, see also Caldwell, Caldwell, Bracher,

& Santow, 1988; Leridon, 1990; Leridon & Villeneuve-Gokalp, 1989; Sweet, 1989; Sweet & Bumpass, 1990b; Wiersma, 1983.)

Trends and Levels

Cohabitation status has not been asked in either the decennial census or the CPS, although beginning with the 1990 census, it will be possible to identify most cohabitors. It has been possible to indirectly identify cohabitors from the composition of households in both the CPS and the decennial census. Two-adult households consisting of unrelated, opposite-sex persons are assumed to be cohabitors. This definition, of course, contains both errors of erroneous inclusion of opposite-sex "roommates" without an "intimate" relationship, and erroneous exclusion of cohabiting couples living in multiadult households. Although the precise level is unknown, this measure is probably accurate enough for assessing both trends and differentials in cohabitation.

According to the March 1988 CPS, 2.6 million couples were cohabiting in the United States. It appears that only about 450,000 couples were cohabiting in 1960; many were older couples in what might better be termed common-law marriages than in cohabiting relationships. The decade of the 1970s was a period of rapid growth in the prevalence of cohabitation, with the number of cohabiting couples increasing from 500,000 at the beginning of the decade to 1.6 million by 1980. The upward trend continued through the 1980s (U.S. Bureau of the Census, 1989, Table A-7).

Four percent of all Americans age 19 and older are currently in a cohabitation relationship. This proportion is higher at the younger ages, with 8% of all persons age 19 to 29 cohabiting. If only unmarried persons are considered, the proportion is, of course, higher—approximately 1 in 10. The proportions are highest among persons age 19 to 34; at those ages about 1 in 7 never-married and about 1 in 4 formerly married persons are currently cohabiting. The rates of cohabitation decrease with increasing age. Less than 5% of unmarried persons in their 50s and about 1% of unmarried persons aged 60 and older are cohabiting (U.S. Bureau of the Census, 1989, Table A-7).

The NSFH was the first American survey to collect cohabitation histories from a cross-section of the population. This permits not only the identification of current cohabitors but also persons who have cohabited in the past but are not currently doing so. It also allows the analysis of the effects of prior cohabitation experience on subsequent behavior, such as the stability of marriage. (Three papers reporting on cohabitation patterns from these data are Bumpass & Sweet, 1989, 1990; Bumpass, Sweet, & Cherlin, 1991. Some findings of these papers are discussed later.)

One quarter of American adults of all ages have cohabited at some time in their lives. The age pattern reflects two different factors: Cohabitation was quite uncommon two decades ago but in recent years has become more common. It is something that occurs primarily either before first marriage or following marriages that terminate at relatively young ages. About one quarter of those persons aged 19 to 24, nearly half of persons age 30 to 34, but only one seventh of persons aged 50 to 59 have cohabited (Bumpass & Sweet, 1989).

Another perspective on the level and trend in cohabitation comes from looking at the proportion of successive first-marriage cohorts who have cohabitation experience before marriage. Of persons marrying for the first time during the first half of the 1980s, 42% had cohabited at some time before their marriage. For first marriages in the period 1975 to 1979, the proportion was 32% while for those in 1965 to 1974, it was only 11%. Most of the persons who cohabited before their first marriage cohabited with their first spouse only. For example, of persons who married in 1980 to 1984:

32% had lived only with the person they married
7% had lived with the person they married and at least one other partner
3% had not lived with the person they married but had lived with some
   other partner
58% had not cohabited before marriage

The proportion of remarrying persons cohabiting between marriages is even higher than the proportion marrying for the first time. In recent years about three fifths of persons entering second marriages have cohabited between their first and second marriages (Bumpass & Sweet, 1989; see also Schoen & Owens, 1990).

Stability of Cohabitation Relationships

In the 1960s, it was common to refer to cohabitors as "shacking up." This term connoted a short-term, temporary, sexual relationship. What can we say about the stability of cohabitation relationships today? To address this question, we have selected first-cohabitation relationships (i.e., first cohabitations that occurred before the person had been married) beginning between 1975 and 1984, using life-table procedures.

The first row of Table 4.2 shows that 62% of persons in first cohabitation relationships are still cohabiting by the first anniversary (Bumpass & Sweet, 1989). By the second anniversary, 36% are still cohabiting, and 9% by the fifth anniversary. The second row adds some further light on the "instability" of these relationships. By the first anniversary, one quarter have terminated as cohabitation relationships by virtue of being converted to marriages. By 3 years, more than half have been converted

TABLE 4.2. Percentage of persons who are still cohabiting with their partner and percentage still with their partner (including being married) at various intervals after beginning cohabitation.

	Percentage by the nth anniversary				
	1	2	3	4	5
Still cohabiting	62	36	23	15	9
Marrying partner	26	42	53	56	59
Still with partner (either married or cohabiting)	83	71	64	59	54

Life-table estimates based on experience of persons entering first-cohabitation relationships between 1975 and 1984.
Note. The data are adapted from Bumpass & Sweet, 1989.

into marriages, and by 5 years nearly three fifths. In fact, only a minority of first cohabitations end by "separation;" the majority end when the partners get married.

The final row of Table 4.2 shows the percentage of persons who are still living with their first partner at successive anniversaries. Five sixths are still together (either married or still cohabiting) after 1 year, half after 3 years, and three fifths after 5 years. Note that the attrition reflected in these data includes not only separations from cohabitation but also separations following marriage.

Differentials

The conventional wisdom in the late 1960s and 1970s was that cohabitation was primarily a phenomenon of college students and of the better-educated population (Henslin, 1980). The NSFH (Bumpass & Sweet, 1989; Bumpass, Sweet, & Cherlin, 1991) data show that it was just the opposite. Cohabitation is now, and has been for the past two decades, more common among persons with less education, and is relatively rare for those with a college education. The growth of cohabitation started earlier and proceeded more rapidly for persons with less than a high school education.

Although blacks are somewhat more likely to experience cohabitation before marriage than whites, this is due to the confounding effects of other characteristics. Net of these characteristics, such as a lower level of education, their rate of cohabitation is about 25% lower than for whites. There is essentially no Catholic–non-Catholic differential in premarital cohabitation. Net of other characteristics, persons who grew up in a one-parent family have a cohabitation rate that is 60% higher than those who did not (Bumpass & Sweet, 1989).

Relationship to Marriage Trends

One of the most striking social demographic changes of the past quarter century is the increase in the ages at which people marry. The average age at first marriage has increased by about 3 years since 1960. Premarital cohabitation, however, also increased rapidly during this same period. Bumpass et al. (1991) have shown that between 1970 and 1985, there was a 28% decrease in the number of person years spent in marriage between ages 18 and 25 but only a 12% decline in the number of person years spent in unions (marriages and cohabiting unions together). Young couples are forming unions and "setting up housekeeping" at nearly the same rate in the late 1980s as in the late 1960s, but nearly half of them are choosing to initially live as partners, rather than as spouses.

Relationship to Marital Disruption

There are two separate ways to think about the relationship of increased cohabitation to marital disruption: on the aggregate level and on the individual level.

At the aggregate level, rising levels of cohabitation may have the effect of reducing the rate of marital disruption. If cohabitation is seen by the participants as a "trial marriage" or if it is something done by people who would like to marry but whose lives are not settled enough to feel that they should get married, then it may be that cohabitation will tend to select out "unsuitable" unions before marriage—in effect, resulting in many couples "divorcing" before they get married. If this is true, the current rate of marital disruption may be lower than it would have been in the absence of the increase in cohabitation. Thus, the slowing of the increase in the divorce rate that has been observed in the early 1980s may be due to this, rather than to an increase in "familism" or an increased commitment to marriage.

On the individual level, what is the effect of having cohabited on subsequent marital stability? Again, one might think that couples who are unsuitable for each other may find that out while cohabiting and never get married. This might suggest that, other things equal, couples who cohabit before they get married would have a lower rate of marital disruption than those who did not. The data suggest that this is not the case. Persons who cohabited before first marriage have a much higher rate of marital disruption than those who did not. If they lived only with their spouse, the rate is 49% higher than for those who did not cohabit; if they lived with someone other than their first spouse, their rate is 84% higher.[3]

---

[3] This includes those who lived with their first spouse and at least one other partner, as well as those who did not live with their first spouse but did live with someone else before first marriage.

These differentials are net of many other characteristics known to be associated with marital disruption. (For other studies of the effect of prior cohabitation on marital stability and marital quality, see Balakrishnan et al., 1987; Bennett, Blanc, & Bloom, 1988; Booth & Johnson, 1988; Thomson & Colella, 1990; Hall, 1990.) There are two alternative explanations for this result. First, there may be something about living together before marriage that affects the survival chances of the marriage. Perhaps expectations about the relationship or behavior patterns develop during the period the couple is cohabiting that are not conducive to the long-term survival of the relationship. We know of no study that gives any indication of what these expectations or behavior patterns might be. Note that they would have to be something that is statistically independent of the structural characteristics that are controlled in the analysis: age, race and ethnicity, education, religious preference, activities early in marriage, and a variety of other characteristics.

The second possibility is that couples who choose to cohabit before getting married are selected on (unmeasured) characteristics that are not conducive to the long-term survival of marriage. That is to say, these couples would have a higher risk of marital instability, even in the absence of cohabitation. They may have a value system that places a relatively lower priority on relationship stability or personality characteristics that are not conducive to cultivating and maintaining strong, enduring relationships. Again, we know of no study that has identified any of these characteristics by showing that when they are present, the effect of having cohabited before marriage on marital instability is attenuated. Again, they would have to be independent of the measured characteristics that are already included in the model. There is some interesting evidence that bears on this relationship. In a study of Canadian marriages, Hall (1990) claims that "secular individualism" accounts for the higher disruption rates of persons with cohabitation experience. The "secular individualism" indicators, however, are measured after the experience of both premarital cohabitation and marital disruption. Sweet and Bumpass (1990b) have shown that young adults with cohabitation experience have less traditional family and sex role attitudes. They suggest that some of this difference may be the result of the experience of cohabitation, but there are some attitudes for which this does not appear plausible, and selectivity is probably the reason. They go on to show that young, never-married adults who expect to, or who desire to, cohabit in the future also have less traditional family and sex role attitudes than those who do not.

Conclusion

The use of representative population samples as well as careful and precise conceptualization and measurement are critical to an understanding of union stability. This includes the calculation of rates with appropriate denominators, proper awareness of issues of sample selection and truncation, and the use of an appropriate measure of the timing of the dissolution of unions. The basic, descriptive work done by social demographers provides the "big picture" into which the results of more intensive studies of smaller, less representative samples can be fit.

The remarkable expansion of both retrospective and longitudinal data and the development and diffusion of methods to deal with them have greatly expanded our understanding of processes of marriage, cohabitation, and marital disruption. To understand contemporary family life, there is a continued need for cross-sectional information on union formation in large-scale surveys such as the CPS. (It is hoped the CPS will begin to collect information on nonmarital as well as marital unions.) It is also important to continue to try to obtain a better understanding of the more subjective aspects of union formation and dissolution: views of marriage, nonmarital cohabitation, and the dissolution of unions. This is something that we attempted, but were only partially successful at, when we designed the NSFH (see Sweet, 1989; Sweet & Bumpass, 1990b). Clearly, there is a need for more longitudinal studies, such as the planned reinterview of the NSFH sample, in order to better understand both antecedents and consequences of marital events and experience.

The increase in nonmarital cohabitation that has occurred in the United States since the 1970s has raised new problems for social demographers interested in marital relationships. We have begun to collect information regarding cohabiting, as well as marital, unions. However, considerable conceptual ambiguity remains. Nonmarital cohabitation does not appear to be functionally identical to marriage. Young adults do not regard them as the same. Clearly, many couples who now choose to cohabit would have married in the social environment of just a few years ago. To the extent that these relationships end in "divorce" before a marriage occurs, they represent unstable "marriages" that were once represented in our data. At the same time, it is also clear that many cohabiting relationships would not have been marriages in earlier times. In some cases, the partners have no intention of marrying each other, while in others, whether to eventually marry or not is an open question. Hence, we know that measures of union stability based on the concept of marriage are not satisfactory, but it is not clear what is appropriate. We can measure the stability of coresidential unions (with or without marriage), but in doing so we must keep clear that such measures represent a conceptual disjuncture with work on "marital" stability.

We have been more successful in documenting the trends in union formation and dissolution than in explaining them. Presently, the level of marital instability in the United States is very high, both by historical standards and in comparison to levels in other industrial countries. Examination of the historical trend over the last century makes it clear that the current pattern is an extension of a long-term trend and not a sharp break with the past. Hence, it seems inappropriate to seek explanation in events since the 1960s or 1970s. Social trends such as the increasing employment of women are undoubtedly linked with increased marital instability, but these changes also have deep historical roots (Davis, 1984) and are best seen as part of the long-term evolution of industrial society (Bumpass, 1990; Sweet & Bumpass, 1987).

While comparison with other industrialized societies suggests that the forces underlying the decreased stability of marital unions have gone further in the United States than in other parts of the world, it is clear that all Western industrial societies have been experiencing the same general trend (see Festy, 1985; Lye, 1989). Hence, it does not seem fruitful to look for the sources of increased marital stability in any particular social policy or in any other distinctive feature of a particular society.

Differentials remain among subpopulations in the rate of marital disruption. However, the trends for all social and economic groups appear to have been upward. Those groups that have relatively low levels of disruption have very high rates in historical perspective. For example, while the rate of disruption among college-educated women is considerably lower than that of women who did not complete high school, the current level is as high as that which Moynihan (1967) labeled "pathological" among blacks in the 1960s. The rise in marital disruption has been pervasive through all industrial societies and, in the United States at least, through all social and economic strata. (This is similar to the trend in fertility. The baby "bust" of the 1960s and 1970s was experienced by all subpopulations to about the same degree and with very similar timing; Rindfuss & Sweet, 1977.)

Thus, the inductive work of social demographers suggests that a theoretical understanding of current high levels of marital disruption must take into account the long-term nature of the trend, the pervasiveness of the trend, and the persistence of differentials by individual characteristics. This suggests a theoretical perspective that would seek to identify critical variables in the long-term process and then to specify how particular circumstances mediate the impact of these variables (Bumpass, 1990). Examples include Ogburn and Tibbitts' (1933) arguments regarding the decreased dependence on family relationships for essential functions and Lesthaeghe's emphasis on individuation and secularization (Lesthaeghe, 1983; Lesthaeghe & Surkyn, 1988; Lesthaeghe & Wilson, 1985).

References

Bacon, L. (1974). Early motherhood, accelerated role transition, and social pathologies. *Social Forces*, *52*(March), 333–341.

Balakrishnan, T. R., Vaninadha Rao, K., Lapierre-Adamcyk, E., & Krotki, K. J. (1987). A hazard model analysis of the covariates of marriage dissolution in Canada. *Demography*, *24*(3), 395–406.

Bennett, N. G., Blanc, A. K., & Bloom, D. E. (1988). Commitment and the modern union: Assessing the link between premarital cohabitation and subsequent marital stability. *American Sociological Review*, *53*(1), 127–138.

Booth, A., & Edwards, J. N. (1985). Age at marriage and marital instability. *Journal of Marriage and the Family*, *47*, 67–76.

Booth, A., & Johnson, D. (1988). Premarital cohabitation and marital success. *Journal of Family Issues*, *9*(2), 255–272.

Bumpass, L. (1984). Children and marital disruption: A replication and update. *Demography*, *212*, 71–82.

Bumpass, L. (1990). What's happening to the family? Interactions between demographic and institutional change. Presidential address, at the annual meeting of the Population Association of America. *Demography*, *27*, 483–498.

Bumpass, L., Castro Martin, T., & Sweet J. (1991). Background and early marital factors in marital disruption. *Journal of Family Issues*, *12*(1), 22–42.

Bumpass, L., & Sweet, J. (1972). Differentials in marital instability. *American Sociological Review*, *37*(6), 754–766.

Bumpass, L., & Sweet, J. (1989). National estimates of cohabitation: Cohort levels and union stability. *Demography*, *26*(4), 615–625.

Bumpass, L., & Sweet, J. (1990). Children's experience in single-parent families: Implications of cohabitation and marital transitions. *Family Planning Perspectives*, *21*(6), 256–260.

Bumpass, L., Sweet, J., & Castro Martin, T. (1990). Changing patterns of remarriage. *Journal of Marriage and the Family*, *52*, 747–756.

Bumpass, L., Sweet, J., & Cherlin, A. (1991). *The role of cohabitation in declining rates of marriage. Journal of Marriage and the Family*, *53*(4), 913–927.

Burch, T. K. (1989). Common-law unions in Canada: A portrait from the 1984 family history survey. In J. Legare, T. R. Balakrishnan, & Roderic Beaujot (Eds.), *The family in crisis: A population crisis?* (pp. 105–120). Ottawa: Lowe-Martin.

Caldwell, J. C., Caldwell, P., Bracher, M. D., & Santow, G. (1988). *The contemporary marriage and fertility revolutions in the West*. Australian Family Project Working Paper No. 3, Research School of Social Sciences, Australian National University, Canberra, Australia.

Carlson, E. (1986). Couples without children: Premarital cohabitation in France. In K. Davis & A. Grossbard-Schechtman (Eds.), *Contemporary marriage: Comparative perspectives of a changing institution* (pp. 113–130). New York: Russell Sage Foundation.

Castro Martin, T., & Bumpass, L. (1989). Recent trends in marital disruption. *Demography*, *26*(1), 37–51.

Cherlin, A. (1981). *Marriage, divorce, remarriage*. Harvard University Press.

Cherlin, A., & McCarthy, J. (1984). *Demographic analysis of family and household structure, final report*. Berhesda, MD: National Institute for Child

Health and Human Development, Center for Population Research. (Contract N01-HD-12802.)

Chi, S. K., & Houseknecht, S. K. (1985). Protestant fundamentalism and marital success: A comparative approach. *Sociology and Social Research*, *69*(3), 351–374.

Cox, D. R. (1972). Regression models and life tables. *Journal of the Royal Statistical Society*, Series B, *34*, 187–220.

Davis, K. (1984). Wives and work: The sex role revolution and its consequences. *Population and Development Review*, *10*(3), 397–417.

Espenshade, T. (1985). Marriage trends in America: Estimates, implications and underlying causes. *Population and Development Review*, *11*(2), 193–245.

Festy, P. (1985). *Divorce, judicial separation and remarriage. Recent trends in member states of the Council of Europe*. Council of Europe Population Studies, No. 17. Strassbourg: Council of Europe.

Frisbie, P. W. (1986). Variations in patterns of marital instability among Hispanics. *Journal of Marriage and the Family*, *48*, 99–106.

Glenn, N. D., & Kramer, K. B. (1987). The marriages and divorces of the children of divorce. *Journal of Marriage and the Family*, *49*, 811–825.

Glenn, N., & Supancic, M. (1984). The social and demographic correlates of divorce and separation in the U.S.: An update and reconsideration. *Journal of Marriage and the Family*, *46*, 563–575.

Glick, P. (1984). Marriage, divorce, and living arrangements: Prospective changes. *Journal of Family Issues*, March, 7–26.

Hall, D. R. (1990). *Secular individualism and divorce: The link between premarital cohabitation and marital dissolution in Canada*. Unpublished paper, Department of Sociology, University of Western Ontario, London, Ontario, Canada.

Heaton, T. (1984). Religious homogamy and marital satisfaction reconsidered. *Journal of Marriage and the Family*, *46*(3), 729–733.

Henslin, J. M. (1980). Cohabitation: Its context and meaning. In J. Henslin (Ed.), *Marriage and family in a changing society* (pp. 223–241). New York: The Free Press.

Hoem, J. (1985). *The impact of education on modern union formation*. Stockholm Research Reports in Demography, No. 27. Stockholm: University of Stockholm.

Hoffman, S., & Holmes, J. (1976). Husbands, wives, and divorces. In G. Duncan & J. N. Morgan (Eds.), *Five thousand American families: Patterns of economic progress* (Vol. 4, pp. 23–76).

Khoo, S. (1987). Living together: Young couples in de facto relationships. Australian Institute of Family Studies Working Paper No. 10, Development Studies Centre, Australian National University, Canberra, Australia.

Kiernan, K. E. (1986). Teenage marriage and marital breakdown. *Population Studies*, *40*, 35–44.

Leridon, H. (1990). Cohabitation, marriage, separation: An analysis of life histories of French cohorts from 1968 to 1985. *Population Studies*, *44*, 127–144.

Leridon, H., & Villeneuve-Gokalp, C. (1989). The new couples: Number, characteristics, and attitudes. *Population*, *44*, 203–235.

Lesthaeghe, R. (1983). A century of demographic and cultural change in Western Europe: An exploration of underlying dimensions. *Population and Development Review*, *9*, 411–436.

Lesthaeghe, R., & Surkyn, J. (1988). Cultural dynamics and economic theories of fertility change. *Population and Development Review*, *14*, 1–45.

Lesthaeghe, R., & Wilson, C. (1985). Modes of production, secularization, and the pace of the fertility decline in Western Europe, 1870–1930. In A. Coale & S. Watkins (Eds.), *The decline of fertility in Europe* (pp. 261–292). Princeton: Princeton University Press.

Lillard, L. A., & Waite, L. J. (1989). *Modelling divorce with the panel study of income dynamics*. Final Report to the Social Security Administration. (Grant No. 10-P-98299-0-01.) Santa Monica, CA: Rand Corp.

Lye, D. N. (1989). Shifting family values and the rise of divorce in developed countries. Paper presented at the annual meeting of the Population Association of America, Baltimore, MD.

McCarthy, J. (1978). A comparison of the probability of the dissolution of first and second marriages. *Demography*, *15*, 345–359.

McCarthy, J. (1979). Religious commitment, affiliation and marriage dissolution. In R. Withnow (Ed.), *The religious dimension: New directions in quantitative research* (pp. 179–197). New York: Academic Press.

McLanahan, S., & Bumpass, L. (1988). Intergenerational consequences of family disruption. *American Journal of Sociology*, *94*(1), 130–152.

Menken, J., Trussell, J., Stempel, D., & Babakol, O. (1981). Proportional hazards life table models: An illustrative analysis of socio-demographic influences on marriage dissolution in the United States. *Demography*, *18*, 181–200.

Michael, R. T. (1978). The rise in divorce rates, 1960–1974: Age-specific components. *Demography*, *15*(2), 177–182.

Morgan, S. P., & Rindfuss, R. R. (1985). Marital disruption: Structural and temporal dimensions. *American Journal of Sociology*, *90*, 1055–1077.

Mott F., & Moore, S. F. (1979). The causes of marital disruption among young American women: Interdisciplinary perspectives. *Journal of Marriage and the Family*, *41*, 355–365.

Moynihan, D. P. (1967). The Negro family: The case for national action. In L. Rainwater & W. L. Yancey, *The Moynihan report and the politics of controversy*. Cambridge, MA: MIT Press.

National Center for Health Statistics. (1973). *100 years of marriage and divorce statistics: United States, 1867–1967* (Series 21, No. 24). U.S. Department of Health, Education, & Welfare, Vital and Health Statistics, Hyattsville, MD.

National Center for Health Statistics. (1978). *Divorces and divorce rates: United States* (Series 21, No. 29).

Ogburn, W. F., & Tibbitts, C. (1933). The family and its functions. In President's Research Committee on Social Trends, *Recent social trends* (pp. 661–708). New York: McGraw-Hill.

Preston, S. H., & McDonald, J. (1979). The incidence of divorce within cohorts of American marriages contracted since the Civil War. *Demography*, *16*, 1–26.

Rindfuss, R., & Sweet, J. A. (1977). *Postwar fertility trends and differentials in the United States*. New York: Academic Press.

Schoen, R. (1988). Practical uses of multistate population models. *Annual Review of Sociology*, *14*, 341–361.

Schoen, R., & Owens, D. (1990) *A further look at first unions and first marriages*. Paper presented at the conference on demographic perspectives on the

American Family: Patterns and prospects, Department of Sociology, State University of New York at Albany.

Schoen, R., & Nelson, V. E. (1974). Marriage divorce, and mortality: A life table analysis. *Demography*, *11*(2), 267–290.

Schoen, R., Urton, W., Woodrow, K., & Baj, J. (1985). Marriage and divorce in 20th century American cohorts. *Demography*, *22*(1), 101–114.

Spanier, G. (1983). Married and unmarried cohabitation in the United States: 1980. *Journal of Marriage and the Family*, *34*, 277–288.

Sweet, J. A. (1977). Demography and the family. *Annual Review of Sociology*, *3*, 363–405.

Sweet, J. A. (1978). Indicators of family and household structure of racial and ethnic minorities in the United States. In *The demography of racial and ethnic groups*, F. Bean & P. Frisbie (Eds.). New York: Academic Press.

Sweet, J. A. (1989). *Differentials in the approval of cohabitation*. NSFH Working Paper No. 8, National Survey of Families and Households, University of Wisconsin, Madison.

Sweet, J. A., & Bumpass, L. (1974). Differentials in marital instability of the black population: 1970. *Phylon*, *35*(3), 323–332.

Sweet, J. A., & Bumpass, L. (1987). *American families and households*. New York: Russell Sage Foundation.

Sweet, J., & Bumpass, L. (1990a). *Religious differentials in marriage behavior and attitudes*. NSFH Working Paper No. 15, National Survey of Families and Households, University of Wisconsin, Madison.

Sweet J., & Bumpass, L. (1990b). *Young Adults' Views of Marriage, Cohabitation, and Family*. Paper presented at the conference on demographic perspectives on the American family: Patterns and prospects, sponsored by the Department of Sociology, State University of New York at Albany.

Sweet, J., Bumpass, L., & Call, V. (1988). *The design and content of the National Survey of Families and Households*. NSFH 1, Center for Demography and Ecology, University of Wisconsin, Madison.

Tanfer, K. (1987). Patterns of premarital cohabitation among never-married women in the United States. *Journal of Marriage and the Family*, *49*, 483–495.

Teachman, J. D. (1982). Methodological issues in the analysis of family formation and dissolution. *Journal of Marriage and the Family*, *44*, 613–621.

Teachman, J. D. (1983). Early marriage, premarital fertility and marital dissolution. Results for blacks and whites. *Journal of Family Issues*, *4*(1), 105–126.

Thomson, E., & Colella, U. (1990). *Cohabitation and marital stability: Quality or commitment?* NSFH Working Paper No. 23, National Survey of Families and Households, University of Wisconsin, Madison.

Thornton, A. (1988). Cohabitation and marriage in the 1980s. *Demography*, *25*(4), 497–508.

Thornton, A., & Rogers, W. (1987). The influence of individual and historical time on marital dissolution. *Demography*, *24*, 1–22.

U.S. Bureau of the Census. (1989). Marital status and living arrangements: March 1988 (Series P-20, No. 433). Washington, DC: U.S. Department of Commerce.

Weed, J. A. (1980). National estimates of marriage dissolution and survivorship. Vital and Health Statistics (Series 3, No. 19 IV) (DHHS Publication No. PHS 81-1403). Washington, DC: U.S. Dept. of Health and Human Services.

Westoff, C., & Ryder, N. (1977). The contraception revolution. Princeton, NJ: Princeton University Press.

White, L., & Booth, A. (1985). The quality and stability of remarriages: The role of stepchildren. *American Sociological Review, 50,* 689–698.

Wiersma, G. E. (1983). *Cohabitation, an alternative to marriage? A cross-national study. Publications of the Netherlands Interuniversity Demographic Institute and the Population and Family Study Centre* (Vol. 9). Boston: Martinus Nijhoff Publishers.

Willis, R. J., & Michael, R. T. (1988). *Innovation in family formation: Evidence on cohabitation in the U.S.* Paper presented at IUSSP Seminar on the Family, the Market and the state in aging societies, Sendai City, Japan.

Wu, L. L., & Tuma, N. B. (1990). Local hazard models. In C. C. Clogg (Ed.), *Sociological methodology* (pp. 141–180). Oxford: Basil Blackwell.

5
Broken Attachments: Relationship Loss From the Perspective of Attachment Theory

Cindy Hazan and Phillip R. Shaver

Loss is an integral part of close relationships. Death, estrangement, and geographical distance often separate us from those with whom we are close. Relationships are continually being constituted and dissolved. If we are truly to understand close relationships, we must not limit ourselves to studying them only during their constitutive phase but also throughout their natural cycle. As there is much to learn from studying attraction and relationship formation (e.g., Berscheid & Peplau, 1983; Berscheid & Walster, 1978), so there is much to learn from studying relationship dissolution (e.g., Duck, 1982; Hill, Rubin, & Peplau, 1976; Levinger, 1976; Weiss, 1975). As Lewin observed, it is when an entity is moving and changing that its dynamics reveal themselves most clearly (cited in Deutsch, 1954). And as Bowlby (1979) suggests in the title of one of his books, to understand human relationships we must examine both "the making and [the] breaking of affectional bonds."

In this chapter, we examine relationship loss from the perspective of attachment theory (Bowlby, 1969, 1973, 1980), as it applies to infants and young children (e.g., Ainsworth, Blehar, Waters, & Wall, 1978; Bretherton & Waters, 1985; Main & Cassidy, 1988; Sroufe, 1983; Waters & Deane, 1985) and as it applies to adolescents and adults (e.g., Hazan & Shaver, 1987, 1990; Kobak & Sceery, 1988; Main & Goldwyn, 1984; Ricks, 1985; Weiss, 1982). Although many relationships qualify as close, we limit our discussion to *attachment* relationships (described more fully later)—the central and most profound class of close relationships, such as those between parents and children and between adult partners.

Attachment theory emphasizes the full cycle of relationships—their formation, maintenance, and dissolution—and the defining features of an attachment relationship include reactions to both the presence and absence of an attachment figure. In fact, it is difficult to discuss the function or dynamics of attachment without considering loss. The behavioral system that regulates attachment feelings and behaviors includes "built-in" responses to loss, and the primary motive for creating attachment theory in the first place was to explain children's reactions to separation from their mothers (Bowlby, 1958, 1969).

The process of mourning a loss is something that most of us take for granted. We are not shocked by a mourner's rage and desperation at the sudden death of a beloved. We anticipate the sadness and despair of the recently widowed. We are not surprised when a newly separated friend has difficulty sleeping or concentrating. To understand loss, however, we must look beneath the surface, see beyond what most of us take for granted. What explains the way we respond?

Our goal in this chapter is to answer this question. We begin with a definition of attachment and an overview of attachment theory, followed by a description of childhood responses to separation and loss. This was attachment theory's major purview in the beginning, and there is still more known about children from an attachment point of view than is known about adults. Next, we consider responses to loss in adulthood, focusing on both bereavement and estrangement, which bear striking similarities to childhood reactions. Following the discussion of normative responses to loss, we describe the major individual differences. This is where some of the most recent research has been done and where a host of answerable questions have yet to be addressed. Finally, we briefly consider loneliness as the natural consequence of relationship loss. Throughout the chapter, we illustrate our argument with excerpts from interviews and various works of literature. Loss has inspired not only grieving but art as well.

Attachment Relationships

According to attachment theory, humans are innately predisposed to form close relationships, and behavior in such relationships is regulated in part by a set of innate behavioral systems. The primary job of the attachment system, at least in infancy, is to regulate proximity to the attachment figure. Using concepts borrowed from control systems theory (e.g., G. A. Miller, Galanter, & Pribram, 1960; Young, 1964), it can be said that the attachment system includes a "set-goal" for proximity. The set-goal functions somewhat like a thermostat: When the room temperature drops below a set temperature, the heat comes on; once the set temperature is reached, the heat goes off. The attachment system is activated whenever distance from the attachment figure exceeds the set-goal for proximity, such as when the attachment figure changes location or disappears from sight, or when environmental conditions change in an unexpected and/or threatening way. Once activated, the system triggers a series of behaviors (e.g., calling, crawling, clinging) that serve to reestablish proximity. Bowlby (1973) refers to these attachment behaviors as "separation protest," and such behavior distinguishes attachments from other kinds of close relationships. As long as an infant is within the set range of the attachment figure, there is no special effort exerted to increase proximity, and attention can be directed elsewhere.

In addition to the separation–protest feature, attachment relationships are functionally distinct from other close relationships. Attachments serve two functions: They provide a "safe haven" to which to retreat (Bowlby, 1969) and a "secure base" from which to engage in activity (Ainsworth, 1967; Ainsworth et al., 1978). A central tenet of attachment theory is that the features and functions of attachment relationships are essentially the same "from the cradle to the grave" (Bowlby, 1977). Other aspects of attachment change dramatically with physical and psychological development. For example, the distance from the attachment figure that can be comfortably tolerated (i.e., the set-goal for proximity) increases steadily from infancy through childhood and adolescence. In addition, psychological closeness takes on increasing importance relative to physical closeness (Main, Kaplan, & Cassidy, 1985), although the need for physical closeness never disappears entirely.

Perhaps the most significant change in attachment between infancy and adulthood is a structural one. Infants and children are attached to their care givers; that is, they use their care givers as havens of safety and secure bases for exploration and protest separation from them. Care givers, however, are not normally attached, in the technical sense, to their infants or children. The relationship is complementary, with attachment figures providing, but generally not receiving, care. In adulthood, attachment relationships are usually more reciprocal, with the partners serving as care givers for, and seeking care from (i.e., being attached to), each other, and also typically involve sex. The prototypical adult attachment relationship is thus structurally more complex, involving the integration of at least three behavioral systems: attachment, care giving, and sexual mating (Shaver, Hazan, & Bradshaw, 1988).

Within an attachment theoretical framework, *love* refers to a relationship that involves one or more of these behavioral systems. Love of parent implicates the attachment system; love of offspring, the care-giving system; and being passionately "in love," the sexual mating system. In other words, attachment, care giving, and sexual mating may be conceptualized as three different *types* of love, or as the *components* of the prototypical adult love relationship. (See Sternberg, 1986, for a similar componential approach.)

In infancy and childhood, the primary attachment figure is usually a parent, most often the mother. By late adolescence or early adulthood, the attachment figure of infancy and childhood is replaced by a peer (Hazan & Hutt, 1990; Weiss, 1982). This does not mean that parents are relinquished as attachment figures. Rather, their position in the hierarchy of attachment figures changes.

The process of becoming attached is strikingly similar for individuals of all ages. First, a potential attachment figure is targeted. Though the characteristics of the target person no doubt vary tremendously across individuals and available partners, attachment theory suggests that this person will be perceived as potentially available, responsive, and "wiser." For infants, this could include any older child or adult, whereas for adults it may include anyone who possesses a valued quality or skill. Efforts are then directed toward maintaining proximity to, and attracting the attention of, that individual (Bowlby, 1979). In infancy and childhood, proximity seeking results mostly from fear, while in adulthood it is primarily motivated by sexual attraction.

Whether the relationship involves an infant–care-giver pair or an adult couple, responsiveness is critically important. It is the primary determinant of the quality of attachment between infants and care givers (Ainsworth et al., 1978) and an important feature of interpersonal attraction among adults (Aron, Dutton, Aron, & Iverson, 1989; Berscheid & Walster, 1978; Rubin, 1973). Responsiveness of the target person usually evokes feelings of joy, security, and confidence; unresponsiveness commonly results in anxiety and obsessive preoccupation (Tennov, 1979). Interactions between individuals who are becoming attached are also similar in infancy and adulthood in that they typically involve extended mutual gazing and unique physical closeness (Robson, 1967; Rubin, 1974; Sroufe, 1983). (See Shaver et al., 1988, for a more complete list of similarities.)

The attached individual gradually contructs a mental representation or "internal working model" of the target person or attachment figure through a process analogous to imprinting. (This may be the purpose of all that mutual gazing and intimate personal storytelling.) This working model includes information about how likely it is that an attachment figure will be accessible and responsive. It is jointly determined by the innate predisposition to form attachments and the experiences one has actually had in attachment relationships (Bretherton, 1987; Main et al., 1985). Bowlby (1973) calls the models "tolerably accurate reflections" of actual experience. Any continuity in the quality of attachments that an individual forms at different ages is assumed to be mediated by these models as they influence social information processing, emotional regulation, and behavior in close relationships.

Responses to Loss During Childhood

When the attachment system is activated and attachment behaviors are triggered, they continue to be engaged until sufficient proximity to an attachment figure has been established. For an average infant on an average day, this can usually be accomplished simply by calling out, crying briefly, or crawling to the care giver. But how does the system respond when the care giver is unavailable for an extended period of time, perhaps indefinitely? It was while observing children in just such situations that Bowlby in the late 1940s and early 1950s first began to formulate his theory.

Much of the early theorizing about childhood grief came from clinical cases of young children housed in residential nurseries in London (Bowlby, 1953; Heinicke, 1956; Robertson, 1953; Spitz, 1953). Many observers were struck by the intensity of the children's initial reactions to separation and were surprised by its lasting effects. In addition, they were impressed by the strong similarity of response across children, which seemed to follow an invariant sequence.

First, there was an initial *protest* response, characterized by anxiety and anger, and a preoccupation with and search for the care giver—behaviors that, under different circumstances, would probably have the desired effect of locating mother or attracting her attention. Despite the fact that the nursery staff was generally competent and willing to provide care, the children were inconsolable. Those who were reunited with their mothers during this phase showed prolonged effects of the separation. For at least several months afterward, the children were unusually anxious and clingy. They sought constant and close proximity to their care givers and were difficult to reassure. Here is an example of a 16-month-old girl, Dawn, who had spent 15 days in a residential nursery:

During the first day Dawn was active and fairly cheerful, apparently unaware of the situation. Next morning, however, she cried desperately for "Mummy, Daddy." For long periods she stood by the door through which her father had disappeared. Attempts by staff to comfort her were to no avail. During the next three days she continued to fret inconsolably and was to be seen much of the time standing near the door. (Bowlby, 1980, p. 421)

Even the *threat* of loss can provoke clingy protest behavior. The following example appears in Bowlby's (1973) volume on separation:

A mother denies using threats and then corrects herself: "No—oh, I tell a lie, I once did—and upset her that much that I've never said it any more." (What did you say?) "Well, she was having an argument with me, and she says to me, 'You don't live here. Hop it!' So I says, 'Oh, well, I can do that! Where's my coat? I'm moving!' So I got my coat from the back, and I was gone. I just stood outside the door, and she cried so bitter, she did. As soon as I came in, she got hold of my leg and wouldn't let go, sort of thing. I'll *never* say it no more." (p. 228)

For the children who were not reunited with care givers, the protest behavior eventually subsided, either from fatigue or from the realization that the behavior was futile. The intense activity eventually gave way to *despair*, a phase characterized by withdrawal, passivity, and depression. Bowlby borrowed from Anna Freud and Dorothy Burlingham (1943) an example of 3-year-old Patrick, a boy who had been taken from his mother on previous occasions and sent to a foster-home, and into a hospital (with measles). At the time of Freud and Burlingham's observations, he was in a residential nursery and separated from his mother, who was physically ill. At first, he insisted vigorously that his mother would come and pick him up, put on his coat, and take him home. Gradually, he substituted highly visible dressing gestures for words. Still later,

what showed as an expressive movement one day was reduced the next to a mere abortive flicker of his fingers. While the other children were mostly busy with their toys, playing games, making music, etc., Patrick, totally uninterested, would stand somewhere in a corner, moving his hands and lips with an absolutely tragic expression on his face. (Bowlby, 1980, p. 12)

If left alone for an extended period of time, most children in the nursery began to come out of depression and despair, began to eat and sleep normally again, and appeared to have recovered. It was only when some of the "recovered" children returned home that this interpretation was called into question. What had looked like adaptation was actually something more like emotional distancing. The children who appeared to have recovered from the separation avoided contact with their care givers. They had entered a psychologically defensive phase which Bowlby called *detachment*.

Owen was aged 2 years and 2 months at the start of what proved to be an 11-week separation. Both during the journey home with his father and after he had entered the house and met mother he remained characteristically numb, silent, and unresponsive. . . . Then, and during the next couple of days, he began some-times to turn to his father; but his mother he continued to ignore. During his second day home he bumped his knee and, when he seemed about to cry, mother at once offered comfort. Owen however passed her by and went to father instead. (Heinicke & Westheimer, 1966, quoted in Bowlby, 1980, p. 21)

Responses to Loss in Adulthood

Although attachment theory is explicitly a life-span theory, for many years, empirical studies of attachment were limited to infants and mothers. This is likely due to Bowlby's emphasis on the importance of the first attachment relationship for the formation of lasting internal working models. His initial formulation of the theory appeared under the title, "The Nature of the Child's Tie to His Mother" (Bowlby, 1958). The exclusive focus on infancy was additionally facilitated by the development of a paradigm for assessing infant attachment (Ainsworth et al., 1978) and the lack of procedures for assessing attachment beyond infancy.

The first efforts to test the life-span implications of attachment theory were made by Parkes (1972) and Weiss (1975). They, like Bowlby, started with loss. Weiss primarily investigated loss due to divorce; Parkes studied bereavement in widows and widowers. Later, Shaver and Rubenstein (1980) demonstrated a link between childhood experiences of loss and subsequent adult loneliness.

Loss That Is Due to Death

Although there is tremendous cultural variation in the rituals and customs surrounding death, the human response to the demise of an attachment figure hardly varies (Gorer, 1973; Marris, 1958; S. I. Miller & Schoenfeld, 1973; Palgi, 1973). The contemporary anthropologist Renato Rosaldo (1989), known generally for talking about cultural differences in emotional reactions, learned about the power and uniformity of grief reactions when his wife unexpectedly died in an accident while they were engaged in fieldwork:

Immediately upon finding her body I became enraged. How could she abandon me? How could she have been so stupid as to fall? . . . Powerful visceral emotional states swept over me, at times separately and at other times together. I experienced the deep cutting pain of sorrow almost beyond endurance, the cadaverous cold of realizing the finality of death . . . the mournful keening that started without my willing, and frequent tearful sobbing. (p. 9)

The way in which adults respond to loss of an attachment figure is not essentially different from the way children, the world over, respond (Bowlby, 1980; Heinecke & Westheimer, 1966; Parkes & Weiss, 1983). After a brief period of numbness in cases of unexpected death, adults normally enter a phase of intense protest behavior. Individuals report feeling agitated, anxious, and preoccupied with thoughts of the lost partner, coupled with a compulsion to search for him or her, as though trying to undo the loss even when it is obviously irreversible. It is not uncommon for individuals to be drawn to places where the partner used to go or even to the partner's gravesite. Lindemann (1944) observed in the widows he studied a marked "restlessness, inability to sit still, moving about in an aimless fashion, continually searching for something to do. There is, however, at the same time, a painful lack of capacity to initiate and maintain normal patterns of activity" (p. 148). Parkes (1972) studied London widows and found them

drawn to places associated with their husband . . . most were reluctant to leave the home where he had lived; they treasured possessions and parts of the house that were especially "his," and tended to return repeatedly to them. . . . One of these terminated a visit to her sister prematurely because she felt that she had left her husband too long. (p. 50)

Widowed partners often find it difficult to inhibit care-giving impulses. Parkes (1972) reported that, "One widow felt concern for her deceased husband whenever the weather was inclement. 'It's terrible if it's raining. It's as if I want to pick him up and bring him home'" (p. 51).

Occasionally, the normal but generally inarticulate yearnings of the bereaved can be expressed in art. In "The Going," written in the months following the death of his wife, Thomas Hardy describes his experiences of searching:

Why do you make me leave the house
And think for a breath it is you I see
At the end of the alley of bending boughs
Where so often at dusk you used to be;
    Till in the darkening dankness
    The yawning blankness
Of the perspective sickens me!

In a letter written by D. H. Lawrence 5 days after the death of his mother, with whom he had had a very close and somewhat disturbed relationship, he says:

I am so miserable without my "matouchka." When I am not in good health my mind repeatedly presents me a picture: no matter what my thoughts are, or what I am doing, the image of a memory floats up. This afternoon, it is just the winsome, wavy grey hairs at my mother's temple, and her hand under her cheek as she lay. (Lawrence quoted in Aberbach, 1989, p. 40)

For most mourners, realization that the loss cannot be recovered results in deep sadness and despair. The intense activity and rumination of the protest phase give way to lethargy and depression. Many widows and widowers report being incapable of getting out of bed, unconcerned about responsibilities or personal appearance, and a general lack of interest in life and other people (Parkes, 1972). The despair lasts an average of a few weeks or months before the process of recovery begins.

From an attachment-theoretical perspective, the goal of healthy mourning is to achieve an adaptive degree of "detachment" from the lost partner and a return to ordinary living. Weiss (1988) argues that the process of recovery from the loss of an attachment figure actually involves three separate processes. First, individuals grieving a lost attachment figure are highly motivated to develop a causal explanation of the loss, the outcome of a process of *cognitive acceptance*. The absence of a satisfactory account of how and why (maybe even whether, as in the case of the wives of soldiers "missing in action") the loss occurred may inhibit further recovery. (For more on the nature and value of accounts of traumatic experiences, see Harvey, Orbuch, & Weber, 1990, and Chapter 10 in this volume.)

If the loss can be understood and accepted cognitively, the groundwork is laid for the process of *emotional acceptance*. For the loss to be emotionally accepted, memories of the partner must be "neutralized" (Weiss, 1988), or "decathected," as S. Freud (1917–1955) put it. Neutralization can be facilitated by recalling memories one by one until habituation to each is achieved or until the memories are no longer paralyzingly painful. The process of neutralization may require many months or years, and vulnerability to momentary remorse or distress may last almost indefinitely. As widows and widowers sometimes say, "You never get over it, you just get used to it" (Weiss, 1988). Anniversaries tend to serve as reminders that the pain may never disappear completely.

Finally, individuals must undergo some degree of *identity change*. This involves developing a new image of the self that reflects the reality of the changed circumstances. To the extent that a person understands and accepts both the loss and its myriad implications, recovery has occurred. It is evidenced in a certain degree of freedom from distress, the ability to attend to the business of life, and a capacity for joy and hopefulness, perhaps even a new relationship. According to one estimate, return to preloss functioning takes, on average, 3 or 4 years (Glick, Weiss, & Parkes, 1974).

Loss That Is Due to Estrangement

When the loss of an attachment relationship results from estrangement rather than death, the sequence of response is very similar, presumably because the unavailability of the partner, for whatever reason, activates the attachment system. Still, responses to estrangement differ in important ways from responses to death.

Unlike death, estrangement is typically a voluntary loss, at least for the "leaver" as opposed to the "left." The process of detachment on the part of the leaver commonly begins in secret (Vaughan, 1986). This allows for a very gradual breaking away, which is undoubtedly less painful than sudden loss. As they contemplate ending the relationship, leavers experience the kind of anxiety that characterizes attachment-system activation. Most report alternating frequently between wanting to separate from the partner and panicking at the thought of losing the relationship. A 30-year-old woman told Weiss (1975, p. 25):

When the idea occurred to me that I could live without Dave and be happier, my immediate next feeling was just gut fear. It's really hard to explain. It was just terror. I would think that you would start feeling happy if you would feel you could maybe make a better life without somebody. But my whole instinct was just fear.

Such vacillation can continue all the way to, and through, the separation. Here is a painfully humorous example from Weiss's study (1975, p. 46):

Wednesday afternoon I had the second of two conferences with my husband and his lawyer and my lawyer and myself. At the end of the second one I told my lawyer that I was not going to do that any more. In preparation for seeing him I had gotten myself as beautiful as I could. And I felt that as long as my husband was in the room, I felt protected, and that it was just the two of us, not the lawyers. And, midnight, I was sitting in bed, eating vegetable soup, my first meal of the day, and I wanted to call him and say, "What a colossal mistake we've made. I only feel together when I'm with you."

Eventually, the panic causes either a revaluing of the relationship and a resolution to stay with the partner, or it gives way to sadness over the realization that the relationship cannot be saved. When loss seems inevitable, the leaver can begin the process of detachment even before the actual separation occurs. Recovery, in this case, also requires both emotional and cognitive acceptance, as well as a change in identity (or working models) to reflect the impending change in relationship status. Identity change can be accomplished by, for example, forming new friendships that exclude the partner, participating in recreational activities that are unlikely to interest the partner, or more subtly, using "I" rather than "we" language (Vaughan, 1986).

The eventual separation often comes as a surprise to the partner. Although the *sequence* of responses is typically similar to what has been experienced by the leaver, it is likely to be much more intense (Vaughan, 1986). The partner who is left behind does not have the same options to "try out" separation or to work on developing a new identity before it is needed.

Another important difference compared with death-related loss is that, in the case of estrangement, the lost attachment is potentially recoverable. When the attachment system is activated, the natural response is to seek proximity to the attachment figure, and this seems to happen whether establishing proximity is possible or not. The fact that an estranged partner may still be attainable can foster not only hope but protracted protest (Weiss, 1975, 1988). Movement toward recovery may thus be hindered. In some cases, chronic activation of the attachment system in the absence of the former partner may result in premature attachment to another person. A likely candidate would be an individual providing support and care during a difficult time.

Recently separated individuals report occasional intense, though short-lived, feelings of euphoria (Bowlby, 1980; Weiss, 1988). For the partner who has been left, this somewhat mysterious deviation from negative emotions tends to follow relatively trivial but successful coping experiences. One man recalled waking at 4:00 in the morning and thinking about his estranged wife:

I couldn't get back to sleep. I got out of bed and made myself follow my morning routine. I straightened out the apartment and washed the dishes. I got dressed and went out. It was still early so I started to walk, instead of taking the bus. It was a brisk, snowy morning, just after dawn. I suddenly felt happy. I had gotten myself through the night. I was going to see people during the day. I was all right. It was a fine world. (Weiss, 1975, p. 54)

For the partner who initiated the separation, euphoria also results from feeling that the self is competent to face the challenges of life alone and from fantasizing about the wonderful life and exciting new relationships that lie ahead.

By the time a couple decides to separate, all former fondness and affection may have eroded. For this reason many newly separated individuals, especially those who initiated the separation, are surprised when they begin to experience intense anxiety and a compulsion to be near the former partner. One of Weiss's subjects traveled across the continent from his estranged wife to see a former girlfriend: "Here I was, three days with someone of the opposite sex, trying to start rebuilding, and I just got overwhelmed with panic at being three thousand miles from Laura" (Weiss, 1975, p. 49). Weiss argues that this very common feeling is due to the persistence of attachment and suggests that an attachment bond can be broken only by an extended period of psychological and/or physical distance.

Psychological Loss and Individual Differences in Attachment

When Bowlby identified the protest–despair–detachment response to loss, he was observing the behavior of children who had been *physically* separated from their mothers. In the first laboratory tests of attachment theory, Ainsworth and her colleagues (1978) discovered that the effects of *psychological* distance are similar.

In studying the quality of attachment between infants and their mothers, Ainsworth identified three primary patterns, one *secure* and two insecure patterns: *insecure–resistant* and *insecure–avoidant*. These patterns were revealed in the infants' behavior in a laboratory "strange situation," where many aspects of attachment were noted, especially the behavior the infants displayed in response to brief separations from mother. Securely attached infants were distressed by the brief separations; they typically abandoned any exploratory activity and cried. When mother returned, however, the securely attached infants were easily comforted and quickly resumed exploration. Insecure–resistant infants showed signs of distress even before separation and on reunion appeared alternately angry and afraid. The typical insecure–resistant infant was too preoccupied with mother to spend much if any time exploring. Infants exhibiting the insecure–avoidant pattern did not appear distressed by the separation and did not seek proximity to mother on reunion. Instead, they focused their attention on the available toys (Ainsworth et al., 1978).

It was possible to explain the three observed patterns of attachment in terms of experience. Before their visit to the laboratory when the infants were 12 months of age, the infant–mother dyads had been naturalistically observed at home on a regular basis. Infants who appeared securely attached in the laboratory had experienced consistent responsiveness from their mothers. In contrast, the insecurely attached infants had not received such consistent or responsive care. Mothers of the insecure–resistant infants had been inconsistent in their responses, sometimes ignoring their infants' bids for closeness, sometimes responding effectively, and sometimes intrusively imposing affection when the infants were engaged in play. Mothers of the insecure–avoidant infants were consistently unresponsive and appeared to find physical contact with their infants aversive.

In terms of attachment theory, the infants' experiences with their attachment figures had taught them what to expect whenever they sought proximity. Such expectations form the basis of internal working models. There is considerable evidence that working models of attachment, like any well-rehearsed cognitive schema, tend to be stable (Erikson, Sroufe, & Egeland, 1985; Hazan & Hutt, 1989; Main et al., 1985; Waters, Wippman, & Sroufe, 1979). Recent research by Main et al. (1985), Kobak and Sceery (1988), and us (e.g., Hazan & Shaver, 1987, 1990) indicates that the same three patterns of attachment also characterize relationship functioning in adolescence and adulthood.

In the case of secure attachment, working models are organized around the expectation that attachment figures will be reliably available and responsive. In the case of insecure attachment, working models are organized around the expectation that attachment figures may *not* be available and responsive; in other words, they are organized around the *anticipation of loss*. The three patterns of attachment reflect the functioning of the attachment behavioral system, as summarized in Figure 5.1. Insecure–resistant, or anxious–ambivalent, infants can be thought of as stuck in a state of attachment system activation, a chronic panic and protest loop. The attachment figure's unpredictable availability keeps the infants hopeful and persistent. In contrast, the behavior of the insecure–avoidant infants is functionally equivalent to defensive detachment. Their primary care givers have been, for all intents and purposes, psychologically absent.

Individual Differences in Response to Loss

Some individuals fail to recover from the loss of an attachment relationship, especially those who are insecurely attached (Bowlby, 1980, 1988). For example, Bowlby (1980) described two forms of "disordered mourning": chronic mourning and the absence of conscious grieving. Chronic mourning is essentially persistent protest accompanied by feelings of anxiety and anger or an inability to overcome depression and despair. It seems likely that anxious–ambivalent adults would be most

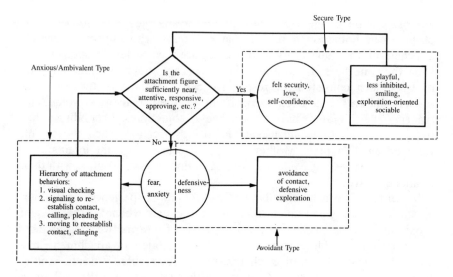

FIGURE 5.1. Dynamics of attachment.

vulnerable to such chronic mourning. This notion is supported by M. Main's (personal communication, 1988) finding that unresolved grief is associated with anxious-resistant or "preoccupied" attachment. The absence of conscious grieving is essentially a premature movement to the detachment phase characterized by pathological self-sufficiency and flat affect. Results from a recent study of the breakup of dating relationships (Simpson, 1990) suggest that avoidant individuals are most prone to premature detachment.

The Probability of Loss

As mentioned, insecure attachment involves the anticipation (and fear) of loss, and ironically it is insecure individuals who are more prone to *experience* relationship losses. Insecurely attached infants experience more rejection from their primary care givers (Ainsworth et al., 1978; Main & Stadtman, 1981), and insecurely attached preschoolers are more likely to be rejected by their peers (Main & Weston, 1981; Sroufe, 1983). Insecure attachment in adulthood is associated with a higher rate of divorce and shorter lived romantic relationships (Hazan & Shaver, 1987). In addition, insecurely attached adults are less competent in providing care to their partners (Kobak & Hazan, 1990), which contributes to relationship dissatisfaction and dissolution.

Just as some people are especially susceptible to broken attachments, breakups are probably more likely to occur at certain junctures in a relationship. It is well-documented that the intense passion that typifies new romantic pairings eventually wanes (Reedy, Birren, & Schaie, 1981; Shaver & Hazan, 1988; Sternberg, 1986). This early passionate phase is what is generally refered to as being "in love" or, as Tennov (1979) calls it, "limerent." Once the passion has faded or subsided, a couple must have something else to keep them together, such as an attachment bond. One might predict that separations would be more likely to occur at the point in the relationship when passion begins to wane. Best estimates are that the passionate phase lasts at most 2 or 3 years (Tennov, 1979), though it must certainly pass more quickly in the case of adolescents, whose average romantic relationship endures a few weeks or months (Hill et al., 1976).

It is interesting to note that while the rate of divorce in Western countries has increased dramatically in recent decades (Burgess, 1981; Norton & Glick, 1979), the profile of divorce has hardly changed at all. There is still a global peak in relationship breakups at 4 years, a phenomenon only half-facetiously labeled the "4 year itch" (Fisher, 1987). It takes 2 to 3 years for passion to fade, and it may take about that long for an attachment bond to be fully formed. In children there is a marked shift in attention away from mother and toward peers at around 3 years of age (Bowlby, 1969). Moreover, Parkes and Weiss (1983) found that divorced individuals who had been married for 2 years or less showed a relative lack of suffering, perhaps an indication that an attachment had not yet been formed.

Loneliness as Protest Without an Object

Weiss (1973) identified two types of loneliness. One type, which he calls social isolation, is the kind of loneliness felt in the absence of a social network or community involvement. The symptoms of social isolation are similar to what children experience when they are without playmates, feelings Rubenstein and Shaver (1982) called "impatient boredom." Weiss calls the other type of loneliness emotional isolation, a feeling one experiences in the absence of an attachment relationship. Its symptoms closely resemble the symptoms of attachment system activation, including anxiety and fear. Loneliness that is due to the absence of an attachment relationship is like protest without an object. Weiss (1973) has pointed out that trying to cure loneliness of the social isolation type with an attachment relationship, or to sooth the loneliness of emotional isolation with new friendships, rarely works. This suggests that recovery from loss, as accomplished by emotional detachment from a lost partner, may serve simply to land one back where one started—in protest, only this time without a specific person toward whom to direct attachment behaviors.

Conclusion

The breaking of an attachment bond evokes distinct feelings and behaviors that vary little across age and culture. The first response is one of panic and often irrational attempts to reestablish contact. When this is not possible, most individuals sadly withdraw and, with time and distance, adjust to the loss and perhaps establish new attachments. The universal nature of human response to close relationship loss is suggestive of inborn predispositions, and one of the pieces of evidence that Bowlby (1980) used to support his claim that attachment is regulated by an innate behavioral system.

It is easy to imagine how the protest–despair–detachment sequence of response to loss would be adaptive. When our basic sense of safety and security is in any way threatened, it makes good sense to drop whatever we are doing and work to reestablish it. But it also makes sense to give up at some point, not to persist to the point of dropping dead from exhaustion but instead to seek comfort and protection elsewhere.

There seems little doubt that close relationships are important for healthy development and adjustment. Unattached individuals are more susceptible to everything from automobile accidents to alcohol abuse (Bloom, Asher, & White, 1978), from dissatisfaction with life (Campbell, 1981) to death from cancer (Goodwin, Hurt, Key, & Sarret, 1987). The grieving and lonely are vulnerable to disease and deterioration, as studies of their hearts and immune systems demonstrate (e.g., Kiecolt-Glaser, Garner, et al., 1984; Kiecolt-Glaser, Ricker, et al., 1984; Lynch, 1977). All this suggests that close relationships satisfy basic human needs, not tremendously different in importance from the need for food and water.

If the function of mourning is detachment, then one can see that loneliness is a useful response. When lonely, we are reminded of our social needs, and we remain somewhat distressed and uncomfortable until we take action to establish a new relationship. Such is the natural cycle of the making and breaking of affectional bonds—a dynamic equilibrium maintained by a behavioral system designed to strike a balance between the costs and benefits of being attached.

Acknowledgment. Preparation of this chapter was facilitated by National Science Foundation grant BSN-8808736.

References

Aberbach, D. (1989). *Surviving trauma: Loss, literature, and psychoanalysis.* New Haven, CT: Yale University Press.

Ainsworth, M. D. (1967). *Infancy in Uganda: Infant care and the growth of love.* Baltimore, MD: Johns Hopkins University Press.

Ainsworth, M. D. S., Blehar, M. C., Waters, E., & Wall, S. (1978). *Patterns of attachment: Assessed in the strange situation and at home.* Hillsdale, NJ: Lawrence Erlbaum.

Aron, A., Dutton, D. G., Aron, E. R., & Iverson, A. (1989). Experiences of falling in love. *Journal of Social and Personal Relationships, 6,* 243–257.

Berscheid, E., & Peplau, L. A. (1983). The emerging science of relationships. In H. H. Kelley, E. Berscheid, A. Christensen, J. H. Harvey, T. L. Huston, G. Levinger, E. McClintock, L. A. Peplau, & D. R. Peterson (Eds.), *Close relationships* (pp. 1–19). New York: Freeman.

Berscheid, E., & Walster, E. (1978). *Interpersonal attraction.* Reading, MA: Addison-Wesley.

Bloom, B., Asher, S. J., & White, S. W. (1978). Marital disruption as a stressor: A review and analysis. *Psychological Bulletin, 85,* 867–894.

Bowlby, J. (1953). Some pathological processes set in train by early mother–child separation. *Journal of Mental Science, 99,* 265–272.

Bowlby, J. (1958). The nature of the child's tie to his mother. *International Journal of Psychoanalysis, 39,* 350–373.

Bowlby, J. (1969). *Attachment and loss: Vol. 1. Attachment.* New York: Basic Books.

Bowlby, J. (1973). *Attachment and loss: Vol. 2. Separation: Anxiety and anger.* New York: Basic Books.

Bowlby, J. (1977). The making and breaking of affectional bonds. *British Journal of Psychiatry, 130,* 201–210, 421–431.

Bowlby, J. (1979). *The making and breaking of affectional bonds.* London: Tavistock.

Bowlby, J. (1980). *Attachment and loss: Vol. 3. Loss: Sadness and depression.* New York: Basic Books.

Bowlby, J. (1988). *A secure base: Parent–child attachment and healthy human development.* New York: Basic Books.

Bretherton, I. (1987). New perspective on attachment relations: Security, Communication, and internal working models. In J. Osofsky (Ed.), *Handbook on infant development.* (2nd ed.) (pp. 1061–1100). New York: John Wiley & Sons.

Bretherton, I., & Waters, E. (Eds.). (1985). Growing points of attachment theory and research. *Monographs of the Society for Research in Child Development, 50*(1–2), v–xi.

Burgess, R. L. (1981). Relationships in marriage and the family. In S. Duck & R. Gilmour (Eds.), *Personal relationships 1. Studying personal relationships* (pp. 179–196). New York: Academic Press.

Campbell, A. (1981). *The sense of well being in America: Patterns and trends.* New York: McGraw-Hill.

Deutsch, M. (1954). Field theory in social psychology. In G. Lindzey (Ed.), *Handbook of social psychology.* Reading, MA: Addison-Wesley.

Duck, S. (Ed.) (1982). *Personal relationships 4: Dissolving personal relationships.* London: Academic Press.

Erickson, M. F., Sroufe, L. A., & Egeland, B. (1985). The relationship between quality of attachment and behavior problems in preschool in a high-risk sample. *Monographs of the Society for Research in Child Development, 50*(1–2), 147–166.

Fisher, H. E. (1987). The four-year itch: Do divorce patterns reflect our evolutionary heritage? *Natural History*, *10*, 22–25.

Freud, A., & Burlingham, D. (1943). *War and children*. New York: International Universities Press.

Freud, S. (1917/1919). Mourning and melancholia. In J. Strachey (1955) (Ed. and Trans.), *The standard edition of the complete psychological works of Sigmund Freud* (Vol. 18, pp. 67–143). London: Hogarth Press. (Original work published 1917)

Glick, I., Weiss, R. S., & Parkes, C. M. (1974). *The first year of bereavement*. New York: Wiley-Interscience.

Goodwin, J. S., Hurt, W. C., Key, C. R., & Sarret, J. M. (1987). The effect of marital status on stage, treatment and survival of cancer patients. *Journal of the American Medical Association*, *258*, 3125–3130.

Gorer, G. (1973). Death, grief and mourning in Britain. In E. J. Anthony & C. Koupernik (Eds.). *The child in his family: The impact of disease and death*, New York: Wiley.

Hardy, T. (1912–1913). The going. In J. Gibson (Ed.), *The complete poems of Thomas Hardy*. (1976) London, England: Macmillan.

Harvey, J. H., Orbuch, T. L., & Weber, A. L. (1990). A social psychological model of account-making in response to severe stress. *Journal of Language and Social Psychology*, *9*, 191–207.

Hazan, C., & Hutt, M. J. (1989, October). *Continuity and change in inner working models of attachment*. Paper presented at the meeting of the Society for Experimental Social Psychology, Santa Monica, CA.

Hazan, C., & Hutt, M. J. (1990). *From parent to peer: Transition in attachment*. Unpublished manuscript.

Hazan, C., & Shaver, P. R. (1987). Romantic love conceptualized as an attachment process. *Journal of Personality and Social Psychology*, *52*, 511–524.

Hazan, C., & Shaver, P. R. (1990). Love and work: An attachment-theoretical perspective. *Journal of Personality and Social Psychology*, *59*, 270–280.

Heinicke, C. M. (1956). Some effects of separating two-year-old children from their parents: A comparative study. *Human Relations*, *9*, 105–176.

Heinicke, C. M., & Westheimer, I. (1966). *Brief separations*. New York: International Universities Press.

Hill, C. T., Rubin, Z., & Peplau, L. A. (1976). Breakups before marriage: The end of 103 affairs. *Journal of Social Issues*, *32*, 147–168.

Kiecolt-Glaser, J. K., Garner, W., Speicher, C., Penn, G. M., Holliday, J., & Glaser, R. (1984, January–February). Psychological modifiers of immunocompetence in medical students. *Psychosomatic Medicine*, *46*, 7–14.

Kiecolt-Glaser, J. K., Ricker, D., George, J., Messick, G., Speicher, G. E., Garner, W., & Glaser, R. (1984, January–February). Urinary cortisol levels, cellular immunocompetence, and loneliness in psychiatric inpatients. *Psychosomatic Medicine*, *46*, 15–23.

Kobak, R. R., & Hazan, C. (1990). *Working models in marital relationships: The role of attachment in communication and relationship satisfaction*. Unpublished manuscript.

Kobak, R. R., & Sceery, A. (1988). The transition to college: Working models of attachment, affect regulation, and perceptions of self and others. *Child Development*, *88*, 135–146.

Levinger, G. (1976). A social psychological perspective on marital dissolution. *Journal of Social Issues*, *32*, 21–47.

Lindemann, E. (1944). Symptomatology and management of acute grief. *American Journal of Psychiatry*, *101*, 141–149.

Lynch, J. J. (1977). *The broken heart: The medical consequences of loneliness*. New York: Basic Books.

Main, M., & Cassidy, J. (1988). Categories of response to reunion with the parent at age 6: Predictable from infant attachment classifications and stable over a 1-month period. *Developmental Psychology*, *24*, 1–12.

Main, M., & Goldwyn, R. (1984). Predicting rejection of her infant from mother's representation of her own experience: Implications for the abused-abusing intergenerational cycle. *Child Abuse and Neglect*, *8*, 203–217.

Main, M., Kaplan, N., & Cassidy, J. (1985). Security in infancy, childhood, and adulthood: A move to the level of representation. *Monographs of the Society for Research in Child Development*, *50*(1–2), 66–104.

Main, M., & Stadtman, J. (1981). Infant response to rejection of physical contact by the mother: Aggression, avoidance, and conflict. *Journal of the American Academy of Child Psychiatry*, *20*, 292–307.

Main, M., & Weston, D. (1981). The quality of the toddler's relationship to mother and father: Related to conflict behavior and the readiness to establish new relationships. *Child Development*, *52*, 932–940.

Marris, P. (1958). *Widows and their families*. London: Routledge & Kegan Paul.

Miller, G. A., Galanter, E., & Pribram, K. H. (1960). *Plans and the structure of behavior*. New York: Holt, Rinehart & Winston.

Miller, S. I., & Schoenfeld, L. (1973). Grief in the Navajo: Psychodynamics and culture. *International Journal of Psychiatry*, *19*, 187–191.

Norton, A. J., & Glick, P. C. (1979). Marital instability in America: Past, present, and future. In G. Levinger & O. C. Moles (Eds.), *Divorce and separation*. New York: Basic Books.

Palgi, P. (1973). The socio-cultural expressions and implications of death, mourning and bereavement arising out of the war situation in Israel. *Israel Annals of Psychiatry*, *11*, 301–329.

Parkes, C. M. (1972). *Bereavement*. New York: International Universities Press.

Parkes, C. M., & Weiss, R. S. (1983). *Recovery from bereavement*. New York: Basic Books.

Reedy, M. N., Birren, J. E., & Schaie, K. W. (1981). Age and sex differences in satisfying love relationships across the adult life span. *Human Development*, *24*, 52–66.

Ricks, M. H. (1985). The social transmission of parental behavior: Attachment across generations. *Monographs of the Society for Research in Child Development*, *50*(1–2), 211–227.

Robertson, J. (1953). Some responses of young children to loss of maternal care. *Nursing Times*, *49*, 382–386.

Robson, K. S. (1967). The role of eye-to-eye contact in maternal–infant attachment. *Journal of Child Psychology and Psychiatry*, *8*, 13–25.

Rosaldo, R. (1989). *Culture and truth: The remaking of social analysis*. Boston: Beacon Press.

Rubenstein, C., & Shaver, P. (1982). *In search of intimacy*. New York: Delacorte.

Rubin, Z. (1973). *Liking and loving*. New York: Holt, Rinehart & Winston.

Rubin, Z. (1974). Lovers and other strangers: The development of intimacy in encounters and relationships. *American Scientist*, *62*, 182–190.

Shaver, P. R., & Hazan, C. (1988). A biased overview of the study of love. *Journal of Social and Personal Relationships*, *5*, 473–501.

Shaver, P. R., Hazan, C., & Bradshaw, D. (1988). Love as attachment: The integration of three behavioral systems. In R. J. Sternberg & M. L. Barnes (Eds.), *The psychology of love* (pp. 68–99). New Haven, CT: Yale University Press.

Shaver, P. R., & Rubenstein, C. (1980). Childhood attachment experience and adult loneliness. In L. Wheeler (Ed.), *Review of personality and social psychology* (Vol. 1, pp. 42–73). Beverly Hills, CA: Sage.

Simpson, J. (1990). The influence of attachment styles on romantic relationships. *Journal of Personality and Social Psychology*, *59*, 971–980.

Spitz, R. A. (1953). Aggression: Its role in the establishment of object relations. In R. M. Loewenstein (Ed.), *Drives, affects and behaviour*. New York: International Universities Press.

Sroufe, L. A. (1983). Infant–caregiver attachment and patterns of adaptation in preschool: The roots of maladaptation and competence. In M. Perlmutter (Ed.), *Minnesota symposium on child psychology* (Vol. 16, pp. 41–83). Hillsdale, NJ: Lawrence Erlbaum.

Sternberg, R. J. (1986). A triangular theory of love. *Psychological Review*, *93*, 119–135.

Tennov, D. (1979). *Love and limerence: The experience of being in love*. New York: Stein & Day.

Vaughan, D. (1986). *Uncoupling: How relationships come apart*. Oxford: Oxford University Press.

Waters, E., & Deane, K. E. (1985). Defining and assessing individual differences in attachment relationships: Q-methodology and the organization of behavior in infancy and early childhood. *Monographs of the Society for Research in Child Development*, *50*(1–2), 41–65.

Waters, E., Wippman, J., & Sroufe, A. (1979). Attachment, positive affect, and competence in the peer group: Two studies in construct validation. *Child Development*, *50*, 821–829.

Weiss, R. S. (1973). *Loneliness: The experience of emotional and social isolation*. Cambridge, MA: MIT Press.

Weiss, R. S. (1975). *Marital separation*. New York: Basic Books.

Weiss, R. S. (1982). Attachment in adults. In C. M. Parkes & J. Stevenson-Hinde (Eds.), *The place of attachment in human behavior* (pp. 171–184). New York: Basic Books.

Weiss, R. S. (1988). Loss and recovery. *Journal of Social Issues*, *44*, 37–52.

Young, J. Z. (1964). *A model of the brain*. London, England: Oxford University Press.

Part III
Process of Relationship Loss

6
The Language of Disengagement: A Face-Management Perspective

SANDRA METTS

The language of disengagement says a great deal about the couple using it. The content of accusations, complaints, pleadings, justifications, and confessions reflect the unique relationship experiences of the partners who speak them. This does not mean, however, that the language of disengagement is without pattern. Because messages must conform to cultural, social, and linguistic constraints, commonality in their structure and function can be discerned across breakups. Moreover, variations in pattern are systematic and can be traced to the influence of antecedent and concomitant variables. In short, the messages that people produce during the very personal moments of their disengagement are amenable to investigation as sociological phenomena.

Part of the commonality in the language of disengagement stems from the fact that, although specifics may vary, disengagement messages are designed to inform the hearer of two pieces of information: (a) The speaker feels diminished, neutral, or negative emotion toward the hearer (e.g., "I don't love you anymore") or toward the hearer as a particular kind of partner ("I don't love you the way a woman should love her husband"), and/or (b) the speaker expects exemption from the role-related obligations that previously existed ("I plan to date other people, you should too" or "I'll sleep in the spare room until I find another place"). Although both pieces of information signal an intent to withdraw from the relationship, a declaration of reduced affection devalues the receiver more directly than does a declaration of role exemption. Although reduced affection can be inferred as a likely motivation for a declaration of exemption, other motivations are also possible, some not directly related to the partner. Thus, the threat to partner's "face" or public image is less direct. Common sense suggests that, unless retaliation is a goal or unless affection was never firmly established, persons would opt for the less threatening message. That is, they would present their intent to disengage as a desire to change the status of role obligations in the relationship rather than as a declaration of changes in affection directed toward their partner.

111

This chapter argues that a preference for face-preserving messages during disengagement is one of several patterns that can be explained by the theory of face and face work posed originally by Goffman (1967). The first section of the chapter presents the tenets and principles of face theory and related constructs such as politeness and accounts. Next, a model is proposed that integrates the research on disengagement strategies with a face perspective.

Face Management

The term *face* refers to the positive social attributes that a person is able to claim during an interaction (Goffman, 1967, 1971, 1981). Because one's face is, in effect, a "self" exposed to public evaluation, a social actor is emotionally invested in its maintenance:

> If the encounter sustains an image of him that he has long taken for granted, he probably will have few feelings about the matter. If events establish a face for him that is better than he might have expected, he is likely to "feel good"; if his ordinary expectations are not fulfilled, one expects that he will "feel bad" or "feel hurt." (Goffman, 1967, p. 6)

Any social actor who feels no commitment to the maintenance of his or her face and can endure its loss without distress is what Goffman calls *shameless*.

In a similar fashion, though less intensely, the social actor becomes emotionally involved in the face of others. This is apparent when a person loses face in an embarrassing situation and observers feel vicarious embarrassment. Such empathy is presumably fundamental to the interconnectedness of the social fabric. In fact, Goffman (1967) remarks that social actors who can watch others lose face and feel nothing are *heartless*.

To the extent that social actors are rational, preferring face gain to face loss, preferring smooth interactions to disrupted interactions, they should collaborate with others in the mutual support of face. The verbal and nonverbal actions that facilitate face management are called face work. According to Goffman (1967), "Face-work serves to counteract "incidents"—that is, events whose effective symbolic implication threaten face" (p. 12). One general class of actions, called *avoidance face work*, functions to prevent or minimize the effects of face-threatening incidents before they happen. A second general class of actions, called *corrective face work*, functions to remediate situations after an incident has occurred.

Avoidance Face Work

Avoidance face work is used in two ways. It is used to prevent face loss from occurring at all, as when a sensitive communicator maneuvers the conversation away from a potentially embarrassing topic. It is also used to minimize face loss that seems likely to occur by framing the face-threatening action in light of extenuating circumstances (e.g., "As your friend, I feel compelled to tell you that . . ."; or "I'm sorry to interrupt you but I'm in a hurry"). Two common linguistic devices used to frame pending face threats are disclaimers (Hewitt & Stokes, 1975) and politeness (Brown & Levinson, 1978, 1987).

Disclaimers

When social actors believe that their behavior may be perceived by others as discrepant with the positive attributes they have previously claimed, they may preface their actions with a disclaimer. *Disclaimers* are conventionalized linguistic devices designed to forestall negative attributions to one's character, competence, integrity, or motives. Hewitt and Stokes (1975) identify five types of disclaimers: *hedging* (indicates uncertainty and receptivity to suggestions; "I may be wrong but . . ."); *credentialing* (indicates that there are good reasons and appropriate qualifications for engaging in a sanctionable action; "I'm your mother and I have every right to read your mail."); *sin license* (indicates that this is an occasion when a rule can be violated without considering it to be an indicator of a character defect; "What the heck, it's Friday"); *cognitive disclaimer* (assurance that even though subsequent behavior may seem strange, it is actually reasonable and under cognitive control; "I know this sounds crazy, but . . ."); and *appeal for suspended judgment* (request to suspend judgment for a possibly offensive act until it has been fully explained; "Hear me out before you get upset").

Politeness

Whereas disclaimers tend to focus on the projected face loss of the speaker, politeness tends to focus on projected loss of the hearer's face (although the speaker's face is implicated in the process of redressing the hearer's face). Brown and Levinson (1978, 1987) speculate that face has two forms: positive face (the desire to be liked and valued; the desire to maintain a positive self-image) and negative face (the desire to be unimpeded and unrestrained; the desire to maintain autonomy and self-determination).

Because face threats are endemic to social interaction, languages contain mechanisms that enable members of a culture to indicate their sensitivity to the face needs of others (Brown & Levinson, 1978, 1987). These linguistic devices are known collectively as politeness. "Positive politeness" is directed toward the positive face needs of a listener. It expresses affiliation through indications that the listener's desires are known and considered important, that he or she is viewed as a member of an in-group, a friend, or a valued other. "Negative politeness" is directed toward the negative face needs of the listener. It offers assurances that a person's freedom will not be curtailed unnecessarily. It is characterized by self-effacement and formality, permitting the listener to feel that his or her response was not obligatory or coerced. Of course, such deference and self-effacement necessarily entails a threat to the speaker's positive face.

The fact that speakers have polite forms available to them for acknowledging the face needs of their hearer does not mean they always use them. Sometimes criticism is delivered bluntly and requests are made directly. According to Brown and Levinson (1978), speakers select an appropriate strategy to cope with an impending face threat by balancing the competing goals of redressing face and accomplishing the task that necessitates the face threat. Using positive and negative politeness are only two of five "strategies" available to social actors when they are considering a face-threatening act (FTA). "Going bald on record" (making the face threat with no redressive action) is the most efficient strategy but the least face preserving. "Going off record" (hinting) is more face preserving than doing the FTA with politeness but is not very efficient. Not doing the FTA at all is the most face-preserving strategy but is also inefficient in accomplishing the task that entailed the FTA. "Going on record" with redressive action (positive or negative politeness) provides a fairly equal trade-off in the competing goals of saving face and maximizing efficiency.

Corrective Face Work

When an offensive action has not been averted or prefigured, a predicament arises. According to Schlenker, predicaments are "situations in which events have undesirable implications for the identity-relevant images actors have claimed or desire to claim in front of real or imagined audiences" (1980, p. 125). Restoring social order and reestablishing impugned identities are accomplished in a ritualized sequence that Goffman (1967) calls the "remedial interchange." The slots or turns that constitute the sequence include a challenge, an offering, an acceptance, and, sometimes, an expression of appreciation (thanks) for a favorable evaluation.

Challenge

When an untoward act has caused participants to lose face, the transgressor may be called to account for his or her behavior. This challenge (also called a *reproach*; Schönbach, 1980) can be encoded in various ways, depending on the features of the predicament. Challenges might be implicit (e.g., silence, or aghast looks) or explicit (e.g., projected apologies, projected excuses, or projected justifications) (McLaughlin,

Cody, & O'Hair, 1983). Challenges might refer to past behavior (e.g., accusing or demanding explanations), to present behavior (e.g., stopping problematic conduct), and to future behavior (e.g., giving advisories) (Morris, 1988). And finally, challenges may be mitigating (i.e., allow the transgressor to save face and diffuse the situation) or aggravating (i.e., exacerbate face loss and intensify the disruption of the situation) (McLaughlin et al., 1983).

Offerings

Three general classes of messages function as offerings: accounts, apologies (or concessions), and refusals. Accounts are attempts to remediate predicaments through reframing of the event or the actor's role in the event. Specifically, justifications deny the pejorative nature of the act (e.g., "There was no harm done" or "It was only a joke"), whereas excuses minimize an actor's responsibility for an untoward act (e.g., "I was busy," or drunk or afraid; "I don't know what came over me"; Scott & Lyman, 1968). Schlenker (1980) identifies a third type of account, defense of innocence, which includes statements that the event did not occur (defense of nonoccurrence) or that the accused did not do it (defense of noncausation).

Apologies both accept responsibility for the untoward act and acknowledge its offensiveness. Minor offenses are typically remedied with a simple apology ("I'm sorry"), whereas more serious offenses elicit more elaborate apologies (Schlenker & Darby, 1981). A fully formed apology expresses an appropriate emotional response to having committed the offense (e.g., guilt, remorse, or embarrassment); indicates awareness of proper conduct; acknowledges that violations should be punished; promises proper behavior in the future; and performs an act of penance and/or offers restitution (Goffman, 1967).

Apologies are frequently combined with other types of offerings. For example, people build sequences of strategies to cope with embarrassment, expressing regret through an apology, attempting to restore order through remediation strategies, and offering an explanation in the form of an excuse (Cupach, Metts, & Hazleton, 1986). Similar patterns occur in conflict situations as well. Holtgraves (1989) found that an apology and an account (usually in the form of an excuse) were the preferred combination to deal with conflict arising from inconsideration or forgetfulness. Holtgraves suggests that the apology–account sequence may be a particularly useful combination because "the speaker can express regard for his/her own face in the account while simultaneously being deferential to the hearer with a concession" (1989, p. 5).

Although accounts and apologies are the preferred (and generally most mitigating) responses to a challenge, social actors can refuse to provide either (Schönbach, 1980). Refusals may consist of a counterreproach, a silent turn, or a turn with no reference made to the act in question (McLaughlin et al., 1983). Refusals may also be expressed as a denial that the accuser has the right to issue the challenge (Schönbach, 1980).

Acceptance

Offerings that are successful in redressing the face loss of participants and restoring social order will be positively valued and, in the case of accounts, "honored" (Scott & Lyman, 1968). The honorability of an account is a function of both the structure of the account and the characteristics of the person providing the account. If an account is structurally "well-formed," it will be consistent with the gravity of the offense and will present reasonable motives. Characteristics of the transgressor that affect the honoring of an account are his or her moral worth, expressed repentance, and status relative to the person calling for the account (Blumstein, 1974).

When an account is not considered legitimate or reasonable, it is rejected. Rejections may lead to additional offerings, to a shift in roles as the rejected person challenges the rejection, or to a deadlock and termination of the interchange (Goffman, 1967). Thus, rejecting an offering can become just as aggravating as refusing to provide an offering.

Summary

The previous discussion suggests that social situations influence messages and that messages reframe situations. This reciprocity is most clearly seen in the rituals of avoidance (politeness) and corrective (remedial interchange) face work. The preference is to avoid face threat when possible and to remediate the situation when it does occur. Unfortunately, the face work required for remediation can present the user with a dilemma: The strategies that most clearly redress the face needs of the other party also most strongly threaten the face needs of the user. The fully elaborated apology, for example, anoints the positive face of the recipient while at the same time threatening the user's positive face needs ("I'm a bad person; please forgive me") and negative face needs ("I promise that I will never do it again; I'll do anything to make it up to you").

As would be expected, messages that redress threats to both recipient's and sender's face needs are difficult to produce. Holtgraves (1989) found that remedial strategies rated "satisfying" and "helpful" to hearer (e.g., concessions) were also rated the more difficult to produce and the least likely to be used. The extent to which a person is (a) willing to engage in face work (to go on record with redressive action) and (b) employ face tactics that are self-deprecating, self-restraining, and elaborated depends on both situated factors (e.g., degree of aggravation in previous turns) and external factors (e.g., relative power or status of other, and severity of offense).

Given the inherently face-threatening nature of disengagement, it is surprising that face theory has not been applied more systematically to the language of disengagement. One attempt to bring face theory into a central position in the study of disengagement is evidenced in the work of Baxter (1984, 1987). She uses face theory as a framework for organizing and interpreting the findings from her extended program of research. To integrate Baxter's work with other research examining the language of disengagement and to situate both within a face-management perspective, the following model is presented. It is hoped that this model not only will facilitate continued efforts to explain existing findings but also will encourage research that generates and tests hypotheses based on face theory.

A Face-work Model of Disengagement

The model presented here integrates avoidance and corrective face work with the disengagement strategies identified in current disengagement research. Two prominent typologies of disengagement strategies are those originating in the work of Cody (1982) and Baxter (1982). These typologies will be summarized briefly and then situated in the model.

Typologies of Disengagement Strategies

Cody (1982) derived 12 "clusters of tactics" from descriptions of relationship terminations provided by college students. These were subsequently reduced (through cluster analysis and multidimensional scaling) to five strategies (Banks, Altendorf, Greene, & Cody, 1987). These are (a) avoidance ("I didn't say anything to the partner. I avoided contact with [him or her] as much as possible"); (b) negative identity management ("I told [him or her] that I was going to date other people and that I thought [he or she] should date others also"); (c) justification ("I fully explained why I feel dissatisfied with the relationship, that it hasn't been growing, and that I believe we will both be happier if we don't date anymore"); (d) de-escalation ("I told [him or her] that I need to be honest and suggested that we break it off for awhile and see what happens"); (e) positive tone ("I told [him or her] that I was very, very sorry about breaking off the relationship").

Baxter (1982) also derived a set of specific tactics from college students' accounts of disengagement and reduced them to a smaller set of four strategies: withdrawal ("I avoided my partner"); positive tone ("I tried to create a good feeling between us"); manipulation ("I asked someone else to tell her"); and directness ("I expressed a desire to leave" and "I fully explained my reasons for wanting to leave"). Wilmot, Carbaugh, and Baxter (1985) provided long-distance couples with 14 tactics taken from an earlier study (Baxter, 1982). These were then factor analyzed, revealing three general "approaches" to terminating a relationship: (a) verbal directness (confront other with completed decision to end the relationship, discuss the relationship with the other); (b) verbal indirectness (express desire to end the relationship with the hope of getting back together; intentionally do things to dissatisfy the partner in hopes he or she will break it off); (c) nonverbal withdrawal (avoid partner; continue to see partner but not quite as often as in the past; while interacting with partner reduce the amount of eye contact).

In subsequent theoretical writings, Baxter (1987) reconfigured both earlier typologies. The result is a more complex structure but one that allows for finer discrimination among tactics and that makes the association with face theory more explicit. Baxter (1985) posits three dimensions that can be used to characterize clusters of disengagement strategies: direct versus indirect, unilateral versus bilateral, and other-orientation versus self-orientation. Baxter sorts previously identified strategies according to these dimensions, yielding six clusters:

1. *Indirect–unilateral:* Withdrawal (lessens intimacy or frequency of contact), pseudo-de-escalation (false declaration of wanting to retain some level of relationship) and cost escalation (make cost of being in relationship high through rude or hostile actions)
2. *Indirect–bilateral:* Mutual pseudo-de-escalation (both partners share in deception that some level of commitment will be retained) and fading away (implicit understanding that the relationship is over)
3. *Direct–unilateral:* fait accompli (simple statement that the relationship is over; no account, no discussion), state-of-the-relationship talk (explicit statement of dissatisfaction and desire to exit in the context of a bilateral discussion of the relationship's problems
4. *Direct–bilateral:* Attributional conflict (conflict not over whether to exit, but why the exit is necessary; placing blame), negotiated farewell (explicit communication about the relationship and its termination; sense-making session without blame)
5. *Self-orientation:* Cost escalation, fait accompli, withdrawal, and attributional conflict
6. *Other-orientation:* State-of-the-relationship talk, pseudo-de-escalation, bilateral pseudo-de-escalation, fading away, and negotiated farewell.

The Model

For any model to be a useful heuristic, it must depict an expected relationship among component units. Figure 6.1 depicts an expected relationship among three components: (a) a condition external to the immediate interaction (i.e., severity of offense); (b) a type of message (e.g., an excuse) or a type of message sequence (negotiated farewell);

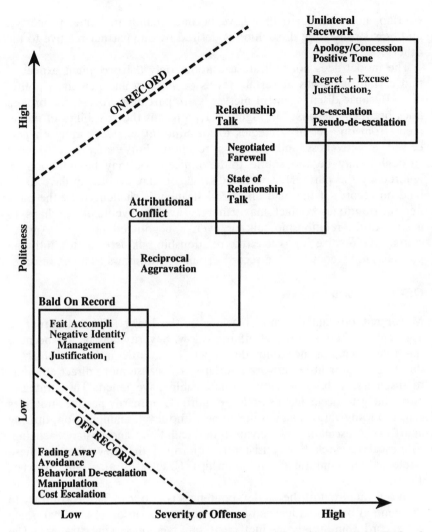

FIGURE 6.1. A face-work model of disengagement. Note: Justification$_1$: Defined by Cody (1982); Justification$_2$: Defined by Scott & Lyman (1968).

and (c) some measure of the social appropriateness of that message or message sequence (i.e., degree of politeness). The fundamental assumption is that as severity of the threat increases, the threat to the offended person's face increases. This increasing threat should result in greater weight being placed on hearer support, thereby increasing the likelihood of a deferential move exhibiting high politeness. The notion of "offense" within the parameters of the model refers to the fact that a relationship is being dissolved. The "severity" of this offense reflects the loss incurred and is a function of several factors, including, for example, how long a couple has been dating or married, the amount of network overlap, how enmeshed they have become (children, home, property), and how strongly the dissolution is desired by one partner relative to the other.

The model does not indicate causation, only that we might expect to find certain messages at certain levels of severity and perceived politeness. Because disengagement messages are part of a process, the broken lines between the boxes in Figure 6.1 represent the possibility of movement from one set of strategies to an adjacent set, depending on perceived effectiveness and partner's reaction. For example, off-record strategies may be too subtle to be noticed (or may be intentionally ignored by the partner), and the disengager may eventually have to go bald on record. If the bald on-record strategy is challenged by the partner, attributional conflict may emerge, leading eventually perhaps to a state-of-the-relationship talk or even a negotiated farewell. And of course, the reverse is possible: the relationship talk deteriorates until one partner simply goes bald on record or finally withdraws as a last resort.

Off-Record Strategies

Movement through the model begins in the lower left-hand corner of Figure 6.1, where severity of offense is low. Severity may be low because the relationship is not fully developed (i.e., little intimacy, of short duration, and/or little network overlap) or because more direct attempts to disengage a fully developed relationship have failed. The strategies most likely to occur in this area are indirect, primarily passive strategies referred to by various names including withdrawal, manipulation, drifting apart, cost escalation, behavioral de-escalation, and distance cueing. Empirical research has consistently confirmed the prevalence of these strategies in nonintimate relationships (Banks et al., 1987; Baxter, 1985).

In this quadrant of the model, politeness is also low. This is contrary to the general premise advanced by Brown and Levinson (1978) that going off record (hinting) is an inefficient but face-preserving strategy. The decision to associate off-record strategies with low politeness in the model is based on the fact that disengagement is a special kind of face-threatening situation. During disengagement, some degree of directness indicates politeness because the disengager is willing to threaten his or her own negative face needs to acknowledge the positive face needs of the other party. According to Baxter (1987), "The other's positive face is threatened under any circumstance, but the threat is probably greatest with Distance Cueing [off-record strategies] for it doesn't even show the basic courtesy of a face-to-face accounting" (p. 207). In addition, Brown and Levinson (1987) discuss exceptions to the general principle of polite indirectness. When inefficiency is more costly than the face threat, for example, Brown and Levinson contend that it is polite to be direct. In the case of disengagement, indirectness promotes ambiguity about the status of the relationship and leaves both partners open to possible embarrassment within their social networks and in future face-to-face encounters.

The assumption that off-record strategies are associated with low politeness is also supported by empirical research, though the support is indirect. No one has assessed perceived politeness when these strategies are used, but related data suggest that they are not perceived favorably by users or recipients. Metts, Cupach, and Bejlovec (1989) found that withdrawal was negatively associated with postdisengagement friendship for the initiator of a breakup. Wilmot et al. (1985) found that when disengagers used withdrawal, they reported that they did not feel good about the breakup and expressed regrets for using that strategy.

One set of off-record strategies, labeled *cost escalation* by Baxter (1985), seems to be particularly low in politeness. In a study of postdisengagement friendship, the person who was broken up with was significantly less likely to remain friends with a former romantic partner when he or she used cost escalation (manipulation) than any other strategy (Metts et al., 1989). Although cost-escalation strategies are intended by the user as a way to avoid confrontation, in practice they simply shift the burden of confrontation to the recipient. The recipient must decide when the increased cost for the relationship is beyond his or her tolerance and, at that point, must issue a challenge to the partner. If an offering is made, the recipient must then evaluate the offering and, if appropriate, must dissolve the relationship. Thus, cost escalation implicates not only the positive face of the recipient (in the use of hostile and/or demeaning actions) but also the negative face of the recipient in that he or she is coerced into orchestrating the disengagement. Ironically, cost escalation is also threatening to the positive face of the user because he or she must create the image of a person not worthy of being a relational partner (Baxter, 1987). Observers would quite likely see the person using cost escalation as both "heartless" and "shameless."

On-Record Strategies

According to Brown and Levinson (1978), speakers do a cost–benefit analysis in deciding to go on record with an FTA. On-record strategies are more effortful and constraining to the user because the range of possible interpretations of his or her behavior is greatly reduced. The lack of ambiguity, however, is also part of the gain in going on record. The user gains clarity through voicing his or her position, avoids attributions of cowardice and manipulativeness, and gains attributions of honesty and outspokenness (Brown & Levinson, 1987). Baxter (1987) notes that on-record strategies demonstrate to the social network that the disengager has displayed concern for the other's face commensurate with the expectations and obligations that accompany close relationships.

On-record strategies, however, are not all equally polite. *Bald on-record* (nonredressed) strategies are blunt and unelaborated statements that the relationship is over. Among these strategies are fait accompli, negative identity management, and justification (as Cody, 1982, defines it). These strategies are indeed efficient and unambiguous. They do indicate enough respect for the relationship and for the partner to confront the dissolution directly. Bald on-record strategies, however, are placed relatively low in politeness on the model because they do not redress the recipient's positive face needs through apologies or accounts, and they do not redress the recipient's negative face by allowing his or her participation in the decision to disengage.

One would expect bald on-record strategies to be used when the speaker believes the relationship is substantial enough to merit a formal exit but not emotionally or structurally enmeshed enough to entail guilt or obligation (low severity of offense). The disengager may also feel exempt from guilt and obligation because the reasons for terminating are attributed to the partner. Banks et al. (1987) found disengagers used negative identity-management strategies to dissolve relationships when they felt the partner was responsible. This leads to the speculation that bald on-record strategies might be used to disengage a relationship subsequent to partner's use of cost-escalation strategies. As Banks et al. observe, "disengagers may feel somewhat justified in the use of a strong, impolite tactic if they believe that the target has behaved in ways which warrant such behavior" (1987, p. 38).

The degree of politeness associated with bald on-record strategies has not been formally assessed, but related findings suggest that it is not viewed favorably. Wilmot, Carbaugh, and Baxter (1985) found that people who used verbal directness to terminate a relationship reported negative emotional reactions to the termination. Wilmot et al. argue that when the self is blunt in terminating, the action apparently boomerangs and produces negative reactions for both user and recipient.

Going on record with redressive action is represented in the model in Figure 6.1 by three boxes. The first is labeled with Baxter's (1985) term *attributional conflict.* As defined by Baxter, attributional conflict indicates that both parties have agreed on the need for dissolution but have not agreed on the reasons why. Although Baxter does not identify specific strategies that might be used in attributional conflict, it is likely that both parties issue challenges as to the other's role in the dissolution. These may provoke aggravating offerings or refusals to account. The resulting pattern is reciprocal aggravation.

One would expect to find attributional conflict episodes in relationships where termination is a relatively severe offense. It is unlikely that a couple would invest the time and effort to identify the cause of dissolution unless the relationship was perceived as a significant loss. Interestingly, the model indicates that politeness is greater for attributional conflict than for bald on-record strategies. This may seem counterintuitive, but it is based on the assumption that bilateral disengagement, even when conflictual, redresses at least the negative face needs of both parties because both participate in the disengagement decision. In addition, because both parties have agreed that dissolution is desirable, the loss of positive face value is less than in unilateral withdrawal.

The second box in Figure 6.1 for on-record with redressive action, *relationship talk*, is also labeled after Baxter's (1985) work and contains the two types of episodes she identified. As with attributional conflict, Baxter did not record specific strategies occurring within these types of episodes, but we can infer that they are more face redressive than in attributional conflict. Not only is the decision to disengage the relationship a bilateral one, but the reasons are not in dispute or are external to the relationship. Baxter (1982) found increased directness with an externally attributed locus of cause when compared to a cause attributed to the relationship parties. Baxter maintains that external attribution is less threatening to the face of the relationship parties. The general absence of face threat and the explicit desire to negotiate a mutually satisfying dissolution of the relationship motivate the association between relationship talk and high politeness and high severity of offense (significant relationship loss) reflected in the model.

The final cluster of strategies is called *unilateral facework* because it contains strategies most explicitly directed to the face needs of the recipient. In these situations, disengagement is desired by one party, and he or she perceives the exit to be a severe offense. The strategies included here are de-escalation, pseudo-de-escalation, and accounts, because they request redefinition (rather than termination) of the relationship. These strategies redress the loss of positive face entailed by the disengager's unilateral decision by expressing continued desire to be in a relationship, to be friends, and to be affiliated. Excuses, excuses plus regrets, positive tone strategies, and apologies all express strong regard for the recipient's positive face through self-castigation and penitence. Excuses also, however, redress the user's need to provide an account for his or her responsibility in the dissolution.

These strategies no doubt occur to some degree in relationship talk episodes. The model isolates them as a cluster of strategies merely to underscore their use in unilateral disengagement. A person desiring disengagement should be willing to employ these strategies when the severity of offense is perceived to be high, either because the relationship was very strongly established and enmeshed or because the resistance of the other induces guilt or fear of retribution. Baxter (1983) found disengagers to use less indirectness and more other-orientation as the prior closeness of the relationship increased. Similarly, Banks et al. (1987) found that disengagers were more likely to use positive tone, de-escalation, or justification when network overlap was high, the relationship was intimate, and postdisengagement friendship was desired. That is, people used positive tone and de-escalation tactics to reduce the level of intimacy in the relationship while attempting to keep some kind of relationship alive, and they did so when the partner was not blamed for the costs in the relationship and there was a chance to increase intimacy at a later time.

These strategies are also associated with high politeness. Apologies and concessions, for example, are considered to be highly deferential (e.g., Schlenker & Darby, 1981; Schönbach, 1980). Holtgraves (1989) found the regret plus excuse to be more satisfying to hearers than any other face-work strategies, and Metts et al. (1989) found that when an initiator used positive tone strategies, the couple was more likely to remain friends after the breakup.

Conclusion

The model described here is a first step toward bringing theoretical coherence to research on the language of disengagement. Its contribution is to explore possible relationships among types of messages (or episodes) and two theoretically relevant variables, severity of offense and degree of politeness. The preliminary relationships presented in the model as well as the juxtaposition of strategies within boxes were derived from a synthesis of theoretical and empirical literature. The accuracy of this representation will have to be tested and the model refined accordingly. Several issues for future research will facilitate this process.

First, a meaningful measure of politeness must be devised. Attempts to locate politeness entirely in the linguistic form of utterances have been criticized (Craig, Tracy, & Spisak, 1986). As Brown and Levinson admit, politeness has a pragmatic as well as semantic aspect; "if the overt content of an utterance is rude, for example, politeness strategies won't necessarily redeem it" (1987, p. 11). Measures of politeness, then, should not be limited to the number or type of face-work elements in a message but should also include assessments of perceived politeness made by people in particular contexts. It is interesting to speculate, for example, whether conventionalized disengagement messages such as "I'm not good enough for you," actually threaten the user's positive face to the degree that might be implied in the linguistic form.

Second, related to the assessment of politeness is determining how to measure degree of aggravation. The substantial body of literature attesting to the fact that speakers exacerbate face loss is clearly relevant to disengagement. It is not clear, however, whether a mitigation–aggravation continuum is isomorphic with, or independent from and merely parallel to, a politeness dimension. Teasing out the qualities of the two types of assessments is an important direction for future research.

Third, a mutually exclusive, equivalent, and exhaustive typology of disengagement strategies should be developed. At present, categories within typologies and categories across typologies are not comparable. For example, some categories refer to an entire episode (attributional conflict, negotiated farewell), whereas other strategies refer to a single type of statement (pseudo-de-escalation, fait accompli). It is not clear to what extent episodic categories also include these single messages or are constituted of a different class of messages.

Nonequivalent categories within a typology pose a problem identified previously by Miller (1982) in regard to Marwell and Schmitt's (1976) compliance-gaining tactics. He observed that the likelihood of use for certain tactics was unaffected by experimental manipulations. He argued that these tactics differ qualitatively from others in the typology. "Threat," for example, allows respondents to call to mind a variety of options from their behavioral repertoire, while "negative self-feeling" (i.e., tell the target that he or she will feel worse about himself or herself if he or she does not comply) allows little choice; a respondent either makes that particular statement or does not. Miller found that the strategies that represented a near dichotomous choice of "use" or "no use" were most sensitive to experimentally induced variation in the independent variables "type of relationship" and "power" of the target.

In addition, nonequivalent categories across typologies make systematizing findings difficult. Consider as illustration the category of "positive tone." In Cody's (1982) typology, positive tone strategies are simply apologies expressing regret at the breakup (i.e., "I said I was sorry that the relationship had to end"). Positive tone strategies in Baxter's (1985) typology are generalized positive orientations toward in partner, "I tried to end it on a positive note and get [him or her] not to have hard feelings." Apologies may be used with this strategy, but other types of messages may be included as well. In addition, the speaker may have intended to create good feeling but may not have been able to operationalize that intention in his or her messages. The noncomparability of typologies slows efforts to generate a parsimonious description of disengagement patterns and to identify how situational, relational, and social variables influence strategy selection.

Fourth, the broadly defined rubric referred to here as *severity of offense* requires specification. Current disengagement research (e.g., Banks et al., 1987) has examined the influence of network overlap, reasons for disengagement, attitudes toward partner's role, and degree of intimacy. In the service of heurism, the model presumed a sort of linear combination of these variables contributing to total severity. In reality, each of these variables merits independent and conjoint examination to determine its relative importance in the degree of severity (or cost) attending a particular dissolution.

Finally, the traditional reliance on college students and premarital couples must be augmented with samples from other populations. Conclusions based on premarital couples may misrepresent the nature of communication in the disengagement process. As a case in point, Baxter (1987) asserts that indirect strategies (off-record hinting) are the most commonly used mechanisms for disengaging. This may be true when relationships are casual and couples can simply "stop dating." It is difficult to imagine, however, that a couple married for 21 years with three children could simply "stop being married" by reducing eye contact and not calling anymore. Partners in established relationships can signal diminished feelings indirectly but cannot declare exemption from role-related obligations and rights without going on record. Data obtained almost exclusively from premarital couples have obscured important distinctions.

References

Banks, S. P., Altendorf, D. M., Greene, J. O., & Cody, M. J. (1987). An examination of relationship disengagement: Perceptions, breakup strategies and outcomes. *Western Journal of Speech Communication, 51*, 19–41.

Baxter, L. A. (1982). Strategies for ending relationships: Two studies. *Western Journal of Speech Communication, 46*, 223–241.

Baxter, L. A. (1983). Relationship disengagement: An examination of the reversal hypothesis. *Western Journal of Speech Communication, 47*, 85–98.

Baxter, L. A. (1984). Trajectories of relationship disengagement. *Journal of Social and Personal Relationships, 1*, 29–48.

Baxter, L. A. (1985). Accomplishing relationship disengagement. In S. Duck & D. Perlman (Eds.), *Understanding personal relationships* (pp. 243–265). London: Sage.

Baxter, L. A. (1987). Cognition and communication in the relationship process. In R. Burnett, P. McGhee, & D. D. Clarke (Eds.), *Accounting for relationships* (pp. 192–212). London: Methuen.

Blumstein, P. W., Carssow, K. G., Hall, J., Hawkins, B., Hoffman, R., Ishem, E., Maurer, C. P., Spens, D., Taylor, J., & Zimmerman, D. L. (1974). The honouring of accounts. *American Sociological Review, 39*, 551–566.

Brown, P., & Levinson, S. (1978). Universals in language usage: Politeness phenomena. In E. Goody (Ed.), *Questions and politeness: Strategies in social interaction* (pp. 56–289). New York: Cambridge University Press.

Brown, P., & Levinson, S. C. (1987). *Politeness: Some universals in language usage.* Cambridge: Cambridge University Press.

Cody, M. J. (1982). A typology of disengagement strategies and an examination of the role intimacy, reactions to inequity and relational problems play in strategy selection. *Communication Monographs, 49*, 148–170.

Craig, R., Tracy, K., & Spisak, F. (1986). The discourse of requests: Assessment of a politeness approach. *Human Communication Research, 12*, 437–468.

Cupach, W. R., Metts, S., & Hazleton, V. (1986). Coping with embarrassing predicaments: Remedial strategies and their perceived utility. *Journal of Language and Social Psychology, 5*, 181–200.

Goffman, E. (1967). On face work. In E. Goffman, *Interaction ritual* (pp. 5–45). Garden City: Anchor Books.

Goffman, E. (1971). *Relations in public: Microstudies of the public order.* New York: Basic Books.

Goffman, E. (1981). *Forms of talk.* Oxford: Oxford University Press.

Hewitt, J. P., & Stokes, R. (1975). Disclaimers. *American Sociological Review*, *40*, 1–11.

Holtgraves, T. (1989). The form and function of remedial moves: Reported use, psychological reality and perceived effectiveness. *Journal of Language and Social Psychology*, *8*, 1–16.

Marwell, G., & Schmitt, D. R. (1976). Dimensions of compliance-gaining behavior: An empirical analysis, *Sociometry*, *30*, 350–364.

McLaughlin, M. L., Cody, M. J., & O'Hair, H. D. (1983). The management of failure events: Some contextual determinants of accounting behavior. *Human Communication Research*, *9*, 208–224.

Metts, S., Cupach, W. R., & Bejlovec, R. (1989). "I love you too much to ever start liking you": Redefining romantic relationships. *Journal of Social and Personal Relationships*, *6*, 259–274.

Miller, M. D. (1982). Friendship, power and the language of compliance-gaining. *Journal of Language and Social Psychology*, *1*, 111–121.

Morris, G. H. (1988). Finding fault. *Journal of Language and Social Psychology*, *7*, 1–25.

Schlenker, B. R. (1980). *Impression management: The self-concept, social identity, and interpersonal relations.* Monterey, CA: Brooks/Cole Publishing.

Schlenker, B. R., & Darby, B. W. (1981). The use of apologies in social predicaments. *Social Psychology Quarterly*, *44*, 271–278.

Schönbach, P. (1980). A category system for account phases. *European Journal of Social Psychology*, *10*, 195–200.

Scott, M., & Lyman, S. (1968). Accounts. *American Sociological Review*, *22*, 46–62.

Wilmot, W. W., Carbaugh, D. A., & Baxter, L. A. (1985). Communicative strategies used to terminate romantic relationships. *Western Journal of Speech Communication*, *49*, 204–216.

7
Dialectical Processes in the Disengagement of Interpersonal Relationships

WILLIAM R. CUPACH

Interpersonal relationships are inherently paradoxical. They afford simultaneously the opportunities for both ecstasy and agony. They create dilemmas, double binds, quandaries, and contradictions for relational partners. Individuals want to be open and honest, but they also want to protect their partner and preserve their own self-image. They want passion and abandonment but not without security and order. Recognition of these various contradictory phenomena has led scholars to import dialectical principles to provide a more complete understanding of the dynamic construction and erosion of relationships (e.g., Altman, Vinsel, & Brown, 1981; Baxter, 1988; Cissna, Cox, & Bochner, 1990; Conville, 1989; Masheter & Harris, 1986; Rawlins, 1983a, 1983b; Rawlins & Holl, 1987, 1988; Wiseman, 1986). In the spirit of this line of work, this chapter is based on the premise that the negotiation of dialectical tension between relational partners is central to the conduct and interpretation of relational life (and death). A dialectical perspective can therefore offer insight into the creation and dissolution of interpersonal relationships.

The notion of dialectics has been defined and elaborated in myriad ways. As applied here, it is conceptualized as a metatheoretical perspective, with categories and assumptions that suggest an emphasis for empirical analysis of social phenomena. Thus, although there presently is not a formal dialectical theory of relationship loss and this chapter is not an attempt to construct a theory so-labeled, dialectical phenomena offer a "substantive conception" of relationship processes (Altman et al., 1981; Bopp & Weeks, 1984). It is hoped that such a conception may eventually provoke and undergird the construction of original relationship theories. The purpose of this chapter is to briefly sketch some of the concepts fundamental to dialectical thinking and to show their relevance to close relationship loss. Although a dialectical approach is applicable to all interpersonal relationships (including friendships, kinships, etc.), the analysis in this chapter will focus primarily on close romantic relationships.

Dialectical Concepts

Dialectical thinking comprises many principles and concepts. As applied to interpersonal relationships, the dialectical perspective is primarily concerned with contradictory impulses that produce relationship change. Thus, it is important to explicate two key dialectical concepts that are particularly relevant to understanding relationships: contradiction and process (Baxter, 1988).

Contradiction

The essence of dialectics is contradiction—the antagonism or tension between two opposing forces. Although these contradictory impulses partially negate one another, they are also interdependent and mutually defining. The oppositional concepts of stability and change, for example, are only fully understood in terms of each other. The idea of revealing information draws meaning from its counterpart, concealing information, and vice versa. Thus, ,dialectical foces derive from elements that are systemically unified as well as oppositional.

Process

Another feature central to dialectical thinking is that oppositional forces are dynamic. They evolve and transform over time. By creating and reflecting change, dialectics represent an appropriate perspective for examining the developmental processes of relationships. Because relationships are ongoing processes (see Chapter 1 of this volume), dialectical analysis places less emphasis on causes and critical events of relationships and gives more attention to the features of transition and transformation produced by dialectical contradictions and characteristics of the process of relating.

Dialectic theorists anathematize the idea that relationships achieve a static equilibrium or homeostasis (Altman et al., 1981; Bopp & Weeks, 1984). Change and stability are in dynamic opposition to one another, and both are essential to interpersonal relationships. This further implies that no a priori judgment can be made regarding the most appropriate or efficient balance between poles of a dialectical contradiction. "Balance" between contradictory poles is idiosyncratically determined within each relationship and its surrounding social milieu and is subject to change.

Dialectical Contradictions in Interpersonal Relationships

Although numerous oppositional tendencies can be observed in interpersonal relationships, three dialectical contradictions in particular have received the most attention by scholars of relationships. These are the oppositional tendencies of autonomy–connection, openness–closedness, and novelty–predictability.

Autonomy–Connection

The very nature of a human relationship constitutes a primary dialectical tension. Indeed, the essence of relating may be thought of as the ongoing tension between autonomy and connection. To form a relationship is to forfeit some autonomy to achieve connection. As Baxter (1990) indicates, however, "too much connection paradoxically destroys the relationship because the individual entities become lost. . . . But too much autonomy paradoxically destroys the individual's identity, because connections with others are necessary to identity formation and maintenance" (p. 70). The autonomy–connection dialectic is therefore, the central relationship contradiction "around which a web of secondary contradictions cohere" (Baxter, 1988, p. 259).

The struggle between autonomy and connectedness has been observed in a variety of relationships, including friendships (Rawlins, 1983a), family relationships portrayed in television situation comedies (Brown & Vaughn, 1987), and romantic relationships (Baxter, 1990; Cupach & Metts, 1988; Goldsmith, 1988). Eidelson (1980), for instance, proposes a curvilinear relationship between interpersonal satisfaction and level of relationship involvement over time based on conflicting motives for affiliation and independence. Similarly, Feldman (1979) presents a model of marital conflict based on the simultaneous but conflicting "needs" of an individual for both autonomy and intimacy. This contradiction is also implied in Askham's (1976) analysis of the tension between maintaining a sense of identity and a sense of stability in marital relationships.

Openness–Closedness

Openness and closedness also make up a dialectical tension embedded in all close relationships (Altman et al., 1981; Baxter, 1988; Rawlins, 1983b). These poles represent the tendencies to both reveal and conceal information. It is axiomatic that the exchange of information is necessary for the development of intimacy in interpersonal relationships (Altman & Taylor, 1973; Berger & Bradac, 1982). At the same time, openness creates vulnerability and presents risks that can threaten partners and their relationship (Bochner, 1982; Parks, 1982). Consequently, although openness is instrumental in the creation and preservation of intimacy, individuals also report falsifying, withholding, and distorting information to protect the self or partner and to preserve the relationship (e.g., Metts, 1989). Perhaps these conflicting tendencies partially explain the curvilinear relationship between self-disclosure and relational satisfaction (e.g., Gilbert, 1976; Jorgensen & Gaudy, 1980).

Novelty–Predictability

Another pair of contradictory impulses exhibited in relationships is the desire for novelty and the desire for predictability (Baxter, 1988; Wilmot, 1987). Predictability allows control and coordination of behavior between relational partners, as well as promoting mutual understanding between partners. Too much predictability, however, can indicate rigid behavioral patterns and can produce boredom in a relationship. Relational partners, therefore, continually confront balancing the dual needs for predictability and unpredictability in their relationship.

These three dialectical pairs—autonomy–connection, openness–closedness, and novelty–predictability—are pervasive in interpersonal relationships and are currently the most frequently cited oppositional tendencies. Other dialectical tensions are likely to be exhibited in relationships as well. For example, Rawlins (1989) identifies the dialectic of affection versus instrumentality in friendships. Cissna and colleagues (1990) discuss the dialectical tension between marital and parental roles within stepfamilies.

Dialectical phenomena may operate at several related, but distinct levels. An *individual* dialectic, for instance, might be reflected in a person's conflicting needs. A person may want to be somewhat autonomous, and at the same time, desire some degree of connection to partner. A *dyadic* dialectic represents the pulls from each partner, such as one individual wanting more autonomy in a relationship, while the partner exhibits a desire to be more interdependent. A *network* dialectic locates tension neither in an individual nor between individuals but rather between the dyad and other social entities such as social network, family, and cultural forces. A couple may experience conflict over the degree of autonomy–connection that is privately experienced in the relationship versus the balance between these poles that must be portrayed publicly for their shared social network.

Dialectics in Disengagement

Dialectical phenomena are recognizable in at least three aspects of relationship disengagement: (1) dialectical contradictions create relational change; (2) certain dialectical patterns characterize relationship breakdown; and (3) dialectical tensions shape the accomplishment of disengagement.

Dialectics and Change

Change is a dialectical concept, not only because it partially defines the meaning of process but also because it stands in unified opposition to stability. Relationships are essentially characterized by change and the ongoing tension between change and stability. As Baxter indicates, dialectical contradictions in interpersonal relationships "form the exigence for communicative action betwen the parties and constitute the basis of change and development in the relationship" (1988, p. 258). Dialectic principles are therefore particularly suited to understanding relationships.

Change is an integral facet of relationship disengagement. Disengagement represents certain types of change in the relationship—including those related to definitions ascribed to the relationship, degree of interdependence between partners, emotions felt, and behaviors enacted. Moreover, a processual view of relationship disengagement sees breakdown, repair, reconciliation, redefinition, termination, and so on, as embedded parts of the larger ongoing process of relating. Relational decline is not merely the reverse order or mirror image of relationship escalation, either perceptually or behaviorally (Baxter, 1983; Tolhuizen, 1986). A complete understanding of disengagement, therefore, requires inspection of the broader holistic context of relationship change and stability, of which disengagement is a part.

The temporal manifestation of dialectical contradictions gives form to relationships in at least two ways: (1) the interaction between change–stability and other dialectical phenomena over time reveals patterns of relationship trajectory, thereby offering a temporal "profile" of each relationship; and (2) the fluctuating nature and functions of dialectical contradictions can be used to define phases or stages of relationship evolution. These two manifestations are considered in the following sections.

Dialectics and the Temporal Profile of Relationships

Altman and colleagues (1981) contend that change and stability in relationships can be analyzed with respect to various other dimensions of social interaction, such as the oppositional tendencies of openness–closedness. They illustrate how "openness and closedness exhibit patterns or cycles of stability and change at different times over the course of a relationship" (p. 131).

Altman et al. (1981) describe stability and change in terms of several features, among them frequency and amplitude. *Frequency* refers to the number of cycles (e.g., of openness and closedness) per unit of time. Thus, high frequency depicts numerous, rapid shifts in openness and closedness between relational partners. Low frequency characterizes a lack of change in patterns of openness and closedness. *Amplitude* pertains to the "relative amount of openness or closedness in a given cycle. Thus high amplitude reflects a large amount of openness (or closedness) during a given period, and low amplitude indicates the opposite" (Altman et al., 1981, p. 131). Frequency and amplitude considered together define a number of potential stability–change patterns in a relationship.

Baxter and Wilmot (1983) tested some of the implications of the Altman et al. (1981) model regarding openness–closedness cycling by having individuals monitor two of their interpersonal relationships for a 2-week period. Participants completed a semistructured diary entry following each conversation (of 5 or more min) with the targeted relationship partners. They found that more developed relationships (measured as perceived closeness at the beginning of the monitoring period) exhibited less frequency and less amplitude of openness–closedness cycling compared to less developed relationships. Further, the frequency of openness–closedness cycling was associated with change in relationship definition (i.e., average perceived change in closeness–distance across all recorded encounters), particularly among more developed rather than less developed relationships. Amplitude of openness–closedness cycling, on the other hand, was more strongly associated with relationship definition change among less developed rather than among more developed relationships.

The findings of Baxter and Wilmot's (1983) investigation are intriguing and provide qualified empirical support for the cyclical phenomenon proposed by Altman et al. (1981). Several extensions of this research should be pursued, including the examination of cycling over a longer period of time; the simultaneous study of cycling of other dialectical stresses (e.g., autonomy–connection); and the explicit comparison of cycling phenomena in relationships advancing versus relationships declining in intimacy.

Dialectics as Markers of Relational Phases

Developmental approaches to interpersonal relationships typically identify stages of relationship growth and decline (e.g., Knapp, 1984; Levinger, 1983; Wood, 1982). Such approaches have been criticized for delineating relationship stages in an atheoretical or tautological fashion (e.g., Bochner, 1984). Alternatively, as Baxter (1988) argues, a dialectical framework provides a theoretical grounding for identification of developmental stages or phases of relationships. In her application of a dialectical perspective to the strategic management of relationships, Baxter (1988) has identified four potential phases of the autonomy–connection contradiction. Using extant literature on communicative strategies, she illustrates that each phase is characterized by the negotiation and management of the secondary contradictions, novelty–predictability and openness–closedness. Importantly, the nature and function of each dialectical contradiction is qualitatively different in each developmental phase.

Phase 1, *autonomy to connection*, is characterized by novelty in the form of psychological uncertainty. At the same time, behavioral predictability is afforded as individuals largely follow familiar and ritualistic scripts that govern appropriate behavior in initial interactions (e.g., Berger & Bradac, 1982). Openness and closedness are balanced through gradual, reciprocated self-disclosures and affinity-seeking behavior that is generally indirect in nature. In phase 2, *autonomy and connection*, predictability is engendered by the mutual creation of private idioms, rituals, and other symbols that characterize the evolving relational culture, while novelty stems from the emergence of nonscripted behavior, the development of idiosyncratic rules for behavior, and the attendant conflict. Openness–closedness is reflected in the continuing self-disclosure necessary for relationship advancement, as well as the identification of taboo topics, and the use of indirect "secret" tests to gain more information and predictability in the relationship. Phase 3, labeled *autonomy–connection synthesis*, is marked by constructive efforts to envigorate and revitalize the relationship through various maintenance and repair strategies. Phase 4, *connection to autonomy* identifies relationships in decline, a topic to be further explored in a subsequent section.

In a therapeutic application of dialectical thinking, Sarnoff and Sarnoff (1989a, 1989b) have identified six stages of marital relationships based on six dialectical challenges occurring over the life span of a marriage. Each stage represents a mutual goal for expanding the relationship, as well as the concomitant opposing defensiveness that potentially thwarts the goal. For example, stage 1—*coupling and concealing*—depicts newlyweds faced with the desire to share intimacy, checked by the fear of vulnerability. Stage 2—*reproducing and retreating*—identifies the potential for expanding the relationship by having children, which can evoke envy by the husband who cannot give birth and resentment for the wife who is constrained by pregnancy.

Unless they realize the dialectical nature of their relationship—the constant struggle between the deep need for love and the equally deep fear of it—spouses are likely to blame each other for the conflicts and tensions no couple can avoid. (Sarnoff & Sarnoff, 1989a, p. 57)

Thus, the authors identify each marital stage and its attendant contradiction with the intent of making spouses aware of such tensions and the behavioral options for managing them.

Dialectics and Relationship Breakdown

To the extent that dialectical tensions drive change and evolution in relationships, they may account for their quality and success and, conversely, their erosion and failure. Because all relationships, by definition, possess dialectical opposition, it is not the mere presence of dilemmas that determines relational quality. Rather, it is the ability to successfully cope with inevitable contradictions.

Management of Dialectical Tension

Cupach and Metts (1988) surveyed college students involved in romantic relationships to assess the occurrence and impact of dialectical forces in relationships. They discovered that the frequency with which dialectical tension was perceived was negatively associated with relational satisfaction. In addition, the degree of personal anxiety and the amount of overt conflict produced by dialectical forces were negatively related to relational satisfaction. These data suggest that when the oppositional nature of dialectical forces becomes particularly salient to relational partners, it can be problematic for the health of the relationship. Moreover, the *recurring* salience of a contradiction (and its attendant stresses) in a relationship likely suggests the inability or unwillingness of one or both partners to successfully cope with dialectical contradictions.

Presumably, the competence of partners to strategically manage dialectical tension is critical (e.g., Baxter, 1988; Bochner, 1984). Baxter (1988, 1990) proposes four general strategic responses to dialectical opposition: selection, separation, neutralization, and reframing. The strategy of *selection* involves choosing actions consistent with one horn of the dilemma or one pole of the contradiction. Individuals may choose openness over closedness, for instance. *Separation* involves either temporal cyclic alternation or topical segmentation of oppositional forces. *Cyclic alternation* includes responding to each pole of the contradiction at different points in time, such as being open for a time, then being closed, then being open again. *Segmentation* deals with each pole of the contradiction with mutually exclusive activity, such as disclosing on some topics but being private about others, or by maintaining relational predictability while incorporating interactional novelty. *Neutralization* entails compromise between opposing tendencies by diluting their intensity. This is accomplished in one of two ways: *moderation* is the use of neutral messages, as in small talk; *disqualification* uses ambiguous or indirect communication that avoids explicit reference to either polarity. *Reframing* involves transcending the contradiction by redefining the poles as nonoppositional. Viewing autonomy as enhancing rather than impeding connection would be an example of reframing.

Baxter (1990) conducted retrospective personal interviews with individuals involved in romantic relationships to explore the presence of dialectical contradiction across various stages of relationship development and the strategic responses employed by individuals to manage the contradictions. Her results indicated that relational satisfaction was positively associated with the use of reframing in coping with autonomy–connection, and negatively associated with the use of disqualification in coping with openness–closedness. In coping with the novelty–predictability contradiction, the use of reframing and segmentation were positively correlated with relational satisfaction while the use of selection was negatively associated with satisfaction.

The management of dialectical tensions is likely to be influenced by the manner in which relational partners perceptually frame the circumstances surrounding the contradictions. Cupach and Metts (1988) conducted interviews of individuals in both married and dating relationships to explore how dialectical tensions were managed on a day-to-day basis. Management was found to be a function of whether dialectical pulls were viewed as cyclical or static. A cyclical view of dialectical tension sees the imbalance as temporary though possibly recurrent. Such a view was associated with proactive and constructive attempts to deal with dialectical tension such as open discussion and negotiation and with attempts to revitalize the relationship by changing behavior (e.g., periodically performing an unexpected behavior to inject excitement into the relationship). A static view of dialectical tension implies a change from perceived balance to perceived imbalance with little hope for future change. Individuals expressing this view of their dialectical tension typically reported being acquiescent (i.e., giving up or giving in to accommodate their partner) or selecting one pole and subverting the other.

Although this study was exploratory and based on a small sample, it suggests an important direction for future research. It would be useful to consider how individual differences in attributional tendencies pertaining to the perception of dialectical contradictions affect dialectical management practices over time and in turn ultimately affect the trajectories and outcomes of relationships.

Dialectical Patterns Symptomatic of Breakdown

Certain observed patterns of dialectical opposition may signal difficulties in the relationship and perhaps may reflect the inability of partners to effectively manage dialectical opposition. For example, Altman et al. (1981) speculate that a relationship in crisis might first be characterized by high frequency and amplitude of openness–closedness in which individuals engage in a rapid succession of intense confrontations and withdrawals. Then, as the relationship continues to decline, so do amplitude and frequency of openness–closedness as individuals interact less frequently and more superficially. Of course, the determination of whether this pattern reflects crisis in a particular relationship would depend on the subjective judgment of the relationship participants and an examination of the baseline pattern of openness–closedness during a "healthy" phase of the relationship.

Another manifestation of relational breakdown is dissynchrony or incongruence of partners' dialectical cycles or temporal profiles. Altman et al. (1981) discuss two kinds of synchrony in interpersonal interaction: temporal and substantive. Extending their discussion of openness–closedness cycling, they indicate that *temporal synchrony* occurs when the relational partners are matched in terms of their accessibility to one another. When one partner is accessible, so is the other partner; when one is closed, the other is similarly closed. Thus, temporal dissynchrony involves mistiming, such as when one partner seeks interaction but the other person is "not receptive to contact" (Altman et al., p. 152).

The *substantive synchrony* of openness–closedness cycles refers to the matching of content. Matching depicts an instance in which partners are coordinated not only in terms of timing of intimacy but in terms of degree of intimacy in interaction. It could also represent openness on the same subject, such as mutual willingness to discuss particular relational problems.

Mistiming and mismatching probably occur in all relationships to some degree. Research could investigate the consequences and differences of various patterns of cycling:

For example, how viable are relationships with long histories of matching or mismatching and timing and mistiming? Do members of viable relationships exhibit better timing and matching than those in unstable relationships? Does continual good timing and matching result in boredom or a stagnating relationship? To what extent do different relationships progress over time toward greater or lesser synchrony? (Altman et al., 1981, p. 154)

Dialectics and the Accomplishment of Disengagement

Dialectical phenomena pervade relationships, produce and symptomize change, and play a role in the breakdown of relationships. They also are ubiquitous in the strategic phases of accomplishing uncoupling. The individual initiating disengagement is faced with several dilemmas surrounding the process of intentionally changing the definition of the relationship. The initiator's primary goal seems to be termination (or negotiated decline) of the relationship, that is, a desire for more autonomy, but continued connection may be desired until the comparison level of alternatives is sufficient to make leaving the current relationship a safe choice (Sprecher, 1988). Moreover, it is typically the case that the initiator still likes some aspects of the partner. This, along with other barrier forces such as guilt and the perceived costs of termination, produces ambivalence (Levinger, 1979; Vaughan, 1986). Indeed, ambivalence can occur even after the final separation when the initiator has had time to actually experience relational life without the former partner (Vaughan, 1986). Alternatively, if the relationship is renegotiated to a friendship, the partner may still be covertly trying to win the initiator back, and the initiator may be tempted because the relationship is running more smoothly. The initiator must inevitably balance the fear of failing again with the same partner, with the fear of failure by defaulting on an opportunity to reconcile the relationship.

The autonomy–connection dilemma is also manifested in behaviors that seem to contradict the goal of termination. Vaughan remarks that

"Some initiators feel an obligation to fulfill their role as caretaker at the very moment that they are trying to put that role behind. They face the competing demands of leaving the partner, while at the same time preparing the partner for the loss" (1986, p. 174). This, of course, also can create a dilemma for the partner as he or she is faced with the competing goals of reconstituting a relational identity versus reconciling with the partner. Hope springs eternal in the presence of a partner who continues to be present and accommodating.

Both the initiator and the partner are faced with openness–closedness dilemmas, specifically regarding disengagement. The initiator faces the challenge of the extent to which the partner should be forcefully and explicitly confronted (see Chapter 6 in this volume). To be blunt is effortful and accrues numerous possible drawbacks. The initiator may feel guilty for hurting the partner, and forcing the issue may cause the partner to become angry and to retaliate in some way. Being direct without regard for the partner's face can also undermine the goal of maintaining a friendship with the partner and can make the initiator appear cruel in the eyes of others. To be indirect to avoid confrontation with the partner is to protract the difficult process of disengagement. This not only prolongs the initiator's agony, but also gives false hope to the partner (assuming the desire to disengage is not mutual). The ambiguity regarding the status of the relationship stemming from indirectness leaves both partners vulnerable to embarrassment in future encounters with each other and with their social networks (Chapter 6).

The partner wishing to maintain the relationship is also faced with the confrontation–avoidance dilemma. On the one hand, she or he will want to engage in self-disclosure with the initiator in an effort to maintain intimacy with the initiator (Baxter, 1979). At the same time, the partner will often avoid confrontation with the initiator regarding disengagement because it may act as a catalyst in producing termination.

Conclusion

Interpersonal relationships are inherently dialectical phenomena, characterized by contradiction and process. A dialectical perspective can enhance the understanding of disengagement in at least three interrelated ways. First, dialectical contradictions are the impetus for change in interpersonal relationships. Because disengagement cannot be extricated from relationship development and transitions in general, understanding change yields insight into what we call *disengagement*. In particular, plotting patterns of change over time provides a temporal profile of relationships. Such profiles may be instrumental in establishing the types of developmental relationship trajectories that coincide with crisis, repair, reconciliation, and redefinition of relationships. Additionally, differences in the characteristic nature of dialectical functioning can be used to delineate phases and stages of relationship development—including those marking breakdown and disengagement.

Second, dialectical contradictions are implicated in the breakdown of interpersonal relationships. The ability to manage oppositional tendencies is critical to relationship satisfaction and is reflected in the synchrony of partners' dialectical cycles.

Finally, dialectical contradictions are manifested in the interactions and ruminations involved in strategically accomplishing relationship disengagement. In addition to reconciling ambivalence about disengaging the relationship, initiators must strike an appropriate balance between openness and closedness that simultaneously permits achieving the goal of disengagement and preserving the face of both the partner and the self. The partner, too, experiences contradictory impulses of trying to maintain the disengaging relationship versus attempting to save face and reconstruct a different relational identity.

The chief value of the dialectical approach presented here is that certain processual features of disengagement ar revealed and emphasized. Much lip service is paid to studying the *dynamic* aspects of relationships and disengagement. Although the development of methodological innovations permits increasingly sophisticated research, we also need to more clearly conceptualize what "process" is an means. A dialectical perspective assists us in modifying the way we *think* about relationships and their disengagement.

Acknowledgments. The author expresses gratitude to Sandra Metts, Terri Orbuch, and Susan Sprecher for providing helpful feedback on drafts of this chapter.

References

Altman, I., & Taylor, D. (1973). *Social penetration: The development of interpersonal relationships.* New York: Holt, Rinehart & Winston.

Altman, I., Vinsel, A., & Brown, B. (1981). Dialectical conceptions in social psychology: An application to social penetration and privacy regulation. In L. Berkowitz (Ed.), *Advances in experimental social psychology* (Vol. 14, pp. 107–160). New York: Academic Press.

Askham, J. (1976). Identity and stability within the marriage relationship. *Journal of Marriage and the Family, 38,* 535–547.

Baxter, L. A. (1979). Self-disclosure as a relationship disengagement strategy: An exploratory investigation. *Human Communication Research, 5,* 215–222.

Baxter, L. A. (1983). Relationship disengagement: An examination of the reversal hypothesis. *Western Journal of Speech Communication, 47,* 85–98.

Baxter, L. A. (1988). A dialectical perspective on communication strategies in relationship development. In S. Duck (Ed.), *Handbook of personal relationships: Theory, research, interventions* (pp. 257–273). London: Wiley.

Baxter, L. A. (1990). Dialectical contradictions in relationship development. *Journal of Social and Personal Relationships, 7*, 69–88.

Baxter, L. A., & Wilmot, W. W. (1983, February). *An investigation of openness-closedness cycling in ongoing relationship interaction.* Paper presented at the Western Speech Communication Association, Albuquerque.

Berger, C. R., & Bradac, J. J. (1982). *Language and social knowledge: Uncertainty in interpersonal relations.* London: Edward Arnold.

Bochner, A. P. (1982). On the efficacy of openness in close relationships. In M. Burgoon (Ed.), *Communication yearbook 5* (pp. 109–124). New Brunswick, NJ: Transaction Books.

Bochner, A. P. (1984). The functions of human communication in interpersonal bonding. In C. Arnold & J. Bowers (Eds.), *Handbook of rhetorical and communication theory* (pp. 544–621). Boston: Allyn & Bacon.

Bopp, M. J., & Weeks, G. R. (1984). Dialectical metatheory in family therapy. *Family Process, 23*, 49–61.

Brown, J. R., & Vaughn, M. A. (1987, November). *Television as social reality: A dialectical analysis of family interactional process in "The Cosby Show" and "Family Ties."* Paper presented at the Speech Communication Association convention, Boston.

Cissna, K. N., Cox, D. E., & Bochner, A. P. (1990). The dialectic of marital and parental relationships within the stepfamily. *Communication Monographs, 57*, 44–61.

Conville, R. L. (1988). Relational transitions: An inquiry into their structure and function. *Journal of Social and Personal Relationships, 5*, 423–437.

Cupach, W. R., & Metts, S. (1988, July). *Perceptions of the occurrence and management of dialectics in romantic relationships.* Paper presented at the Fourth International Conference on Personal Relationships, Vancouver, Canada.

Eidelson, R. J. (1980). Interpersonal satisfaction and level of involvement: A curvilinear relationship. *Journal of Personality and Social Psychology, 39*, 460–470.

Feldman, L. B. (1979). Marital conflict and marital intimacy: An integrative psychodynamic-behavioral-systemic model. *Family Process, 18*, 69–78.

Gilbert, S. J. (1976). Empirical and theoretical extensions of self-disclosure. In G. R. Miller (Ed.), *Explorations in interpersonal communication* (pp. 197–215). Beverly Hills, CA: Sage.

Goldsmith, D. (1988, May). *A dialectic perspective on the expression of autonomy and affiliation in romantic relationships.* Paper presented at the International Communication Association convention, New Orleans.

Jorgensen, S. R., & Gaudy, J. C. (1980). Self-disclosure and satisfaction in marriage: The relation examined. *Family Relations, 29*, 281–287.

Knapp, M. L. (1984). *Interpersonal communication and human relationships.* Boston: Allyn & Bacon.

Levinger, G. (1979). A social exchange view on the dissolution of pair relationships. In R. L. Burgess & T. L. Huston (Eds.), *Social exchange in developing relationships* (pp. 169–193). New York: Academic Press.

Levinger, G. (1983). Development and change. In H. H. Kelley, E. Berscheid, A. Christensen, J. H. Harvey, T. L. Huston, G. Levinger, E. McClintock, L. A. Peplau, & D. R. Peterson (Eds.), *Close relationships* (pp. 315–359). San Francisco, CA: Freeman.

Masheter, C., & Harris, L. M. (1986). From divorce to friendship: A study of dialectic relationship development. *Journal of Social and Personal Relationships, 3,* 177–189.

Metts, S. (1989). An exploratory investigation of deception in close relationships. *Journal of Social and Personal Relationships, 6,* 159–179.

Parks, M. R. (1982). Ideology in interpersonal communication: Off the couch and into the world. In M. Burgoon (Ed.), *Communication yearbook 5* (pp. 79–107). New Brunswick, NJ: Transaction.

Rawlins, W. K. (1983a). Negotiating close friendship: The dialectic of conjunctive freedoms. *Human Communication Research, 9,* 255–266.

Rawlins, W. K. (1983b). Openness as problematic in ongoing friendships: Two conversational dilemmas. *Communication Monographs, 50,* 1–13.

Rawlins, W. K. (1989). A dialectical analysis of the tensions, functions, and strategic challenges of communication in young adult friendships. In J. A. Anderson (Ed.), *Communication yearbook 12* (pp. 157–189). Newbury Park, CA: Sage.

Rawlins, W. K., & Holl, M. R. (1987). The communicative achievement of friendship during adolescence: Predicaments of trust and violation. *Western Journal of Speech Communication, 51,* 345–363.

Rawlins, W. K., & Holl, M. R. (1988). Adolescents' interaction with parents and friends: Dialectics of temporal perspective and evaluation. *Journal of Social and Personal Relationships, 5,* 27–46.

Sarnoff, I., & Sarnoff, S. (1989a, October). The dialectic of marriage. *Psychology Today,* pp. 54–57.

Sarnoff, I., & Sarnoff, S. (1989b). *Love-centered marriage in a self-centered world.* New York: Hemisphere Publishing.

Sprecher, S. (1988). Investment model, equity, and social support determinants of relationship commitment. *Social Psychology Quarterly, 51,* 318–328.

Tolhuizen, J. H. (1986). Perceived communication indicators of evolutionary changes in friendship. *Southern Speech Communication Journal, 52,* 69–91.

Vaughan, D. (1986). *Uncoupling: How relationships come apart.* New York: Vintage Books.

Wilmot, W. W. (1987). *Dyadic communication* (3rd ed.). New York: Random House.

Wiseman, J. P. (1986). Friendship: Bonds and binds in a voluntary relationship. *Journal of Social and Personal Relationships, 3,* 191–211.

Wood, J. T. (1982). Communication and relational culture: Bases for the study of human relationships. *Communication Quarterly, 30,* 75–83.

8
Developmental Perspectives on Relationship Loss

ROSEMARY BLIESZNER and JAY A. MANCINI

Examination of relationship loss from a developmental perspective invokes at least two behavioral science traditions, that of life-span developmental psychology and that of life-course analysis in sociology. Both are fairly recent conceptual frameworks in the histories of their respective disciplines. The life-span development approach had its origins in biologically based developmental psychology. It emerged when researchers discovered that stage-oriented, fixed sequence, hierarchical principles of development, although useful for describing and explaining children's growth patterns, do not apply well to the diversity observed in adulthood and old age. Similarly, life-course analysis in sociology evolved as researchers acknowledged that historical and cultural changes affect social structure, which in turn influences the trajectories of peoples' lives. Both approaches address differences within and between people over time and attempt to explain how, when, and why change occurs and how individuals adjust to it.

Framers of the life-span development approach focused on aspects of *individual* development such as personality and cognition. Similarly, initial work within the life-course perspective was concerned with the effects of age stratification on individual opportunity, the influence of history and culture on status achievement in various domains, and so forth. More recently, social scientists, aware of the nonstatic nature of close relationships, have begun to take a developmental view of *relationships*. That is, they have adopted a process orientation to close-relationship analysis (see Chapter 1 in this volume).

Rossi (1989) recently called for a distinction between the terms *life span* and *life course* that is not tied to disciplinary boundaries but rather emphasizes the focus of study. She suggested that *life span* designates length of time, whereas *life course* refers to examination of either changing statuses across the years or processes of individual development. Both life-span and life-course conceptions of development and change apply to relationship loss. Relationships exist for various periods of time, and their length is likely to affect the process and outcome of relationship loss.

Moreover, the life stage, concurrent roles, cognitive capacity, personality traits, and other characteristics of individuals are also likely to influence the experience of relationship loss, as is the historical period in which the relationship partners live.

In this chapter we apply both life-span and life-course concepts and principles to the analysis of relationship loss. The discussion focuses on three conceptual frameworks that have evolved from an integration of psychological and sociological concerns about lives over time. First, the critical life events literature offers insights into relationship loss as a process having antecedents and consequences, rather than being a static happening. This perspective highlights the connection between variables such as the timing and sequencing of relationship loss and the subsequent adjustment to it. Second, because most people live most of life in a family context of one sort or another, family development theory is pertinent. This perspective alerts relationship scholars to role sequences and relationship changes or losses that are associated with typical patterns of family living across the life cycle. Third, research on the meaning of relationships in peoples' lives, such as Weiss's (1974) theory of the provisions of relationships, suggests the kinds of relationships that are crucial for maintaining psychological well-being and avoiding the effects of relationship loss.

We use these approaches to exemplify the application of developmental perspectives to the study of relationship loss by (a) reviewing the major tenets and principles of each perspective, (b) applying these principles to relationship loss, and (c) pointing out new research questions about relationship loss that emerge from these traditions. These theoretical perspectives reflect three levels of analysis, increasing in complexity from concern with the individual (critical life-events framework), to the family group (family development concepts), to the larger social network (social provisions theory). Although each perspective is discussed separately in the chapter, each incorporates elements of the others and reminds us that study of relationship loss requires integration of knowledge about individual development, social behavior, and close relationships, all of which are affected by a sociohistorical context that is in constant flux.

Critical Life Events Approach

Baltes and Nesselroade (1979) theorized that three major influence systems affect development. The first two are normative ontogenetic or age-graded influences—those experienced by most people at a predictable stage of life—and normative evolutionary history-graded influences—or those occurring at a certain period of time and affecting all persons regardless of their age. These two antecedents of development parallel the sociological concepts of life time and historical time

(Neugarten & Datan, 1973). The third set of influences consists of non-normative life events, or those that occur at unpredictable times with respect to life stage and are not necessarily experienced by everyone. Each category of influences is important to development, and the three systems interact with each other over the life span. Relationship loss falls into the third group of influences, noncustomary events.

A focus on life events and the ways individuals respond to them emerged from the work of social scientists concerned with stress and adaptation to it, particularly with respect to role transformations. Life events as stressors are defined as processes, rather than static occurrences, that involve both historical and concurrent antecedents, an array of variables that mediate the experience of the event, and adaptive or maladaptive consequences (Hultsch & Plemons, 1979). Responses to life events vary according to characteristics such as the ways individuals define events—whether they are subjective or objective, gains or losses, controllable or uncontrollable, anticipated or unanticipated; the extent to which events occur on time or off time with respect to age norms; whether or not the sequence of events in a person's life follows a typical pattern; the amount and types of change required by the event; and how many events occur concurrently or closely together (Hultsch & Plemons, 1979; McCubbin & Patterson, 1983). Outcomes are also influenced by such properties as whether the occurrence of an event is strongly or weakly correlated with chronological age, whether many or few people experience it, and whether the probability of its occurrence is high or low (Brim & Ryff, 1980).

Relationship loss can be analyzed as a particular life event having antecedents, processes through which it takes place (e.g., Chapters 6 and 7 in this volume), and consequences for the individual experiencing it (e.g., Chapters 10 and 11 in this volume). Relationship loss can be objective, as perhaps divorce or death may be, or more subjective, such as when a person wonders if a friendship is declining in intimacy. Whereas the ending of many relationships is likely to be defined as a loss that is detrimental to well-being, certain endings may be perceived as beneficial: termination of a marriage characterized by physical violence, for instance, or relinquishment of a burdensome care-giving role with the death of the ill party. These latter examples also illustrate the condition that relationship loss can be either voluntary and controlled by at least one of the partners (divorce) or involuntary and uncontrollable (death, or the decline in intimacy that often accompanies an illness such as Alzheimer's disease, cf. Blieszner & Shifflett, 1990). Adjustment to relationship loss will vary according to whether it occurs on time, as in the case of becoming widowed in old age, or off time, becoming widowed in young adulthood. Another important dimension is the amount of anticipatory socialization that one experiences before the relationship loss. Frequent moves may prepare a person for changes in friend networks, whereas the death of a sibling in a car accident may be much more difficult to endure.

Some relationship losses, such as divorce or widowhood, signify role transitions, whereas others, such as having a friend move away or a pet die, do not. As with other events and role transformations, some relationship losses are highly correlated with age (death of spouse, siblings, friends); some are moderately associated with age (divorce, death of parents); and some are not correlated with age, occurring throughout life (friendship ending because of conflict or relocation).

The probability of relationship loss varies with cohort membership, the causes of loss, and the number of role partners within a relationship category. To illustrate each of these conditions, cohort placement suggests that the death of one's grandparents and parents is highly probable, whereas the death of one's child is not. Many people are likely to experience termination of friendships as a result of diverging interests, relocation, conflict, or death (typical causes); relatively few will encounter the end of a friendship because of the incarceration of one partner in the friendship (uncommon cause). In the category of romantic relationships, individuals are more likely to experience breakup with casual dating partners (more numerous) than with spouses (less numerous).

Another set of factors that influences the experience of relationship loss is the position of this event in relation to others occurring concurrently or proximately in time. A loss occurring out of the normative sequence, the death of one's child before the death of one's parent, for instance, may be more difficult to adjust to than a loss that happens in the perceived proper order, such as the death of an older sibling before the death of a younger one. Also, most people find it harder to cope when several events occur close together than when they have time to recover between crises. A relationship loss combined with either another problematic relationship change or with some other life event might be especially troublesome to bear. Weiss (1975) and Johnson (1989) reported that individuals who separate from or divorce their marital partners often experience subsequent difficulties in other relationships, such as with their parents, in-laws, siblings, or friends. These significant others may fail to show sympathy, try to interfere with the divorce plans, offer unwanted advice or critiques of the estranged partner, shun the separated or divorced person, or act in other ways that diminish the quality of the relationship and compound the stress experienced by the person with marital problems. Similarly, Steinman (1979) recounted a case in which the death of a woman's father reactivated old conflicts with her mother, which led to increased dissension with her husband, nearly resulting in divorce.

Consideration of relationship loss from the life-events perspective leads to a variety of new research questions. One important issue is that typical relationship losses, such as death or divorce, usually have been studied alone, without regard to the context in which the loss occurs. For example, although gerontologists are likely to ascertain the physical health status of bereaved persons and correlate health with the outcome variable that interests them, they are unlikely to ask what other individual, family, or network changes have occurred near the death of the loved one. A second potential research focus is on unusual types or aspects of relationship loss and how they affect the persons involved. An illustration of this approach is recent examination of the impact of parental divorce on the relationship between grandparents and grandchildren, which broadens the earlier focus on the distressed couple (e.g., Johnson, 1988; Wilson & DeShane, 1982).

Another area of inquiry has to do with comparisons of relationship losses at different parts of the life course. For instance, although the literature includes studies of friendship in childhood, adolescence, adulthood, and old age, relatively few of them examine why friendships end, and none use the same methods and variables to compare termination of freindship across age groups. Similarly, there are no longitudinal comparisons of friendship decline across one or more persons' life. These kinds of studies would reveal new data on the nature and meaning of friendship across the life course as well as on how people end friendships and how they cope with such losses. Sibling, parent–child, and spousal relationship losses could also be examined longitudinally to yield more insight into the effects of these events on persons' well-being over time.

Finally, the critical life-events perspective suggests the value of studying the effect of early experiences with relationship loss on coping with similar losses later on in life. Tesch (1989) provided a discussion of the influence of early social and friendship experiences on later life friendship; this analysis could be extended to the topic of relationship loss over time.

As suggested previously, it is somewhat artificial to examine critical life events aside from the broader social context of a person's life. A very significant part of that context is the family group, within which many of life's major happenings occur. In the next section, we review the family development approach and show how it can be applied to study of relationship loss.

Family Development Theory

A long-standing theory in the family studies field is called *the family development approach*, and its goals are to describe and explain processes of change in families. Development is defined as "an underlying, regular process of differentiation and transformation over the family's history" (Mattessich & Hill, 1987, p. 437). Family development theory includes a focus on concepts involving the systemic aspects of family life, concepts relating to family structure, and concepts pertaining to orderly sequences of family roles. The most complete summaries of this framework are found in Aldous (1978), Mattessich and Hill (1987), and Rodgers (1973).

Interdependence, selective boundary maintenance, ability to adapt to change, and *task performance* describe the family system. Any one family member neither lives nor acts separately from others in the family; each is involved in a web of relationships (interdependence). Each family is partially receptive to outside influences and develops an identity and history (selective boundary maintenance). The family adapts to the needs of its individual members, as well as to those of the society; in the process of adaptation, new behavior patterns emerge and old patterns are modified (the ability to adapt to change). A family must behave in particular ways so that survival is guaranteed; performing critical tasks is functional for the family and for the society (task performance). Among the critical tasks discussed in the family development framework are socialization for roles within the family, preparation for roles outside of the family, the maintenance of family morale, and the motivation of family members to perform their roles.

In this developmental approach there are three family structure concepts: *position* (a location within a group); *role* (expectations of behaviors and feelings that accompany a position); and *norms* (rules for behavior that guide conduct). Several terms involve orderly sequence: *positional career, role sequence,* and *family career.* Over time, the role content of a family position changes (positional career), and the normative content of a role changes (role sequence). In addition, the positional careers of family members combine to form a family career. The family developmental framework is concerned with family process: "The process of family development involves a regular, ordered sequence of changes within the family as a system that occurs as an adaptation to the needs and demands of the family members and of society" (Mattessich & Hill, 1987, p. 452).

The family development approach is dynamic with regard to the society, the group, and the individual. This framework contends that a family is always linked with the larger society and that some family roles are thereby linked to nonfamily roles. It also assumes that behavior expectations come from the family group itself and that the process of socialization is one of making roles between individuals in the family. And finally, the framework suggests that individual personalities shape the family and are shaped by the family.

Family development theory suggests new areas of inquiry pertaining to relationship loss. First is the consideration of the web of family ties, that is, the level of interdependence. How is loss managed by the family whose individual members are closely connected? How are the coping patterns different or similar for people in a family marked by emotional distance? Are close relationships necessarily more vulnerable? Inter-dependence suggests reciprocal involvement and support; therefore, loss, particularly unanticipated loss, may be especially disruptive to the every-day life of the one who experiences it.

Second, how is family identity affected by relationship loss; does such a loss make the boundary surrounding a family more or less permeable? A family's vision of itself is highly dependent on who is in the family, so that change in family membership may alter that picture suddenly and drastically. Certainly, a family's history is forever changed when a mem-ber is lost, because then part of understanding that history and reflecting on it is placed in the context of how change has occurred.

Third, the question of what happens to behavior patterns comes into play. Some families (and some individuals) exhibit a great deal of behav-ioral continuity even though relationship loss occurs, whereas others develop new behavior patterns. As an example, the loss of a parent or a child means that whatever typical interaction had occurred is no longer possible. If spending time together on weekends was typical, after loss, the time will have to be spent in some other way. How this influences adaptation or adjustment has interesting implications for those working with individuals and families. Not only will the person who is left have a changing definition of self with regard to the lost relationship but he or she also will be prevented from using time in a way that may have been long-standing.

Fourth, how is the performance of critical family tasks altered by relationship loss? In some cases of loss, change in task performance is quite obvious. If the chief breadwinner is no longer a member of the family, fulfillment of that task suddenly is not accomplished. In other instances that involve emotional life, this question is not so easily answered. For example, the organizer or the empathizer in the family group might not be as readily recognized as the breadwinner.

Fifth, how is the family career affected when a member is lost? Does the pattern of positional careers follow the same trajectory as before, or does it change? When a family member is lost, a repositioning of roles and responsibilities occurs. Consequently, what would have been a "normal" course for a particular family is likely to change. One example is in the case of a spouse who must change employment patterns because a husband or wife has died. These alterations may include whether one is employed full- or part-time, whether a job changes from requiring a great deal of travel to necessitating little travel, or whether employment occurs during the day or the evening.

Last, if development is ordered and sequential, what is the range of problems that may occur when disruption that is due to relationship loss occurs? (Cf. Hogan's 1981 analysis of outcomes associated with different patterns of life transitions in education, work, and marriage.) This can be examined in terms of an individual's development (e.g., a child's personality) or a family's development (e.g., if the primary source of financial support is lost).

Questions like these could be applied to a wide variety of family role loss topics (job loss, death of a child, death of a parent,widowhood, separation and divorce, situations of abuse) and to the entire length of the family career. Comparisons among the types of family relationship losses and across periods of the family life cycle would build a more comprehensive understanding of the ways diverse families accommodate to normative and nonnormative changes.

One of the sources of assistance in adjusting to change, for individuals and family groups alike, is the larger social network. In the following section, we consider a developmental perspective on social support and relationship loss.

Theory of Social Provisions

Robert Weiss (1969, 1974, 1987) has elaborated a theory of social provisions that attempts to integrate the role that various relationships play in a person's mental well-being. His perspective on social provisions was developed within the context of loneliness, and his early observations came from work with Parents Without Partners support groups. Weiss's initial interest was in whether particular relationships functioned in specific ways (functional specificity) or whether most relationships performed any number of functions (the fund of sociability). Important relationship functions identified by Weiss (1974) are *attachment*, that is, feelings of intimacy, peace, and security as found in relationships with spouses and very close friends; *social integration*, a sense of belonging to a group with whom one shares common interests and social activities; *reliable alliance*, knowing that one can count on receiving assistance in times of need, a function often provided by kin; *guidance*, having relationships with persons who can provide knowledge, advice, and expertise; *reassurance of worth*, a sense of competence and esteem obtained typically from work colleagues; and *opportunity for nurturance*, being responsible for the care of others, such as one's children.

In studies of adult development, this theory has been applied to mental and physical health (Cutrona & Russell, 1987) and to family and friend relationships (Long & Mancini, 1989; Mancini, 1984; Mancini & Simon, 1984). Cutrona and Russell (1987) noted that the provisions in Weiss's framework touch on aspects of self-esteem, affectional ties, and problem-solving in situations of stress.

The significance of the various provisions might vary from person to person and from one life stage to another, but availability of all of them is essential for healthy development. In fact, the theory contends that the absence or loss of the relationship provisions leads to particular forms of distress. For example, if relationships that provide feelings of attachment are lost, a person experiences anxiety and the loneliness of emotional isolation. The loss of social integration leads to boredom, the feeling that one is not imbedded in a larger group, and the loneliness of social isolation. Loss of a sense of reliable alliance is experienced as vulnerability and the perception of abandonment. If needed guidance or advice cannot be obtained, a person becomes anxious and uncertain. If no one provides reassurance of worth or competence, low self-regard results, and without opportunities for nurturing and being responsible for someone else, a person is apt to feel that life is meaningless. Although each of these provisions and opportunities is somewhat distinct, each shares the thread of feeling connected with others.

The Weiss (1974, 1987) conceptualization holds considerable promise for understanding how social networks function over the individual and family life cycles and for understanding reactions to relationship loss because it encompasses both the functions of social networks and the negative outcomes of relational deficits or losses. The framework appears especially appropriate for helping to explain the linkage between social interaction and psychological health as people proceed through the life course and experience changes in or losses of close relationships.

The theory does not, however, elaborate with any precision how relationship changes or losses affect social provisions. For example, does a person who gets divorced but still has an intimate friend manage to retain more of a sense of attachment than a divorced person who has no truly close friend? Reciprocally, the conditions under which social provision loss may occur even though relationships endure have not been given attention. For instance, disagreement among siblings may cause them to withdraw the kind of support from each other that leads to a sense of reliable alliance, but the relationship continues to exist nonetheless. In addition, Weiss (1974, 1987) did not distinguish between (a) the consequences of a relationship deficit obtaining because a certain category of persons was never present in the individual's social network and (b) the consequences associated with loss of a relationship that once existed. Literature on never-married versus divorced or widowed adults, however, suggests that it is easier to find a substitute for the social provisions offered by a typical relational partner, such as spouse, than to cope with loss of a relationship (Barresi & Hunt, 1990).

An important area of future inquiry with regard to social provisions and relationship loss concerns the role that life course may play. Over the life course, what is the relative importance of the social provisions for personal adjustment? As an example, is attachment equally important for young adults and for older persons? How does the provision concerning reassurance of worth wax and wane as a person ages? and so on for the other provisions. Is a pileup of social provision deficits more difficult to withstand than loss in one category at a time?

Because of age stratification in social relationships and age-related events such as relocation, retirement, failing health, or death of a significant other, older adults may be especially vulnerable to loss of close relationships and their associated social provisions. Thus, gerontologists have become interested in exploring the extent to which one category of close relationship can be substituted for another (e.g., Simons, 1983–1984); Weiss's (1974, 1987) perspective provides a theoretical framework for guiding further research on this matter.

A second area of investigation involves the manner in which a relationship is lost. Relationship loss can be by design or intent or may be entirely out of one's control. In any case, the general research question would be how particular provisions of relationships are variously affected by how relationship loss occurs. Is it more difficult to find replacement sources of provisions when they are lost unexpectedly than when a person engineers the relationship loss (perhaps seeking out alternate sources in advance of the termination)?

A third avenue of inquiry involves how relationship replacement occurs and, by extension, how replacement of sources of social provisions occurs. Several interesting questions surround replacement. For one, how is the rapidity of replacement of social provision sources related to which social provision is at deficit because of relationship loss? In addition, what are the conditions under which such replacement occurs; in particular, what role does the prepotence of a social provision play in whether new relationships are formed? For instance, the loss of the source of social integration may be more than compensated for because of the power of the reassurance of worth provision.

Research on questions such as these extends examination of relationship loss to the level of the network of social support providers available to individuals as they proceed through life. This network, as conceptualized in the theory of social provisions, is both a source of potential relationship losses and subsequent support deficits and a source of assistance in coping with such problems.

Conclusion

Whether the research focus is on the forms of support provided by the social network, the dynamics of family structure and interaction, or the occurrence of significant events in one person's life, a developmental perspective acknowledges the reciprocal interplay between individual stage of life, social and familial context of relationships, and historical period. Most current research on relationship loss does not overtly incorporate these elements. To use Blank's (1982) analogy, we have more a set of black and white snapshots of different relationship losses at specific points in time—colleagues as a result of retirement, friends as a result of going off to college, spouse as a result of divorce or death—than a colored moving picture that captures the full range of relationship loss experiences over the course of life.

The developmental approaches to theorizing about relationship interaction and relationship loss, considered together, suggest additional more general questions than those posed in the preceding discussion. For instance, how does relationship loss vary over the life span? What variables associated with an individual's level of personal development—especially in the arenas of cognitive abilities and personality factors—affect the antecedents, processes, and outcomes of relationship loss? Reciprocally, how does coping with relationship loss at different ages influence development of the person? How do early experiences with relationship loss affect later ones? When relationship loss is voluntary, do the processes that people use to disengage from close relationships change from age group to age group? Do individuals use the same or different processes to disengage from different types of close relationships within their own networks?

Turning from individual to social structural factors, another array of general questions becomes apparent. How do gender, ethnicity, social class, residential location, marital status, and other such variables affect the experience of relationship loss? What is the influence of many versus few opportunities for replacement of the lost relationship on likelihood of ending a particular association or on adjustment to relationship loss?

Elements of time are also important in understanding relationship loss. How long does it take to adjust to loss of different types of relationships? Does the age at which a loss is experienced affect adjustment time? What is the difference between immediate, short-term coping and longer term adjustment to losses such as the death of one's parents or spouse? Is there a difference between coping with a traumatic loss that occurs as a result of a natural disaster, when many others experience similar losses, and one that happens on a more individualized basis? How might the antecedents, processes, and consequences of relationship loss vary over historical time?

Finally, a developmental outlook acknowledges that, with the exception of death, relationship loss does not occur to just one person. Nevertheless, existing studies of relationships such as those between siblings or friends tend to include the perspectives of only one of the partners. Studies of conflict in or termination of these types of relationships that capture the views of both members of the dyad are rare (see Lloyd, 1990, for a dyadic analysis of conflict in dating relationships). Is adjustment to loss of a relationship easier when both people define the reasons for termination similarly than when they have disparate views of their problems? Is it easier when the desire for termination is mutual? In their study of reactions to divorce, Spanier and Thompson (1984) found that men and women who were left by their spouses had a more difficult time coping with marital loss than those who participated in the decision to separate. Finally, what can we learn about relationship loss from cases in which one member of the dyad believes the association has ended while the other considers it to be continuing?

The challenge facing relationship scholars now is to truly integrate a life-span and life-course perspective of individual development with a relationship level of analysis that focuses on process. Conceptual frameworks associated with study of critical life events, family development, and social provisions suggest many fruitful avenues of research for the future.

Acknowledgments. The authors gratefully acknowledge the research assistance of Carol J. Pfaffly.

References

Aldous, J. (1978). *Family careers: Developmental change in families.* New York: Wiley.

Baltes, P. B., & Nesselroade, J. R. (1979). History and rationale of longitudinal research. In J. R. Nesselroade & P. B. Baltes (Eds.), *Longitudinal research in the study of behavior and development* (pp. 1–39). New York: Academic Press.

Barresi, C. M., & Hunt, K. (1990). The unmarried elderly: Age, sex, and ethnicity. In T. H. Brubaker (Ed.), *Family relationships in later life* (2nd ed., pp. 169–192). Newbury Park, CA: Sage Publications.

Blank, T. O. (1982). *A social psychology of developing adults.* New York: John Wiley & Sons.

Blieszner, R., & Shifflett, P. A. (1990). The effects of Alzheimer's disease on close relationships between patients and caregivers. *Family Relations, 39,* 57–62.

Brim, O. G., Jr., & Ryff, C. D. (1980). On the properties of life events. In P. B. Baltes & O. G. Brim, Jr. (Eds.), *Life-span development and behavior* (Vol. 3, pp. 367–388). New York: Academic Press.

Cutrona, C. E., & Russell, D. W. (1987). The provisions of social relationships and adaptation to stress. In W. H. Jones & D. Perlman (Eds.), *Advances in personal relationships* (pp. 37–67). Greenwich, CT: JAI Press.

Hogan, D. P. (1981). *Transitions and social change: The early lives of American men.* New York: Academic Press.

Hultsch, D. F., & Plemons, J. K. (1979). Life events and life-span development. In P. B. Baltes & O. G. Brim, Jr. (Eds.), *Life-span development and behavior* (Vol. 2, pp. 1–36). New York: Academic Press.

Johnson, C. L. (1988). Active and latent functions of grandparenting during the divorce process. *The Gerontologist, 28,* 185–191.

Johnson, C. L. (1989). Divorce-related changes in relationships: Parents, their adult children, and children-in-law. In J. A. Mancini (Ed.), *Aging parents and adult children* (pp. 33–44). Lexington, MA: Lexington Books.

Lloyd, S. A. (1990). A behavioral self-report technique for assessing conflict in close relationships. *Journal of Social and Personal Relationships, 7,* 265–272.

Long, J. K., & Mancini, J. A. (1989). The parental role and parent–child relationship provisions. In J. A. Mancini (Ed.), *Aging parents and adult children* (pp. 151–165). Lexington, MA: Lexington Books.

Mancini, J. A. (1984). Leisure lifestyles and family dynamics in old age. In W. H. Quinn & G. A. Hughston (Eds.), *Independent aging: Family and social systems perspectives* (pp. 58–71). Rockville, MD: Aspen.

Mancini, J. A., & Simon, J. (1984). Older adults' expectations of support from family and friends. *Journal of Applied Gerontology, 3*, 150–160.

Mattessich, P., & Hill, R. (1987). Life cycle and family development. In M. Sussman & S. Steinmetz (Eds.), *Handbook of marriage and the family* (pp. 437–469). New York: Plenum.

McCubbin, H. I., & Patterson, J. M. (1983). The family stress process: The Double ABCX Model of adjustment and adaptation. *Marriage and Family Review, 6*, 7–37.

Neugarten, B. L., & Datan, N. (1973). Sociological perspectives on the life cycle. In P. B. Baltes & K. W. Schaie (Eds.), *Life-span developmental psychology: Personality and socialization* (pp. 53–69). New York: Academic Press.

Rodgers, R. H. (1973). *Family interaction and transaction.* Englewood Cliffs, NJ: Prentice-Hall.

Rossi, A. S. (1989). A life-course approach to gender, aging, and intergenerational relations. In K. W. Schaie & C. Schooler (Eds.), *Social structure and aging: Psychological processes* (pp. 207–236). Hillsdale, NJ: Lawrence Erlbaum.

Simons, R. L. (1983–1984). Specificity and substitution in the social networks of the elderly. *International Journal of Aging and Human Development, 18*, 121–139.

Spanier, G. B., & Thompson, L. (1984). *Parting: The aftermath of separation and divorce.* Beverly Hills: Sage Publications.

Steinman, L. A. (1979). Reactivated conflicts with aging parents. In P. K. Ragan (Ed.), *Aging parents* (pp. 126–143). Los Angeles: The University of Southern California Press.

Tesch, S. A. (1989). Early-life development and adult friendship. In R. G. Adams & R. Blieszner (Eds.), *Older adult friendship: Structure and process* (pp. 89–107). Newbury Park, CA: Sage Publications.

Weiss, R. S. (1969). The fund of sociability. *Trans-Action, 6*, 36–43.

Weiss, R. S. (1974). The provisions of social relationships. In Z. Rubin (Ed.), *Doing unto others* (pp. 17–26). Englewood Cliffs, NJ: Prentice-Hall.

Weiss, R. S. (1975). *Marital separation.* New York: Basic Books.

Weiss, R. S. (1987). Reflections on the present state of loneliness research. In M. Hojak & R. Crandell (Eds.), Loneliness: Theory, research, and applications [Special issue]. *Journal of Social Behavior and Personality, 2*, 1–16.

Wilson, K. B., & DeShane, M. R. (1982). The legal rights of grandparents: A preliminary discussion. *The Gerontologist, 22*, 67–71.

Part IV
Consequences of Relationship Loss

9
Marital Dissolution and Family Adjustment: An Attributional Analysis

JOHN H. GRYCH and FRANK D. FINCHAM

Marital dissolution leads to a series of transitions and stressors that may continue to affect individual and family functioning for years after the formal divorce decree (Emery, 1988; Hetherington, Stanley-Hagen, & Anderson, 1989; Wallerstein, 1983).[1] How families adjust to the dissolution of the marriage is affected by many factors, including financial strains, relocation, and the demands of new social roles (Emery, 1988). In addition to changes in life-style, family members face several psychological tasks during this transitional period. This chapter focuses on one such task, understanding why the marriage failed.

Clinicians and researchers have acknowledged the importance of coming to terms with marital dissolution by understanding its causes and implications. For example, Weiss (1975) has stated that the process of explaining divorce gives structure to the events leading up to the separation so that "they can be seen as outcomes of identifiable causes and, eventually, can be seen as past, over, and external to the individuals' present self" (p. 15). Explanations constructed for the dissolution of the marriage, however, do not necessarily foster positive postdivorce adjustment. In fact, Newman and Langer argue that "individuals may actively promote or exaggerate their own feelings of self-recrimination and their difficulties adapting to divorce by the manner in which they think about or explain their divorces" (1981, p. 224).

The belief that understanding the causes of marital dissolution is critical for coping has given rise to a small but growing research literature that documents the attributions or explanations that adults (e.g., Fletcher, 1983; Harvey, Wells, & Alvarez, 1978; Newman & Langer, 1981) and children (e.g., Kurdek, 1986; Wallerstein, 1983) make for divorce. Although these studies show that adults and children actively attempt to

---

[1] *Marital dissolution* is used to denote a process that begins with a decision to separate and often continues to the point when a divorce is obtained. For ease of presentation, we use the terms *marital dissolution*, *separation*, and *divorce* as synonyms.

understand the separation, the role that attributions may play in post-divorce functioning received little attention. This is an important omission because attributions for events have been linked to individuals' cognitive, affective, and behavioral responses to the events. Attributions for marital dissolution therefore may have far-reaching consequences.

In this chapter we explore the contribution of an attributional perspective to understanding postdivorce adjustment for family members. Toward this end, we address three primary questions: What are the functions and consequences of attributions made for marital dissolution? How are the attributions of children and adults likely to differ? How might attributions relating to marital dissolution affect family functioning? We turn now to the first of these questions.

Functions and Consequences of Attributions for Marital Dissolution

Attribution research, the study of explanations or causes of events, has dominated the social psychological literature since the 1970s (for a review, see Hewstone, 1989). Much of the research on this topic has been guided by a few influential models that describe the determinants or antecedents of attributions (Kelley & Michela, 1980). As the attention of attribution researchers turned increasingly to applied issues in the 1980s, the need to understand the functions and consequences of attributions has become more apparent.

The functions and consequences of attributions have been a salient feature of attribution research on close relationships (for reviews see Bradbury & Fincham, 1990; Harvey, 1987). In the context of relationships characterized by high levels of interdependence, explanations for the causes of behavior may serve to maintain or even cause relationship distress by accentuating the impact of negative partner behaviors and minimizing the impact of positive behaviors (Bradbury & Fincham, 1990). It is likely, however, that the salience of this function changes over the course of the relationship; attributional activity is most common at the beginning and end of relationships (Fincham, 1985; Harvey, 1987). Weiss (1975) reports that marital separation is particularly likely to induce a search for explanations and notes a ruminative quality in spouses' thinking about the divorce: "Again and again they review what went wrong, justify or regret the actions they took, consider and reconsider their own words and those of their spouses" (p. 14).

Although prominent in relationship research, the functions and consequences of attributions have been examined almost exclusively in regard to relationship satisfaction and, to a lesser extent, behavior. The broader functions of attributions, identified by Heider (1958) and reiterated by several subsequent writers (e.g., Hewstone, 1989; Snyder &

Higgins, 1988), have remained largely unexplored. In the remainder of this section, we discuss two functions of attributions in the context of marital dissolution and examine their consequences for adaptation.

Functions of Attributions

Attributions are likely to serve two primary functions. Explanations for the causes of events can lead to a sense of *control* over the events and can also serve to protect or enhance one's *image*. In regard to the latter function, it is important to distinguish between an internal audience, the self, and an external audience because the parameters that influence the focal concern of each, *self-esteem* and *self-presentation*, are likely to differ. Each of these functions is likely to be operative in making attributions for marital dissolution.

Control Function

Understanding the cause(s) of divorce can promote a sense of control in two important respects. First, explanations structure the complex and previously inexplicable factors that led to dissolution of the marriage, thereby giving individuals "cognitive control" over events that may have seemed beyond their control at the time. Second, by understanding the factors that led to the divorce, one may be able to anticipate, and in some cases, control these factors in the future. Depending on whether the causes of the divorce are seen as changeable or unchangeable, attributions may promote either optimism or pessimism regarding future relationships.

The control function is likely to differ for the spouse initiating the divorce and the spouse who is asked for a divorce. Attributing the failure of the marriage to one's spouse may help motivate an individual to leave the marriage (Newman & Langer, 1981), whereas the initial reaction of the spouse who is left may be to protect self-esteem and to attempt to regain a sense of control in a situation in which a major decision essentially has been made for him or her (Wallerstein, 1983). In contrast, Hewstone (1989) suggests that spouses who decide to end the marriage may tend to take responsibility for the divorce at the time of the breakup but over time will tend to perceive their spouses' failings as the primary cause as a means of rationalizing or justifying their decision.

Because children do not have input into the decision to divorce, they are particularly likely to experience a lack of control over marital separation. Divorce is rarely welcomed, especially by young children, even when the marriage has been conflictual and unhappy (Kurdek, 1986). Moreover, children's understanding of the causes of the separation is limited by their level of cognitive development and lack of knowledge concerning many of the factors that may have contributed to marital problems (see following section on development). Thus, it may be very difficult for children to understand veridically their role in the divorce and to establish a sense of control over what happened.

Image Function

Attributions for divorce may remain private or they may be communicated to others. The attributions for private and public audiences may vary as different factors may promote a sense of well-being for each type of attribution. For example, it may be functional for a spouse to denigrate his or her partner when thinking about the failure of the marriage (e.g., "The marriage failed because he is a lazy, selfish person incapable of mature, emotional sharing") but not to make such thoughts public except under special circumstances (e.g., in psychotherapy, when confiding in a close friend). Attributions that follow social conventions and are therefore socially acceptable (e.g., "We drifted apart without realizing it. When we tried to get it together again, it was just too late and so we decided to split up") are likely to be offered publically. In either case, the attributions can serve to promote a positive self-image.

Private attributions may function primarily to protect self-esteem. Numerous studies have shown that individuals tend to attribute successes to internal factors such as ability but tend to attribute failure to external factors, such as task difficulty (for reviews see Bradley, 1978; Tetlock & Levi, 1982). This "self-serving bias" is likely to result in individuals' perceiving their spouses or situational factors as the primary causes for the dissolution of the marriage. Several studies investigating attributions for divorce have provided evidence for this hypothesis (Cupach & Metts, 1986; Fletcher, 1983; Kitson & Sussman, 1982; Newman & Langer, 1981). In each study, divorced adults assigned more responsibility for their divorce to their ex-spouses than to themselves. Similarly, Harvey et al. (1978) found that many of the explanations of divorcing adults focused on fixing blame and adjusting (usually lowering) evaluations of their partner. It should be noted, however, that individuals do not always seek to avoid responsibility for negative events (see Janoff-Bulman & Lang-Gunn, 1988; Shapiro, 1989); the effects of blaming one's self versus others is discussed in more detail in the next section.

Public attributions are most likely to be affected by concerns regarding self-presentation. The explanation provided to others need not be the same as one's privately held explanation. Instead, it is likely to be affected by concerns regarding the presentation of a particular image, the facilitation of the relationship with the listener, and the norms of communication. For example, some individuals may wish to elicit comfort or pity from friends and relatives, whereas others may expressly wish to avoid pity, and the types of attributions communicated are likely to influence such responses. The ability to control one's self-presentation and thereby shape the responses of others may be an important factor in enhancing the well-being of some individuals. Thus, the function served by public self-presentation is ultimately tied to the goal of protecting one's self-image. Finally, attributions communicated within the family can also be influenced by self-presentation. This is particularly noteworthy in regard to explanations that parents give to children for the divorce. Such explanations are an important source of information about who is responsible for the breakup of the family and therefore may be important determinants of children's own attributions.

In sum, explanations for the dissolution of the marriage can serve at least two functions in adjusting to divorce. They can help individuals to attain a sense of control over the separation and shape one's self-image and public image. However, the attributions made by an individual may be more or less likely to promote these functions. In the next section we consider how attributions may affect one's sense of control and self-image and the implications this may have for adjustment to divorce.

Consequences of Attributions

Although very little research exists concerning explanations for marital dissolution and postdivorce adaptation (for an exception, see Newman & Langer, 1981), attributions differ in the extent to which they foster a sense of control and positive self-image and therefore are likely to affect coping with the separation. Most explanations for marital dissolution provide structure to the events causing the divorce, but not all attributions promote the view that the causes of the divorce are "past, over, and external to the individual's present self" (Weiss, 1975, p. 15). On the contrary, some attributions may lead individuals to believe that their marriage failed for reasons that will continue to be present after the divorce. By examining how attributions may affect an individual's sense of control and self-image, the influence of attributions on coping can be illuminated.

A sense of control is most likely to be increased by attributions that identify internal, changeable causes for the failure of the marriage. Such attributions place the power of change within the individual because they reflect the view that, although one contributed to marital problems, one has the capacity to act differently in the future. Factors that are seen as unchangeable, particularly if they are seen as externally caused, are more likely to lead to the belief that one cannot control the occurrence of similar negative events in the future. Self-image is most closely linked to the degree to which individuals blame themselves for the breakup of the marriage. Believing that they are responsible for the divorce and that they could or should have behaved differently is likely to lead to self-blame and a lowered self-image, whereas avoiding self-blame is likely to protect one's self-image. It may appear that the attributions that promote these two functions are incompatible. That is, internal attributions increase a sense of control but also make self-blame more likely, whereas external attributions protect one's self-esteem but may lead to a sense of powerlessness (also see Shapiro, 1989). However, it is important to note that internal attributions and ascription of self-blame are not synonymous (see Fincham & Jaspars, 1980; Shaver, 1985). An *internal attribution* refers to the perceived locus of the cause of an event, whereas *blame* is an evaluative judgment reflecting the belief that an individual acted improperly and had the capacity to act differently. Although attributing the cause to an internal factor is a necessary precursor for blaming one's self, it does not invariably lead to self-blame. For example, a spouse could conclude that his or her behavior added to marital problems but that under the circumstances he or she could not have acted differently and therefore does not blame himself or herself for the separation.

Explanations for marital dissolution are likely to be complex, and both spouses may be implicated as causes of the divorce. Although the majority of spouses report that their partners are primarily to blame for the separation, most also accept some responsibility for marital problems (Fletcher, 1983; Kitson & Sussman, 1982). Individuals may blame their spouse for the divorce but also may recognize their own role in contributing to marital problems and thus may believe that they have control over the course of future relationships.

To understand more fully how attributions for marital dissolution may affect individuals' adjustment, it is necessary to consider their simultaneous influence on the control and image functions. Therefore, we describe a typology, represented in Table 9.1, that considers the degree to which attributions promote both a sense of control and a positive self-image. Although each of these functions is best understood as a continuum, for ease of presentation they will be categorized as either "high" or "low." Similarly, as one individual rarely receives complete blame for divorce, discussion of the object of blame refers to the *degree* to which individuals blame themselves versus their spouse.

TABLE 9.1. Typology representing the relation between attributions and the control and image functions.

Image	Control	
	Low	High
Low	Object of blame	Object of blame
	Self	Self
	Unchangeable cause	Changeable cause
High	Object of blame	Object of blame
	External factors	Relationship
	Unchangeable cause	Changeable cause

Low Control, Low Self-Image

Attributions that are self-blaming and identify the cause of marital dissolution as unchangeable are the most maladaptive type of attribution because they promote neither a sense of control nor a positive self-image. For example, individuals may conclude that the marriage broke up because they are unlovable or inadequate. This type of attribution reflects causes that are internal and stable. Janoff-Bulman (1979; Janoff-Bulman & Lang-Gunn, 1988) termed this type of attribution "characterological self-blame" and argued that it is likely to lead to a sense of personal deficiency and a feeling of increased vulnerability to the recurrence of similar negative events. Individuals who blame themselves for the failure of their marriage and do not believe that they can change may experience low self-esteem, shame, and perhaps depression. These attributions are likely to promote the belief that future relationships also will be unsuccessful and may lead to pessimism or even hopelessness about the future. In addition, individuals who focus on such personal inadequacies as the cause of divorce may experience decreased confidence in their ability to cope effectively with postdivorce transitions.

Low Control, High Self-Image

Attributions that turn the focus of blame for the divorce away from the self are more likely to protect one's self-image. This may be particularly important in the months immediately following the separation because of the host of challenges and stressors that must be confronted at that time. However, individuals who perceive the causes of the divorce as resting primarily in external circumstances or other people may experience a diminished sense of control. For example, if the spouse is seen as responsible for the separation, then the fate of future relationships also may be seen as depending on the behavior of the other individual. Consequently, individuals who blame their spouse or some external factor for the separation may maintain good self-esteem but may experience uncertainty or pessimism concerning future relationships. Explanations that place the blame for the divorce wholly within the spouse may be difficult to maintain, however, because they raise the question of why the individual married such an inadequate person in the first place. Consequently, the self is likely to be implicated as a cause of the breakup as well.

High Control, Low Self-Image

Explanations that focus on internal, changeable factors such as immaturity promote a sense of control but may lead to a low self-image. Although this type of attribution may produce self-blame and low self-esteem, it reflects the belief that change is possible and thus may foster a sense of efficacy and optimism for the future. Thus, self-blame is not necessarily maladaptive. Research on victims of violent crimes, accidents, and disease similarly suggests that self-blame may be adaptive under some circumstances. Attributing negative events to internal, unstable factors, termed *behavioral self-blame* (Janoff-Bulman, 1979), can be adaptive because it promotes the belief that individuals can control future occurrences of the event by changing their behavior. If problems in the past relationship are seen as solvable, individuals are likely to develop optimistic expectations for future romantic relationships (Harvey, Weber, Galvin, Huszti, & Garnick, 1986).

High Control, High Self-Image

Attributions that avoid self-blame and imply a changeable cause of the marital problems promote a positive self-image and a sense of control and thus are likely to have the most positive implications for postdivorce adjustment. Perhaps the best example of this type of attribution is an attribution that focuses on problems in the relationship itself rather than on either individual. Dyadic or relationship attributions recognize that both partners contribute to the marriage and acknowledge the powerful role that situational and environmental factors acting on the relationship may have played in the divorce (Newman & Langer, 1981). Because the problems existed only in the context of a particular relationship, a new relationship is not likely to have the same problems.

Even though avoiding all responsibility for the divorce may protect self-esteem, failure to acknowledge one's role in the divorce may prevent individuals from gaining a thorough understanding of the causes of the marital problems and from becoming aware of changes one can make to ensure that future relationships are more successful. In contrast, attributions that blame one or the other spouse "suggest that stable, personal deficiencies are at the heart of relationship problems and that partners can 'fail' at relationships and/or cause each other's total satisfaction or dissatisfaction" (Newman & Langer, 1988, p. 168). Thus, explanations that identify a dyadic, changeable cause for the divorce are less likely to damage self-esteem and more likely to foster optimism for the future than those focusing on internal or uncontrollable factors.

Empirical evidence supporting the adaptability of relationship attributions is provided by Newman and Langer (1981). They studied 66 women who had been divorced for 1 to 3 years and grouped the women into those who perceived their spouse as the main cause of the divorce ("spouse attributions") and those who believed that the cause of the divorce rested in the relationship itself ("interactive attributions"). It is noteworthy that none of the women in the sample perceived themselves as the primary cause of the divorce. Newman and Langer (1981) found that a greater proportion of women who made spouse attributions, as compared to those who made interactive attributions, were unhappy, less optimistic, and saw themselves as socially inactive. In addition, a greater proportion of these women tended to perceive themselves as lower in confidence, less socially skilled, unlikely to be successful, and to believe that others are better than they are. Similarly, in a 6-month follow-up, women who made interactive attributions reported that they were happier and tended to feel more positively about their ex-husbands.

This research indicates that women who perceived the primary cause of their divorce as located in the relationship reported better adjustment than those viewing their spouses as the primary cause. Although it is not clear from this correlational design whether interactive attributions lead to more positive outcomes or if better adjusted women make interactive attributions, the findings suggest that attributions for divorce are linked to postdivorce adjustment in adults. However, because no women who perceived themselves as primarily responsible for the divorce were included in the sample, the implications of self-blame for coping with divorce remain unknown. Studies examining the relation between attributions and adjustment at different time points following divorce are needed to provide further information about the effects of different types of explanations for divorce.

Although our focus has been on adults' attributions and coping with marital separation, we believe that attributions have similar functions for children. Differences in how children and adults perceive divorce, however, are likely to affect the nature and consequences of their explanations, and in the next section we consider in more detail children's attributions for divorce and their implication for coping with marital dissolution.

Children's Attributions for Divorce

Perhaps even more so than for adults, divorce creates considerable confusion and uncertainty for children. Their ability to understand why the divorce occurred has been identified as an important element in the process of coping with this stressful event (e.g., Kurdek, 1986; Wallerstein, 1983). For example, Wallerstein and Blakeslee (1989) have argued that understanding the divorce is the first of seven tasks that children must work through in adjusting to a divorce, and the attributions they make have implications for several of the other tasks, including dealing with loss of a parent, resolving anger, working out guilt following the divorce, and developing romantic relationships of their own.

Issues of control and image are likely to remain salient for children as well as adults. However, because children's role in the divorce differs greatly from that of their parents, the consequences of particular attributions are likely to be different than for adults. Children usually are not responsible for the dissolution of a marriage and have little control over the events leading to the separation, and therefore, attributions that acknowledge their lack of control may be most adaptive (see Folkman, 1984). For children, attaining a sense of control over the divorce involves understanding that they are not responsible for its occurrence. In addition, it may be functional for children to perceive the cause of the divorce as unchangeable. The hope that their parents will reunite is common in children, and clinicians consider acceptance of the finality of the divorce as a sign of effective coping (e.g., Kurdek, 1986; Wallerstein, 1983). Thus, although attributions that acknowledge some responsibility for divorce and see its cause as changeable may facilitate coping in adults, attributions that absolve children of responsibility and recognize the permanence of the divorce are most likely to protect the self-image of children and help them cope with the changes in the family.

Although children's adjustment after divorce may be facilitated by this sort of explanation, it requires a level of cognitive sophistication that younger children may not possess. Children's understanding of divorce is constrained by their cognitive developmental level and limited awareness of many of the factors that may have contributed to the separation. As a result, the content of their explanations may be very different than adults' and may often reflect inaccurate perceptions of the causes and implications of the divorce. This problem is compounded by the failure of many parents to discuss the divorce with their children (e.g., Young, 1983).

The importance of helping children attain an accurate understanding of the divorce, and in particular, avoiding self-blame, is stressed by therapists and clinical researchers (e.g., Gardner, 1976; Wallerstein, 1983; Weiss, 1975). However, research investigating the degree to which children actually blame themselves for divorce is inconsistent. Whereas some studies report that young children in particular are prone to blame themselves for marital separation (Neal, 1983; Wallerstein & Kelly, 1980; Young, 1983), other studies find that children of all ages generally do *not* assume responsibility for the divorce (Kurdek, Blisk, & Siesky, 1981; Warshak & Santrock, 1983).

One factor that may account for these discrepant findings is the amount of time elapsed since the divorce, a variable associated with children's postdivorce adjustment (Emery, 1988). The studies reporting that children do not blame themselves for divorce assessed the children an average of $2\frac{1}{2}$ to 4 years after the divorce, whereas those finding self-blame assessed the children either at the time of separation or within 18 months following the separation. It is plausible that self-blame is most common around the time of the separation and tends to dissipate over time as children gain a better understanding of the role of parental incompatibility and conflict in the marriage. In fact, Wallerstein and Kelly (1980) argue that almost all children blame themselves for the divorce at first.

Although most children may initially feel some responsibility for the divorce, their ability to form more veridical appraisals of the causes of the separation will be strongly influenced by their level of cognitive development. To understand more fully how children of different ages may perceive the causes of divorce, we examine children's explanations in the context of their social-cognitive development.

Cognitive Development and Children's Attributions

Accurate understanding of divorce requires certain cognitive skills, including the ability to make appropriate causal and responsibility attributions, to take the perspective of the others, and to distinguish between intentions and outcomes (Kurdek, 1986; Kurdek & Berg, 1987). These skills are gained gradually over the course of development, and many young children have not acquired them. Although preschoolers do make causal inferences about events, they have little awareness of distal causes of events (e.g., past behavior, personality); tend to focus on physical, rather than psychological, causes; and may not realize that stable causes have implications for the future (e.g., Allen, Walker, Schroeder, & Johnson, 1987; Rholes & Ruble, 1984; for a review see Miller & Aloise, 1989). Preschoolers also tend to overattribute intentionality, seeing all human behavior as intended (Miller & Aloise, 1989). By age 5, children can distinguish between intended and unintended outcomes, although in a less sophisticated way than older children, and tend to judge only voluntary acts as intentional (Shantz, 1983). Moreover, children of this age often do not recognize that their parents have a marital relationship independent of their relationships with the child (Fu, Goodwin, Sporakowski, & Hinkle, 1987).

Because of their relatively immature cognitive capabilities, divorce may be a fundamentally different event for young children than for older children or adults. Preschoolers tend to perceive divorce in terms of one parent physically leaving the family—and the child—and do not realize that the separation is due to problems between the parents that do not involve them (Kurdek, 1986; Wallerstein, 1983). They may have particular difficulty understanding that even though a parent intends to leave the marriage, he or she does not intend to leave the child. In trying to understand why one parent is leaving, young children may tend to focus on things that they have done to make the parent unhappy and may be likely to feel responsible for divorce (Kurdek, 1986; Neal, 1983). Thus, preschool-aged children are likely to be more confused about the causes and meaning of divorce than are older children, and this uncertainty may lead to fears of being rejected or abandoned by both parents (Hodges, 1986; Wallerstein, 1983). In addition, young children may not distinguish between privately held and publically communicated attributions. However, they tend not to tell their friends about the divorce, which suggests that they may be concerned that others will perceive them as "different" (Kurdek & Berg, 1983).

As children grow older, their causal inferences become more sophisticated, and they make increasing reference to intentions, thoughts, and dispositions as causes of behavior (Shantz, 1983). Their ability to take another's perspective increases, and they are better able to distinguish the intention of an act from its consequences. Even though early elementary school-aged children may still interpret divorce in personal, egocentric terms, they are also likely to recognize the varied factors that lead to marital dissolution and to make more appropriate causal attributions than are preschoolers. For example, elementary school-aged children begin to report that factors such as parental incompatibility can lead to divorce (e.g., Warshak & Santrock, 1983). Elementary school-aged children thus are less likely than preschoolers to blame themselves for the divorce. Instead, they tend to focus the blame on one or both parents (Young, 1983) and may become angry with their parents for breaking up the family. These children, however, still may worry that their behavior somehow contributed to parental problems (Kurdek, 1986; Wallerstein & Kelly, 1980). Even if they do not blame themselves for causing the divorce, children may feel responsible for inconsistent or infrequent visits by the noncustodial parent (Neal, 1983) and may fear being rejected or replaced by the absent parent (Wallerstein, 1983).

Increasing cognitive sophistication leads to more adult-like attributions for the separation. Children in middle school and junior high school frequently explain parental divorce in terms of "internal" or psychological causes and tend not to blame themselves for the divorce. Wallerstein (1983), however, notes that a clear understanding of the causes of the divorce can cause distress for children as well, observing that "the stress of the divorce is greatly increased by the child's accurate perception that the parents are the agents of his distress, and that they have become such agents voluntarily" (p. 270). Consequently, older children may feel strongly ambivalent toward one or both parents (Kurdek, 1986), or may blame one parent for the divorce and perceive the other parent as a victim (Wallerstein, 1983), and may experience anger at their parents that is more intense and long-lasting than that of younger children (Wallerstein, 1983). As children grow older, they also are more likely to be sensitive to the image they project to others and aware of communication norms and therefore may begin to publicly explain the divorce in terms that differ from their privately held attributions.

In sum, research on the development of attributional thinking suggests that young children may be prone to blame themselves for divorce but that this tendency decreases as children become increasingly aware of others' perspectives, psychological causes of behavior, and the nature of the marital relationship. Although children of different ages may differ in their understanding of divorce, to date an association between children's age at the time of divorce and their level of adjustment has not been found consistently (Emery, 1988; Kurdek, 1987). Children of different ages may experience different types of problems when their parents divorce, but it does not appear that a particular age group is more vulnerable to developing adjustment problems than another.

Most of the research on children's and adults' explanations for divorce has focused on *intra*personal consequences of attributions, that is, on the implications that attributions have for an individual's adjustment to divorce. However, attributions have *inter*personal effects as well, and in the final section of the chapter, we consider how explanations for marital dissolution may affect family relationships after the divorce.

Explanations for the Divorce and the Family System

The attributions made for marital dissolution may influence functioning in the divorced family both directly and indirectly. As discussed previously, attributions are often communicated and can be used to present a particular image to others. The explanations that individuals communicate to other members of the family thus may directly affect their perceptions of the causes of the divorce and of other family members. Individuals' privately held attributions may affect family interaction indirectly, by influencing their attitudes and behavior toward other family members.

Because children are often confused about the causes and implications of separation, parents can play an important role in helping them understand what is happening to the family. By discussing the reasons for the divorce, parents may shape the children's understanding of the divorce and may help them adapt to the changes occurring in their lives. However, parents' efforts to explain the separation to their children may not always be beneficial. In some cases, explanations communicated to children may serve the parent's rather than the child's interest. A parent may wish to promote a certain image with the child in order to "win" the child's affection and support. For example, parents may blame their spouse for causing the separation and may deemphasize their own role in the divorce. Although this may help to build an alliance between the parent and child, it may alienate the child from the other parent and may lead either to decreased contact with the parent or increased parental conflict over visitation. In this case, a coping strategy that may help the parent may be quite harmful for the child.

Children's explanations for the separation may also affect parents' adjustment to the divorce. Children are likely to be angry with the parent that they blame for the divorce, and Weiss (1975) notes that it can be devastating to a parent to become the object of their child's hostility. Children's anger may evoke guilt over the parent's role in the divorce, particularly if the parent initiated the divorce, or may lead the parent to avoid contact with the child. Children who are angry with the custodial parent may defy the parent's attempts at discipline and may create conflict in the home, whereas anger directed at the noncustodial parent may lead to opposition to visitation and resistance of that parent's attempts to maintain their relationship. Moreover, anger and resentment toward a parent may continue for a long time and may affect parent–child relationships even after the child becomes an adult (Wallerstein & Blakeslee, 1989; Weiss, 1975).

Attributions that are not communicated to others may also affect interactions between family members after the divorce. Blaming one's spouse for the divorce is likely to lead to hostility between the parents that may have a negative effect on both their relationship and on the children's postdivorce adaptation. For example, hostility between the parents may lead to tension and conflict over such topics as custody and visitation arrangements. Interparental conflict continuing after divorce has been linked to child adjustment problems in a number of studies (e.g., Hetherington, Cox, & Cox, 1982; Long, Slater, Forehand, & Fauber, 1988; Shaw & Emery, 1987). In contrast, interactive or relationship attributions have been found to relate to positive perceptions of one's spouse following divorce (Newman & Langer, 1981) and maintaining a good relationship between the spouses after separation is likely to facilitate the postdivorce adaptation of both parents and children.

Conclusion

In this chapter we have focused on the role that adults' and children's explanations play in adjusting to a particular type of close relationship loss[2] Our analysis indicates that attributions serve two primary functions in helping individuals cope with marital separation: They enable individuals to attain a sense of control over the factors causing the divorce and to maintain a positive self-image. The types of attributions most likely to promote these functions, however, may differ for adults and children. For adults, attributing marital problems to factors within the relationship and perceiving these problems as changeable in the future may be most adaptive, whereas it may be beneficial for children to recognize that they are not responsible for the divorce and that it is likely to be permanent. Attributions are also likely to affect relationships between family members after divorce. Certain attributions may increase hostility and conflict,

---

[2] Although attributions are also likely to be important in coping with other losses, we believe that unique characteristics of divorce limit the extent to which this analysis can be applied to distinctly different types of relationship losses. For example, whereas the death of a spouse or parent also is likely to elicit attributional processing, divorce and death differ on several important dimensions relevant to attributions (Wallerstein, 1983). For example, unlike death, divorce is voluntary for at least one spouse, the partner is not gone permanently, and it is a direct result of problems between spouses. Thus, issues of intentionality and blame generally are more prominent in the case of divorce.

both between spouses and between parents and children, whereas others may promote more harmonious interactions.

It is important to note that our analysis does not apply simply to a discrete event but recognizes that divorce is a transition that takes place over time. In attempting to understand what led to the dissolution of the marriage, individuals continue to modify their understanding of what happened long after the divorce is final. The salience of each function of attributions may also change over time. For example, the need to protect self-esteem may be paramount when the decision to separate is made and therefore spouse-blaming attributions may be most prevalent at that time. Thus, it is most accurate to consider attributional activity as part of the process of adjusting to divorce than as a single conclusion drawn by the individual. In this way, attributions are similar to accounts, which are story-like explanations that include "packages of attributions" (Harvey, Orbuch, & Weber, 1990; Hewstone, 1989; see also Chapter 10, in this volume). The recent attention given to accounts bodes well for future research on attributions for marital dissolution.

Acknowledgments. Frank Fincham was supported in the preparation of this chapter by a Faculty Scholar Award from the W. T. Grant Foundation and by Grant R01 MH44078-01 from the National Institute of Mental Health.

References

Allen, J. L., Walker, L. D., Schroeder, D. A., & Johnson, D. E. (1987). Attributions and attribution-behavior relations: The effect of level of cognitive development. *Journal of Personality and Social Psychology, 52,* 1099–1109.

Bradbury, T. N., & Fincham, F. D. (1990). Attributions in marriage: Review and critique. *Psychological Bulletin, 107,* 3–33.

Bradley, G. W. (1978). Self-serving biases in the attribution process: A reexamination of the fact or fiction question. Journal of Personality and Social Psychology, *36,* 56–71.

Cupach, W. R., & Metts, S. (1986). Accounts of relational dissolution: A comparison of marital and nonmarital relationships. *Communication Monographs, 53,* 311–334.

Emery, R. E. (1988). *Marriage, divorce, and children's adjustment.* Newbury Park, CA: Sage.

Fincham, F. D. (1985). Attributions in close relationships. In J. H. Harvey & G. Weary (Eds.), *Attribution: Basic issues and applications* (pp. 187–203). Orlando, FL: Academic Press.

Fincham, F. D., & Jaspars, J. M. F. (1980). Attribution of responsibility: From man-the-scientist to man-as-lawyer. In L. Berkowitz (Ed.), *Advances in experimental social psychology* (Vol. 12, pp. 81–138). New York: Academic Press.

Fletcher, G. J. O. (1983). The analysis of verbal explanations for marital separation: Implications for attribution theory. *Journal of Applied Social Psychology, 13,* 245–258.

Folkman, S. (1984). Personal control and stress and coping processes: A theoretical analysis. *Journal of Personality and Social Psychology*, *46*, 839–852.

Fu, V. R., Goodwin, M. P., Sporakowski, M. J., & Hinkle, D. E. (1987). Children's thinking about family characteristics and parent attributes. *Journal of Genetic Psychology*, *148*, 153–166.

Gardner, R. (1976). *The parents' book about divorce*. New York: Doubleday.

Harvey, J. H. (1987). Attributions in close relationships: Research and theoretical developments. *Journal of Social and Clinical Psychology*, *5*, 420–434.

Harvey, J. H., Orbuch, T., & Weber, A. L. (1990). A social psychological model of account-making in response to severe stress. *Journal of Language and Social Psychology*, *9*, 191–207.

Harvey, J. H., Weber, A. L., Galvin, K. S., Huszti, H. C., & Garnick, N. N. (1986). Attribution in the termination of close relationships: A special focus on the account. In R. Gilmour & S. Duck (Eds.), *The emerging field of personal relationships* (pp. 189–201). Hillsdale, NJ: Lawrence Erlbaum.

Harvey, J. H., Wells, G. L., & Alvarez, M. D. (1978). Attribution in the context of conflict and separation in close relationships. In J. H. Harvey, W. J. Ickes, & R. F. Kidd (Eds.), *New directions in attributional research* (Vol. 2, pp. 235–260). Hillsdale, NJ: Lawrence Erlbaum.

Heider, F. (1958). *The psychology of interpersonal relations*. New York: Wiley.

Hetherington, E. M., Cox, M., & Cox, R. (1982). Effects of divorce on parents and children. In M. E. Lamb (Ed.) *Nontraditional families: Parenting and child development* (pp. 233–288). Hillsdale, NJ: Lawrence Erlbaum.

Hetherington, E. M., Stanley-Hagen, M., & Anderson, E. R. (1989). Marital transitions: A child's perspective. *American Psychologist*, *44*, 303–312.

Hewstone, M. (1989). *Causal attribution*. Oxford: Basil Blackwell.

Hodges, W. F. (1986). *Interventions for children of divorce*. New York: Wiley.

Janoff-Bulman, R. (1979). Characterological versus behavioral self-blame: Inquiries into depression and rape. *Journal of Personality and Social Psychology*, *37*, 1798–1809.

Janoff-Bulman, R., & Lang-Gunn, L. (1988). Coping with disease, crime, and accidents: The role of self-blame attributions. In L. Y. Abramson (Ed.), *Social cognition and clinical psychology* (pp. 116–147). New York: Guilford Press.

Kelley, H. H., & Michela, J. L. (1980). Attribution theory and research. *Annual Review of Psychology*, *31*, 457–503.

Kitson, G. C., & Sussman, M. B. (1982). Marital complaints, demographic characteristics, and symptoms of mental distress in divorce. *Journal of Marriage and the Family*, *44*, 87–101.

Kurdek, L. A. (1986). Children's reasoning about parental divorce. In R. D. Ashmore & D. M. Brodzinsky (Eds.), *Thinking about the family: Views of parents and children* (pp. 233–276). Hillsdale, NJ: Lawrence Erlbaum.

Kurdek, L. A. (1987). Children's adjustment to parental divorce: An ecological perspective. In J. P. Vincent (Ed.), *Advances in family intervention, assessment, and theory* (Vol. 4, pp. 1–31). Greenwich, CT: JAI Press.

Kurdek, L. A., & Berg, B. (1983). Correlates of children's adjustment to their parents' divorces. In L. A. Kurdek (Ed.), *New directions in child development* (pp. 47–60). San Francisco: Jossey-Bass.

Kurdek, L. A., & Berg, B. (1987). Children's beliefs about parental divorce scale: Psychometric characteristics and concurrent validity. *Journal of Consulting and Clinical Psychology*, *55*, 712–718.

Kurdek, L. A., Blisk, D., & Siesky, A. E. (1981). Correlates of children's long-term adjustment to their parents' divorce. *Developmental Psychology, 17,* 565–579.

Long, N., Slater, E., Forehand, R., & Fauber, R. (1988). Continued high or reduced interparental conflict following divorce: Relation to young adolescent adjustment. *Journal of Consulting and Clinical Psychology, 56,* 467–469.

Miller, P. H., & Aloise, P. A. (1989). Young children's understanding of the psychological causes of behavior: A review. *Child Development, 60,* 257–285.

Neal, J. H. (1983). Children's understanding of their parents' divorce. In L. A. Kurdek (Ed.), *New directions in child development: Vol. 19. Children and divorce* (pp. 3–14). San Francisco: Jossey-Bass.

Newman, H. M., & Langer, E. J. (1981). Post-divorce adaptation and the attribution of responsibility. *Sex Roles, 7,* 223–232.

Newman, H. M., & Langer, E. J. (1988). Investigating the development and course of intimate relationships. In L. Y. Abramson (Ed.), *Social cognition and clinical psychology* (pp. 148–173). New York: Guilford Press.

Rholes, W. S., & Ruble, D. N. (1984). Children's understanding of dispositional characteristics of others. *Child Development, 55,* 550–560.

Shantz, C. U. (1983). Social cognition. In J. Flavell & E. Markman (Eds.), *Handbook of child psychology: Vol. 3. Cognitive development* (pp. 495–555). New York: Wiley & Sons.

Shapiro, J. P. (1989). Self-blame versus helplessness in abused children. *Journal of Social and Clinical Psychology, 8,* 442–455.

Shaver, K. G. (1985). *The attribution of blame: Causality, responsibility, and blameworthiness.* New York: Springer-Verlag.

Shaw, D. S., & Emery, R. E. (1987). Parental conflict and other correlates of the adjustment of school-age children whose parents have separated. *Journal of Abnormal Child Psychology, 15,* 269–281.

Snyder, C. R., & Higgins, R. L. (1988). Excuses: Their effective role in the negotiation of reality. *Psychological Bulletin, 104,* 23–35.

Tetlock, P. E., & Levi, A. (1982). Attribution bias: On the inconclusiveness of the cognition-motivation debate. *Journal of Experimental Social Psychology, 18,* 68–88.

Wallerstein, J. S. (1983). Children of divorce: Stress and developmental tasks. In N. Garmezy & M. Rutter (Eds.), *Stress, coping, and development in children* (pp. 265–302). New York: McGraw-Hill.

Wallerstein, J. S., & Blakesee, S. (1989). *Second chances: Men, women and children a decade after divorce.* New York: Ticknor & Fields.

Wallerstein, J., & Kelly, J. (1980). *Surviving the breakup: How children and parents cope with divorce.* New York: Basic Books.

Warshak, R. A., & Santrock, J. W. (1983). The impact of divorce in father-custody and mother-custody homes: The child's perspective. In L. A. Kurdek (Ed.), *New directions in child development: Vol 19. Children and divorce* (pp. 29–46). San Francisco: Jossey-Bass.

Weiss, R. S. (1975). *Marital separation.* New York: Basic Books.

Young, D. M. (1983). Two studies of children of divorce. In L. A. Kurdek (Ed.), *New directions in child development: Vol. 19. Children and divorce* (pp. 61–70). San Francisco: Jossey-Bass.

10
The Account-Making Process:
A Phenomenological Approach

ANN L. WEBER

Participants in a summer Elderhostel course on grief were invited to complete open-ended questionnaires about their personal experiences in responding to the loss of an important close relationship. Here is an excerpt from the account provided by a 67-year-old man[1]:

The loss was of an infant son who died after one day of life. The loss was particularly painful because of his being our first child. The cause was premature birth (5 months) and insufficient lung development. Today the child would have a good chance of being saved, this was 1963. This was the hardest thing I have had to go through and being asked by our pastor to baptize him, somewhat alone at the home—people do not come to visit an infant apparently—picking out the clothes he would wear, seeing the near-perfect (to me) features and finally the funeral was a soul wrenching experience. . . . We still think of the event on March 1 and wonder what our 26-year-old son would be like. . . .

This man's story was one of the very few responses that specified a relationship other than a marriage as a central loss. Most of the 40 Elderhostelers—all 60 years of age or older—chose to describe memories of the loss, through death or divorce, of a husband or wife. A few commented, almost abashedly, about the difficulty of coping, even now, with having lost a parent (as though such an "expectable" loss should be easier to deal with than the loss of one's child or spouse).

---

[1] This excerpt and others identified as written by Elderhostel participants come from my files. Most were written in response to an open-ended survey distributed to Elderhostel students—men and women at least 60 years of age—enrolled in a class on dealing with intimacy and relationship loss in the summer of 1989. All names of individuals and locations have been changed to protect the privacy and anonymity of the respondents who provided this information. While spelling and punctuation are edited for clarity, the language and wording of responses is preserved verbatim. Omissions, indicated by ellipsis points, were made for the sake of brevity or clarity. Excerpts not otherwise identified or referenced are from these Elderhostel reports in my files.

Another respondent, a 66-year-old woman, provided an account of her response to the "loss" of her husband through Alzheimer's disease, although he was still living when she wrote about it:

I was angry, and that obstructed my other relationships. I couldn't believe that this was happening to such a good man. It wasn't fair. The damn platitudes and fundamental sayings brought my anger to the surface in a profane way. I expressed some spicy words about such feelings. One in particular that continues to haunt me is, "There is a purpose for everything." Well, I wish to God that God would let me in on the purpose because I sure as hell don't see how or why it has happened to him. It happened, not to me, but to him. . . . I must admit the finality of his illness probably "wiped me out" more than anything that has ever happened to me. He's physically here, but the disintegration of his personality and his body . . . has been very difficult to accept. I no longer see him as frequently. I go on longer trips such as this Elderhostel—I find myself consuming myself with activity and *busy*-ness. . . . The coping will continue until he dies, and I have a feeling there may be a sense of relief that he doesn't have to live in that way anymore. I have hurt so long and cared so long and felt helpless so long that I will be glad when it's over—I do try to be able to talk about him as it was and to be able to express my situation without being morbid. People who take the time to let me know they care about me in my grief are probably the best antidote for my suffering.

While most respondents' stories of spousal loss detailed the ravages of illness or the tragedy of sudden death, such stories usually included acceptance of the inevitability of death and some gratitude for a good life together or comfort in the recognition that others had sustained similar losses and understood the emptiness and sadness of bereavement. The following excerpt is unusual in that it chronicles a loss through divorce. Dorcas, a 62-year-old woman, recalls with surprisingly fresh anger and confusion the pain and injustice of her loss; here is her response in its entirety:

The loss through divorce of my second husband [3 years ago] is one that I am still trying to understand. In some ways I am still grieving, even though I have made a good recovery and believe I am happier and wiser than I was before. . . . Len and I met in 1974 in a car pool of five persons who commuted 40 miles to work . . . I had been divorced 3 years; Len was married, unhappily. He took me out to lunch and a passionate romance developed. He took a new job [in another state], but instead of taking his wife with him, he told her he wanted a divorce, and I moved [with him]. When he got his divorce, he arranged for us to be married as soon as the law allowed, to the day. That was 1977. For 8½ years we had what I thought was a good marriage, even a superior one. He and I were very good friends, so comfortable with one another. We talked a lot. We took great trips together. Where our interests diverged, we freely let each other do our own thing. Len hated confrontation and let me have my way most of the time. I really liked that.

We had some problems. Our sex life, which had been wonderful before marriage, became boring. We each thought it was the other's fault. We also had some money problems. I had more money than he, and I think he was threatened by it, although Len has never admitted this. The biggest problem, I think, was that Len undervalued and disapproved of me. He undervalued my intelligence. He disapproved of my disinterest in homemaking. When I developed cancer less than a year after our marriage, he could hardly have been less concerned about me or my illness. That was a terrible shock, but I made excuses for him. I just couldn't admit how little I meant to him.

In January 1986 Len was on a "business trip," which began to look very peculiar when numerous lies surfaced. When he returned he told me he had found his long-lost high-school sweetheart whom he had dated about 5 months at age 15, until her father broke them up. They had no contact for 46 years, although Len could easily have located her had he tried. But he claimed he had always been secretly in love with her, which explains, I guess, that dream-like daze that was such a noticeable and puzzling aspect of his personality. Three days with Nancy was all he needed. He demanded a divorce. Nancy was already packing her things. I thought about it a few minutes. Suggested counseling. He refused. I knew I didn't want to live with him anymore. So I agreed. Actually, I was delighted to give him a divorce. I was elated, euphoric. It was as if *I* had asked *him* for one. The bizarreness of it all carried me along. Truly, there was a lot of humor in it.

But gradually I became angry. Len refused to talk with me about what had gone wrong. All he would say was "nothing went wrong," "no serious problems," etc., etc. He had no interest in helping me achieve closure on the relationship. He just walked away and never looked back. So easy for him! Our life together had meant nothing. He told others he had never loved me. The years we had spent together, what meaning did they have? I suffered a loss of self-esteem.

Nancy and I happen to see each other occasionally. We each had our motives for doing this. I hoped she could help me understand, work through, find meaning in what had happened. But she was unwilling or unable to. I shouldn't have expected it. Len's children were helpful. They liked me, disapproved of what their father did, made me feel like a desirable person. That helped a lot. Len's sister and I are still good friends. To maintain a relationship with his family for some reason is important to me, though his children are becoming less so.

On the whole, I think I am coping well. I am active in a different church and its singles group. I have more friends now than I had before. I have a new home and have fixed it up attractively. I have a new dog and cat. I do volunteer work. I travel. In many ways I'm truly a different person. Yet I am still trying to figure out what went wrong; still trying to make sense of those years we spent together. I still grieve from time to time over the loss of the relationship. I still have fond memories of some of the things we used to do, especially the trips we took together. I am still in the process of getting back the self-esteem I lost when Len walked out.

Dorcas's account has been cited in its entirety because it assembles with style and candor the many different features and qualities that may characterize an account: an introductory statement that acknowledges the storyteller's audience; a brief (well-reviewed) history of the relationship's early stages; a reflection on the factors that led to eventual dissolution, the "fatal flaws" that were there all along but that only became clear in retrospect; a chronicle of her reactions to separation, including denial, euphoria, anger, sadness and confusion; a report of her efforts to cope and her recent strategies for dealing with grief; and most pointedly, the unending hunger for meaning. Indeed, Dorcas's story is amazingly complete, considering that, at the time she wrote it, her Elderhostel course on grief had not yet covered such concepts as stages of grief or strategies for coping, much less coached her in producing an account that addressed these themes.

This chapter is about approaching a "phenomenon" such as this woman's account of her divorce experience in such a way as to preserve and respect its elements *and* its totality, as *she* has presented it, and as it is *meant* to be accepted and interpreted. This is the phenomenological perspective. In contrast, a traditional positivist approach to Dorcas's account would mandate breaking it down into its components, such as self-assertions and attributions. Recent developments in video technology even make it possible for us to record such stories with all visual cues and verbal qualities intact, ripe for content analysis and coding. Presumably, the goal of such objectification would be to reduce the messy, out-of-order form of the reported account to a simpler series of statements and utterances. We could then identify one or more purposes the account serves for its author, for example, to present herself in a sympathetic light or as a capable survivor, or to label her present confusion and loneliness more acceptably as the consequence of undeserved loss and pain. Finally, we could assess her account's value and efficacy in doing its "job." Is her self-esteem significantly higher than that of a griever who has not formulated a self-excusing account? Are her coping skills measurably greater than those of a less articulate survivor of divorce? Is she freer of health problems than she would be if she repressed or stifled her account-making activity? In sum, a traditional scientific approach to this account might view the account as a means to an end, a package of ingredients, each with its own anodyne, a vehicle for social interaction and discourse whose story-like qualities are attractive but merely accidental, epiphenomenal rather than essential.

In contrast, I argue in this chapter that the form of one's account *is* phenomenal, important, an event to be marked if not *the* event most deserving of our interest in intimacy and loss. Accordingly, accounts and account making are best approached from the phenomenological perspective, *as well as* (not instead of) from the traditional view of analytic, interpretive, positivist science. In sum, to cite the broad Gestalt principle, the whole is greater than the sum of its parts: Dorcas's account of her marriage and divorce is more than a checklist of reactions and stages. The "more" that is not grasped by traditional analysis may be better appreciated by a "synthesis." The phenomenological perspective offers one kind of synthesis. In the rest of this chapter, I first review the nature of accounts and account making and examine the phenomenology of relationship loss and account making. Finally, I review the meaning of account making in response to relationship loss.

Relationship Accounts and Account Making

An account is a story-like narrative or explanation of one's experience, such as in a personal relationship, emphasizing the characters and events that have marked its course. An account may be oral or written in form and may unfold as a relatively loose "packaging" of attributions made about one's partner or the relationship or as a more elaborate, structured self-presentation in which such attributions are embedded and interwoven with other messages (Harvey, Weber, Galvin, Huszti, & Garnick, 1986; Weber, Harvey, & Stanley, 1987). One's relationship account may be formulated (at some marginal level of consciousness) by an ongoing process from the first moment the relationship is seen as "crystallized" in the account maker's mind. (Because the account is entirely subjective, the "relationship" itself may be a one-sided fantasy on the part of the account maker, what Sternberg [1988] calls "infatuated love" and similar to what Tennov [1979] calls "limerence.")

In the course of the relationship, one formulates a "master account," which is the "whole story" of the relationship, a running commentary–narrative developed by collecting separate chapters or episodes about specific occasions and events. This master account comes to subsume several subaccounts, such as stories about first meetings, significant shared history, moments of conflict, and chronicles of successful or unsuccessful efforts to cope with trauma or stress. Such ongoing, master-account formulation is more process than product. The reported account itself (or one version or aspect thereof) is manifested only when events or stressors have triggered its "release." (See also Chapter 1 in this volume, regarding the view of relationship loss as a process.)

A real-life example of this sudden release of a seemingly fully formed account is provided by the report of one women, Emily Ann, in a letter she wrote to a friend after the sudden death of her former lover, Tony. Some years before, Emily Ann and Tony had amicably ended their romantic relationship but stayed close friends across time and life changes. Years passed: Emily Ann moved to another city, Tony began a new relationship and married; they all kept in touch. Emily Ann was planning her own wedding when she learned that Tony and his new wife had both been killed suddenly in a freak automobile accident. She was unable to travel to attend the funeral and wrote the following in the letter to their mutual friend:

Grief, yes, I was certainly suffering from the grief of Tony's death. Even as I write these words I do not believe it fully. . . . You all know very well how close [he] and I were for so so many years. We dated for four years, then off and on for two more. He made several quiet trips . . . to see me [after I had moved here]. We made our peace from lovers to friends years ago. And close friends we were, indeed. He knew me before I even went to college. I was 18 and he was 24. He helped me grow up, showed me the world, gave me worth and dignity when I was a shy [provincial] girl with little idea of self-worth and no sophistication what-soever. He taught me love, worth, and helped me grow up gently and wisely. He was my first love and my first friend from outside my narrow little [hometown]. He accepted me fully before I even accepted my own background. Tony was Tony: sweet, constant, cheerful, and a friend to all. We were terribly in love for a very, very long time.[2]

The history of their relationship pours out as though it had been fully contemplated, interpreted, and organized for some sort of presentation long before this letter of bereavement was occasioned. Emily Ann does not have to "start from scratch" to collect her thoughts and explain her feelings to her friends. Her account is available to her, on her mind, "at the ready." Learning of Tony's sudden, untimely death acted as a trigger or releaser for this encapsulated but rich history of their relationship.

Accounts contain poignant and obvious Gestalt qualities and can give the account maker a sense of closure, a better understanding, or a sense of control over the events related (Weber et al., 1987). The fabric of an account may consist largely of memories, often with a distinct "flashbulb" quality of clarity and detail (Harvey, Flanary, & Morgan, 1986). Accounts can condense and refresh all the wealth of affect associated with an intimate relationship and its disruption or loss, as well as facilitating the possibility of emotional catharsis when those feelings are relived (Harvey, Orbuch, & Weber, 1990; Weber et al., 1987). After reflecting on the past, the account maker may "swivel" in time, able to turn to the future to project expectations—or firm resolutions—about future relationship experiences and challenges ahead. Thus, a college student who attributes a recent breakup to "communication problems" in his past relationship indicates that, in any future liaisons, he "expects" to put more energy into better communication with his partner (Harvey, Agostinelli, & Weber, 1989).

The Account-Making Process

Most recently, my colleagues and I have explored the process of account making as a response to stress or trauma, especially relationship conflict or loss (Harvey et al., 1990). In the model we propose, an adaptation of the work of Horowitz (1986), the stress–response sequence includes the following order of stages:

---

[2] This letter, passed on by the writer, is retained in my files.

1. *Traumatic event*: involving shock (feeling overwhelmed, numb)
2. *Outcry*: involving emotional expression (panic, exhaustion, despair, hopelessness)
3. *Denial*: early stage of account making, possibly involving escapism (avoidance, isolation)
4. *Intrusion*: continued or initial account making, involving flooded states (distraction, obsessive review)
5. *Working through*: intensified account making, confiding with close others
6. *Completion*: completion of the "story," acceptance, possession of coping skills
7. *Identity change*: behavioral expectations formulated in line with the account.

In this model we (Harvey et al., 1990) suggest that *failure* to engage in account making will incur several negative consequences, including problems of failing to work through one's loss (e.g., psychosomatic illnesses related to denial); failing to complete the coping process (e.g., prolonged grief or anxiety); and failure to learn or adapt by developing a new identity in response to the loss (e.g., reiterated stress, exhaustion, or fixation of a maladaptive response pattern). In sum, we argue that account making is a useful, healthy, adaptive strategy within the stress–response sequence. One's account, far from being an epiphenomenon or a kind of "frippery" associated with grief or stress, is an essential process of coping with the stresses and losses inevitable in any life touched by intimacy and hope. The production of the account, therefore, is an essential, natural, phenomenal process.

The Phenomenology of Relationship Loss

Phenomenology, as a perspective, is almost overwhelming in its outreach as well as its origins. Phenomenology should not be a restriction of perspective but an enrichment of it. Misiak and Sexton (1973) define "phenomenological" psychology broadly as "any psychology which considers personal experience in its subject matter, and which accepts and uses phenomenological description" (p. 40). A "phenomenon" is literally an "appearance," a subjective experience from the descriptive perspective of the experiencer. In practical terms, phenomena—the appearances of things—are to be contrasted with the *things themselves*. A positivist science like experimental psychology seeks to understand truth *through* its manifestations in appearances, to get *past* the mask or clutter of experience *to* essence. Phenomenology, in contrast, appreciates the essence-as-experience and sees the "mask or clutter" as phenomenally real and worthy of understanding. Appearance, to be sure, is not everything—but it is *something*.

Consider an example of the positivist–phenomenology distinction in the business of conducting accounts research. Accounts are most practically collected as oral or written reports, volunteered by willing retrospectors. Accounts of relationship loss are typically provided by lone survivors of relationships, whose partners are deceased or otherwise unavailable to both the account maker *and* the accounts researcher. The account of a breakup, therefore, is likely to be one-sided in terms of explanations, accusations, and biases. Does this one-sidedness present a crippling problem to the future of work on accounts and attributions? A colleague at a recent social psychology conference summarized many criticisms of accounts research when he phrased his concerns thus: "If you only have *one* survivor's version of the breakup, how do you know you have an accurate, or even a fair, story? Shouldn't you try to track down the other person, get his or her account, and compare their stories to see if they verify each other?"

The term *verify* captures the positivist assumptions—the bias—of such criticisms of accounts research. From a positivist point of view, the basic question to ask about accounts is what they *tell* us about the *real* event, the breakup itself. The positivist assumes that there is a real event, the breakup, whose objective nature exists and can be learned or inferred through various sources, including the self-reports of the former partners. By sifting through partners' reports, coding for meaning and correcting for error or distortion, the intrepid researcher can get at the truth of the events and can draw conclusions about relationships in general. Such a truth-seeking investigation is inquestionably an interesting and worthwhile line of research, focusing on the issues surrounding the real versus the imagined causes of breakup. It suggests that partners will have different perspectives depending on such questions as who left whom, whether the breakup was sudden or gradual, whether other parties were involved, and so on. (The work of Hill, Rubin, & Peplau, 1976, is recommended as representative of efforts in this direction.) These positivist assumptions, however, tend to sidestep the experiences and events themselves by focusing on getting *past* the phenomena (appearances) to objective events that are assumed to be more "real."

In contrast, a phenomenologist's response to this criticism points out that, although accounts are indeed versions of "real" events and sequences, they are also important *as presented*. People are not merely *capable* of composing stories of their loss experiences; research indicates that they *present* such stories, like the examples cited here, composed and at the ready. The stories and the story-telling *process* themselves are real; these "appearances," these subjective interpretations of events, are psychologically real to the experiencers and story-tellers themselves. If we wish to learn about the realities of personal relationships, we would do well to pay attention to such natural forms these realities take on. Phenomenology does not take for granted the objects it studies but rather poses questions about their very existence and the *meaning* of their existence (Gurwitsch, 1966). Rather than assuming that an individual will compose an account of his or her relationship and the experience of its loss, we instead question its very basis: For example, *how* is it that he or she *has this story*—however brief, sketchy, or distorted—*ready to tell* when we ask? We have previously observed that accounts are often surprisingly accessible, as if they were close to the surface of the account-maker's consciousness, ready to be dressed and served up to a variety of listeners or readers (Harvey & Weber, 1982). We may then pose other questions: *What is the meaning* of this "readying" activity on the part of the account maker? *What is the purpose* of this story-producing process? Accounts may serve many functions, may have several varied "careers" (Weber et al., 1987). The phenomenological philosopher Maurice Merleau-Ponty has asserted the functional value of understanding experience subjectively:

Anger, shame, hate and love are not psychic facts hidden at the bottom of another's consciousness: they are types of behavior or styles of conduct which are visible from the outside. . . . To create a psychology of anger is to try to ascertain the meaning of anger, to ask oneself how it functions in human life and what purpose it serves. (Merleau-Ponty, 1964, pp. 52–53)

The works of phenomenological philosophers like Max Weber, Edmund Husserl, Albert Schutz, and their students focus again and again on themes and concepts that are familiar to psychologists, especially in the Gestalt tradition: meaning, intentionality, experience, motivation, subjectivity, and psychological reality (Gurwitsch, 1966; Hekman, 1983; Merleau-Ponty, 1963, 1964; Misiak & Sexton, 1973; Rogers, 1983; Rosenberg, 1986; Schmidt, 1985; Schutz, 1970; Spurling, 1977). In particular, the phenomenological perspective is brought into psychological inquiry through the work of Kurt Lewin (1935, 1936). Lewin's concept of the "life space" emphasized the mutuality of the transaction between personhood and environment. In his equation $B = f(PE)$ (*Behavior* is a *function* of the *Person–Environment* situation), Lewin meant life space (PE) to consist in the totality of possible events, "the total of possible and non-possible ways of being" (Lewin, 1936, p. 14). Thus life space can and very often does include what may not be objectively "true" but is nonetheless meaningful for the individual perceiver. "What is real is what has *effects*" (Lewin, 1936, p. 19). Real influences on human action may include aspects of person and environment that are not contemporaneous, such as memories and past experiences. One's choices and course of action can be affected by what one believes to be true—such as one's own account, however biased or "unverified," of a recent relationship loss—whether it is objectively true or not.

Is there some kind of "naive phenomenology" that can be tried on by nonphilosophers who wish to appreciate appearances for themselves as

well as for the glimpses they give of what they contain? In the intro-
duction to his text, *The Individual in a Social World*, the late Stanley
Milgram poignantly expresses the value of such a perspective even to an
experimentalist:

The source for the experiments in this volume is neither textbooks nor abstract
theory, but the texture of everyday life. They are imbued with a phenomenological outlook. Even so apparently technical a study as "The Lost Letter Technique" begins with the imagined experience of encountering such a missive, the
consciousness of choice which the letter stimulates, and the ultimate resolution of
conflict tendencies in a decisive and measureable act. (Milgram, 1977, p. 1)

Milgram proposes a useful, pragmatic strategy for reaping the benefits
of the phenomenological perspective on social events and actions that
are traditionally viewed through the positivist prism. We can begin by
appreciating the *meaning* and the *meaningfulness* of, for example, an
account and the account-making process that produces it. We can set
aside for the moment questions about the account-maker's error or the
distortion caused by the story-teller's defensive or wounded point of view.
For the time being, we can concentrate our interest and concern on the
energy channeled into account making, the hints the account provides us
about its purpose and effectiveness, and the criteria the account maker
uses to judge how to begin, what to say, and when to finish.

For a concrete application of this phenomenological method, return to
the third account example provided earlier in this chapter, the story
written by Dorcas about her relationship with her husband Len before he
left her for Nancy and her experiences in coping with her feelings there-
after. What are the feelings and tone Dorcas conveys, from line to line, in
her story? What do we think of her, or of Len or Nancy, as we read it?
What are we *meant* to think? How does she end her account? Does she
"leave" us on an optimistic or a despondent note? What characterization
does she offer of herself in her new identity and her life after divorce?
These are some of the questions we can ask from a phenomenological perspective. If we feel adventurous, we might even ask "meta-
phenomenological" questions: Is this report the same story Dorcas would
tell a friend, a *good* friend, a therapist? When she is alone or with people
who are not accounts researchers and is not responding to direct questions about her "breakup story," are there still story-like elements—plot,
structure, characterizations—to be found in her letters and discourse?

The implications of the phenomenological perspective for methodology
are likely to be aversive for most social scientists: This is certainly a very
messy approach. We may say what we will about old-fashioned numbers
crunching: Quantification, at least, reduces lengthy exposition or bad
grammar to neat columns of information. Content analysis is helpful in
shunting half-phrases and obscure allusions into a few discrete, meaning-
fully labeled categories. Can one "appreciate" the subjective impact of an

account without becoming mired in and overwhelmed by its irreducible verbiage? (See also Chapter 2 in this volume, for an examination of the challenges of integrating methodology with theory in understanding relationship loss.) I argue here not to *supplant* traditional methods with a murkier, more empathetic perspective. Rather, I argue in favor of augmenting traditional "clean" methods with additional strategies that are sensitive to preserving the form and intentions of such accounts as provided by the account makers. For example, when reporting the nature of attributions embedded within a breakup account, researchers should provide not only a table of tallies within categories of utterances but also one or more examples of the accounts *as provided*. The whole is greater than the sum of its parts; the account is more than a string of attributions or self-justifications. That elusive "more" may not be articulable, but its sense should be made as available to those who read the report as it was to the researchers themselves.

The Phenomenology of Account Making in Response to Relationship Loss

A phenomenological perspective on account making, most simply stated, might be equivalent to the *account-maker's* perspective. How does the account maker compose and intend his or her account? To accept it "as intended," we must consider the account-maker's intentions and motives. One implication of this perspective is that the effects of account-making can be either intended or *un*intended. For example, there is evidence that account-making can have therapeutic consequences for the account maker, ranging from more efficient coping with loss to alleviation of psychosomatic symptoms of stress (Harvey et al., 1990; Harvey, Weber & Orbuch, 1990). From a phenomenological point of view, we cannot consider such consequences to be motivating unless they are psychologically real to the account maker. In other words, does a grief-stricken survivor of divorce or spousal death tell her story *because* she knows that doing so will be beneficial to her mental and physical health? Or does she rather feel compelled to talk or write about her experiences for more personal or less articulable reasons? What ineffable, non-content-analyzable qualities of the account-making process can be revealed to us from a phenomenological perspective? Research and examples already collected yield several avenues of interest.

Remembering

In writing her account for the Elderhostel project, a 60-year-old woman indicates that this is not the first time she has written about her experiences in coping with her grief:

The death of my first husband, [when I was] 44, was the most devastating experience of my life. He was 49, and died suddenly. . . . My first husband and I were extremely close. He was 30 when we married and I was 25. It was the first marriage for both of us. . . . I went to the cemetery where my husband was buried quite often at first, then it tapered off. I wrote down my feelings. I wrote and wrote and wrote—things I couldn't discuss with others. I talked about my feelings a lot too.

An important sense conveyed by this account fragment is the "automatic" nature of account making, the naturalness and even compellingness of writing down or talking out one's story as a way of coping, of figuring out what has happened, and what it means. This writing–telling process may be so natural and facile simply because the fabric of accounts is largely memory, available at some preconscious level of thought, just below the surface of social awareness. These memories may be sought, dug out, reconstructed for purposes of wishful thinking, sense making, or self-presentation to others. On the other hand, relationship memories are often powerful enough to rise unbidden and intrude on present thinking. Harvey, Flanary, and Morgan (1986) collected descriptions of a variety of "vivid" memories of past loves from their adult respondents. Subjects' verbatim reports about their recall of emotionally significant past relationship ranged from terse, unpleasant images ("He took someone else home in front of me") to longer, more descriptive, story-like explanations:

We were lying in bed at the end of the weekend. We both were aware that the end was upon us, but we had waited until the end of his visit to talk about things. I remember lying there stiff, with the sun streaming in the window, telling him what I wanted from a marriage and how I doubted he was willing to fulfill that expectation. I lay there wanting him to say I was wrong but knowing that he wouldn't. He just turned, looked at me sadly, and said "You're right." (Harvey, Flanary, et al., 1986, p. 368)

Another reason for the just-below-the-surface accessibility of accounts and vivid relationship memories is their relevance to present patterns and future expectations. In urging research on the meaning of family conversations, Edwards and Middleton (1988) observe that remembering is inextricably intertwined with relating:

In the perspective outlined here, the connection between remembering and relationships looks both ways. Relationships are a determinant of remembering, providing criteria of significance . . . and providing also a forum for the process itself. . . . In the other direction, remembering is a determinant of relationships. Relationships can be defined, negotiated, redefined, consolidated, disputed, through conversations about the past. Arguments and agreements occur about what has really happened, who said what and when, and with what intent; glosses are put upon the past, with the aim of defining the present and future paths that a relationship might take. (Edwards & Middleton, 1988, pp. 4–5)

Meaning

Memories may be the fabric of accounts—accurate or not—but they may be woven into a variety of functions. Recall the rhetorical questions posed by Dorcas in reflecting on the end of her marriage: "Our life together had meant nothing. . . . He told others he had never loved me. The years we had spent together, what meaning did they have?" Consider also the interaction between good and bad memories in the following account of a 67-year-old woman recounting her painful divorce and its aftermath:

I can honestly say that today I am a resourceful person, a warm and caring person, without *any* bitterness. I am retired, living alone in my little house and very involved with family and a few friends. Oddly, I am not into church activities. I do help individuals when I can . . . but I can't say I'm a "do-gooder."

I am a very happy person, truly, at this stage of my life. I do remember good things about our marriage—some of the funny things, the sweet, thoughtful gestures. I also remember the very bad times, but I don't dwell on them.

I remember being carried over the threshold of each new apartment or house with each move. I remember a Christmas stocking tied to the foot of my hospital bed after the birth of our first child on Christmas eve. My feelings now are, weren't we lucky to have had so much once. Perhaps now at 67 I'm remembering more often.

The very composition of this account—by emphasizing the detail of specifically *good* memories—appears to be a part of the identity-forging process. The account maker makes self-references as if to underscore her positive development and lack of bitterness: "I am . . . warm and caring. . . . I am a very happy person." These self-descriptions have a particular meaning when considered *in context* with the larger story of her loss and her admission that she *does* remember extremely painful times "but I don't dwell on them." The *meaning* of her present, hard-won self-confidence and contentment can be clear only against the ground of her painful, confusing loss. This is the kind of Gestalt quality possible from a phenomenological perspective.

Accounts may function as vehicles for meaning in several ways. For example, accounts can be very efficient vehicles for meaning via attributional analyses. In relating the "what happened" of one's past relationship, the account maker is free to extemporize and guess about the "why" and "how." Such attributional analyses may help one to cope with the trauma of divorce (Chapter 9 in this volume) or may help one to "get over" the pain of a breakup and the obsession with the ex-partner (Harvey, Weber, Yarkin, & Stewart, 1982).

In the last account, the account maker emphasizes the value and beauty of early, pleasant memories, events that occurred long before the painful divorce. Thus, one way of isolating or constructing meaning seems to be by reassuring oneself that "it was good once." In the next account, the rememberer longs to get past the more recent painful images in order to refresh her memories of better images of her late husband. Here, the meaning she seeks (rather than constructs) is that pain fades and truth—goodness—endures. Rose, a 61-year-old woman, first explains that her husband, Eli, had suffered a stroke that left him brain-damaged and physically immobilized for 9 years until his recent death:

Of course I am still coping. Grief is an ongoing process. I will never stop. He died 3 months before our 40th wedding anniversary, and although friends asked me out (we were married on Christmas Day), I chose to spend my anniversary *with him*. I reread our old love letters and giggled at some of the recollections. I watched reels of movie film of our wedding and honeymoon, and this made me feel good, because once again I was able to see him as young and strong and handsome and not as the wasted, sickly person I remembered for the last 9 years. I still think of him as the dependent, debilitated individual of more recent years. I haven't gotten beyond those mental images as yet. I hope some day I will.

In both of these accounts, meaning is either constructed or sought in the form of catharsis or narrative characteristic of accounts.

Finally, another way in which accounts function as vehicles for meaning is through themes. In many grief-prompted accounts, account makers describe what they specifically miss about their lost partners, such as companionship, advice, passion, or acceptance. Very often, this litany of longings will culminate in a conclusion about what the relationship provided, and therefore, what it "meant." Consider the transition from missing to meaning in the following excerpts from the account of a 75-year-old woman whose husband had died suddenly 3 years before:

The fact that plagued me the most about Ben's death was that there was not time to even say "goodbye." My only real consolation was that this was the way he had expressed he would like to die when the time came. . . .

I miss discussing things I see and read with him. I still cut out articles I think he would have been interested in and then send them to my children at a later date. He helped me to broaden my horizons about many things, but I in turn taught him many things too.

The theme of this account, then, might be "teaching," a common allusion both in retrospective accounts and new attractions. The usefulness of the concept of "themes" as forms of meaning in personal stories has been noted by the anthropologist Sharon R. Kaufman in her work on the life stories and recollections of elderly persons (1986). Insofar as the search for themes is more a content "synthesis" than a content "analysis," it relies on phenomenological methods.

Identity

Close relationship loss has undeniable impact on one's role and identity (see Chapter 11 in this volume). In our model, previously described, of account making as a response to stress or the trauma of loss (Harvey et al., 1990), we concluded that one completes the stress–response sequence *and* the account-making process by developing a new sense of identity. Within an account, this process may be inferred in changes in self-reference or in claims of a new reliance on self-determined standards, as in the account of this Elderhosteler, a 67-year-old widow:

I think of my husband often. Up until recently, when I had to make a decision, I would ask myself, "What would he have done?" Now I find myself acting on my own instincts and knowledge. Family and friends still refer to how he impacted on their lives, and that makes me feel good. The pain of the loss is gone, after 3 years, but I remember him lovingly and wish he were here.

Identity and identity change are revealed through inferences into accounts; this is a good example of the subtleties that might be teased out by a phenomenological perspective. Identity statements are likely to be interwoven with or embedded in relationship retrospections, because an account is as much a self-story as it is a relationship story. In their work, applying personal construct theory to relational trajectories, Neimeyer and Neimeyer (1985) observe that personal identity and interpersonal relationships are intimately interconnected. One relies on one's partner for social comparison, validation, and reality checking. Relationships, like identities, are better understood as processes than as states (Duck & Sants, 1983). The account, a poor substitute for a now-unavailable former partner, must likewise become a tool, a dark mirror, for the identity process, and itself is a work in progress rather than a finished story.

Stories

Finally, in composing and relating their own accounts, account makers reflect the myths of their cultures and the images of their own cherished fairly tales and dreams. It is unlikely that any experimental approach can leave intact the language or rhythm that gives a story-like quality to an account. Content analyses will yield handy lists of criteria, or aptly labeled frequency columns, or coding schemes that may prove applicable in other settings and contexts. But content analyses cannot codify the poetry of an account. Consider the challenge of analytically interpreting the following excerpt, the conclusion of Rose's account, first cited previously, of the death of her husband Eli after a long, debilitating illness:

One thing has given me some good feelings. I named a star after Eli, registered with the International Star Registry, on record at the Library of Congress. I have a map of the location of that star and a framed certificate. Best of all, when I look up into the heavens, I know Eli is up there somewhere, not as a spirit or an angel but as a shining star that I often speak to. The shining star he always was in my life.

Conclusion: Phenomenology and Accounts

Stories are interesting; good pedagogy, speech making, and social influence all make use of parables, fables, reminiscences, and fairy tales. Popular culture in the last decade seems to be enjoying a renaissance of the story form of literature (Harvey, Weber, & Orbuch, 1990). Not everyone can tell a *good* story or tell a story *well*. Yet most of us rely on the story form to help us impose structure and order on our experiences, revitalize our memories, or at least *make sense* of our world. This sense-making dynamic is easily lost by any perspective that takes the story or the story-telling process for granted. By definition, a phenomenological perspective looks *at*, but does not scrutinize or eviscerate, things as they are, or are presented.

As a result of losing a relationship, perhaps especially when the lost partner is no longer accessible as an other, an individual formulates and relates an account in the process of reacting to, acknowledging, and coping with the loss. In many ways, the process of account making is a strategy for coping. The account itself is a vehicle or matrix for sub-strategies, including attributions, self-justifications, self-presentations, and audience manipulations. An account, however, is not *merely* a strategy or a stringing together of scriptal elements. Especially to the account maker, the account is an end in itself, a work in progress, a natural event with personal and social meaning. The phenemonological perspective can seem at best alien and at worst compromisingly messy and cumbersome to the social scientist eager to get at the reality of loss. Insofar as "reality" is conferred by the experiencer, the story-teller, and not by the observer, the phenomenological perspective is an important enrichment to the relationship researcher. We have reason to feel reluctant about getting any closer to the experiences of our subjects. Close relationship loss is eventually a universal experience, a great leveler. We can hardly reassure ourselves that "it won't happen to us." By appreciating the subjective view of such losses and the stories people (including ourselves) tell about them, we wipe clear a window on these events and realize they are much closer than we had thought. The meaning to be found in others' stories of loss is as familiar and poignant as the stories we ourselves compose, waiting our turn to tell them.

References

Duck, S. W., & Sants, H. K. A. (1983). On the origin of the specious: Are personal relationships really interpersonal states? *Journal of Social and Clinical Psychology*, 2(1), 27–41.

Edwards. D., & Middleton, D. (1988). Conversational remembering and family relationships: How children learn to remember. *Journal of Social and Personal Relationships*, 5(1), 3–25.

Gurwitsch, A. (1966). *Studies in phenomenology and psychology*. Evanston, IL: Northwestern University Press.

Harvey, J. H., Agostinelli, G., & Weber, A. L. (1989). Account-making and the formation of expectations about close relationships. In C. Hendrick (Ed.), *Review of personality and social psychology: Vol. 10. Close relationships* (pp. 39–62). Newbury Park, CA: Sage.

Harvey, J. H., Flanary, R., & Morgan, M. (1986). Vivid memories of vivid loves gone by. *Journal of Social and Personal Relationships*, *3*(3), 359–373.

Harvey, J. H., Orbuch, T. L., & Weber, A. L. (1990). A social-psychological model of account-making in response to severe stress. *Journal of Language and Social Psychology*, *9*(3), 191–207.

Harvey, J. H., & Weber, A. L. (1982, July). *Attribution in the termination of close relationships: A special focus on the account*. Paper presented at the international conference on personal relationships, Madison, WI.

Harvey, J. H., Weber, A. L., Galvin, K. S., Huszti, H. C., & Garnick, N. N. (1986). Attribution in the termination of close relationships: A special focus on the account. In R. Gilmour & S. Duck (Eds.), *The emerging field of personal relationships* (pp. 189–201). Hillsdale, NJ: Lawrence Erlbaum.

Harvey, J. H., Weber, A. L., & Orbuch, T. L. (1990). *Interpersonal accounts: A social psychological perspective*. Oxford, England: Basil Blackwell.

Harvey, J. H., Weber, A. L., Yarkin, K. L., & Stewart, B. E. (1982). An attributional approach to relationship breakdown and dissolution. In S. Duck (Ed.), *Personal relationships 4: Dissolving personal relationships* (pp. 107–126). New York: Academic Press.

Hekman, S. J. (1983). *Weber, the ideal type, and contemporary social theory*. Notre Dame, IN: University of Notre Dame Press.

Hill, C., Rubin, Z., & Peplau, L. A. (1976). The end of 103 affairs. In G. Levinger & O. C. Moles (Eds.), *Separation and divorce*. New York: Basic Books.

Horowitz, M. J. (1986). *Stress response syndromes* (2nd ed.). Northvale, NJ: Jason Aronson.

Kaufman, S. R. (1986). *The ageless self: Sources of meaning in late life*. New York: New American Library.

Lewin, K. (1935). *A dynamic theory of personality*. New York: McGraw-Hill.

Lewin, K. (1936). *Principles of topological psychology*. New York: McGraw-Hill.

Merleau-Ponty, M. (1963). *The structure of behavior*. Boston: Beacon Press.

Merleau-Ponty, M. (1964). *Sense and non-sense*. Evanston, IL: Northwestern University Press.

Milgram, S. (1977). *The individual in a social world*. Reading, MA: Addison-Wesley.

Misiak, H., & Sexton, V. (1973). *Phenomenological, existential, and humanistic psychologies*. New York: Grune & Stratton.

Neimeyer, G. J., & Neimeyer, R. A. (1985). Relational trajectories: A personal construct contribution. *Journal of Personal and Social Relationships*, *2*(3), 325–349.

Rogers, M. F. (1983). *Sociology, ethnomethodology, and experience*. Cambridge, UK: Cambridge University Press.

Rosenberg, J. (1986). *The thinking self*. Philadelphia: Temple University Press.

Schmidt, J. (1985). *Maurice Merleau-Ponty: Between phenomenology and structuralism*. New York: St. Martin's Press.

Schutz, A. (1970). *On phenomenology and social relations*. Chicago: University of Chicago Press.

Spurling, L. (1977). *Phenomenology and the social world*. Boston: Routledge & Kegan Paul.

Sternberg, R. (1988). *The triangle of love*. New York: Basic Books.

Tennov, D. (1979). *Love and limerence*. New York: Stein & Day.

Weber, A. L., Harvey, J. H., & Stanley, M. A. (1987). The nature and motivations of accounts for failed relationships. In R. Burnett, P. McGhee, & D. D. Clarke (Eds.), *Accounting for relationships: Explanation, representation and knowledge* (pp. 114–133). London: Methuen.

11
A Symbolic Interactionist Approach to the Study of Relationship Loss

Terri L. Orbuch

Introduction

Social psychologists in sociology are often concerned with the reciprocal impact of social structure and individual behavior (House, 1977; House & Mortimer, 1990; McCall & Simmons, 1978; Stryker & Statham, 1985). In a seminal chapter in the third edition of *The Handbook of Social Psychology*, Stryker and Statham (1985) state:

There is relatively strong agreement among sociologically trained social psychologists on the defining principle of their portion of the larger discipline (social psychology); namely, social life is structured, and this structure is important to the development of the social person and to the production of social behavior. (p. 311)

My colleagues and I have argued previously that people are inexorably driven to search for meaning when confronted with relationship loss (Harvey, Orbuch, & Fink, 1990; Harvey, Orbuch, & Weber, 1990; Harvey, Weber, & Orbuch, 1990; see also Chapter 10 in this volume). The meaning individuals assign to a relationship loss may play a restorative role in many types of grief work after loss. We deal best with loss when we have worked through its meaning for ourselves and have confided that meaning to close, empathic others. At first glance, the pursuit of meaning by individuals confronted with relationship loss may not fulfill the goal of a social psychologist in sociology as defined by Stryker and Statham (1985). In other words, as a sociologically oriented social psychologist, can one address how social structure impacts on the meaning individuals attach to their experiences of relationship loss, and how such meaning, in turn, affects social structure (e.g., development of a new network of association after divorce). The question of how social structure might impact on the meaning individuals assign to their relationship losses is the major question of this chapter.

The theoretical perspective labeled as *social structural symbolic interactionism* is an integrative framework of both symbolic interactionism and role theory and is a most useful framework for social psychologists interested in the impact of social structure on individual behavior. In addition, it provides a useful approach for examining relationship loss and how social structure can impact on the consequences and meaning of the loss for the individual. The symbolic interactionist perspective is by no means the only theoretical perspective within which to study these effects, but it is the specific aim of this chapter to examine how social structure, specifically through the concepts of roles, identities, and role identities, influence the meaning individuals attach to their close relationship loss.

Relationship Loss

Close relationships are essential to the physical and psychological well-being of individuals (Berkman & Syme, 1979; Campbell, Converse, & Rodgers, 1976; Freedman, 1978; Lynch, 1977; review by Peplau & Perlman, 1982). Thus, it is not surprising to find that when individuals experience the loss of an intimate relationship, the transition from being a member of a couple to being a separate entity not defined in connection to that couple can be very stressful. On the Holmes and Rahe Life Change Scale (1967), which is designed to measure levels of stress produced by specific life changes, the three most stressful life changes are changes that involve uncoupling or a transition from being a member of a couple to being a single person. According to the scale, the death of a spouse, a divorce, and marital separation are the three most stressful life changes.

This uncoupling process can be stressful partly because of the loss associated with the termination of the relationship. This loss may include the loss of a person's emotional and material investments in the relationship (Johnson, 1982; Rusbult, 1983) and the loss of a social network connected to the couple (Johnson, 1982; Milardo, 1987). In addition, and more specific to the focus of this chapter, the loss of a relationship may include the loss of an identity associated with the couple (Duck & Lea, 1983).

Vaughan (1986) defines the uncoupling process in terms of its relevance to identity change:

... a process where two people must disentangle not only their belongings but their identities. In a reversal of coupling, the partners redefine themselves, both in their own eyes and in the eyes of others, as separate entities once again. Uncoupling is complete when the partners have defined themselves and are defined by others as separate and independent of each other—when being partners is no longer a major source of identity. (pp. 5–6)

In sum, a major consequence of a relationship loss may be that the individual must engage in "identity transformation"; the individual must redefine who he or she is in relation to other people. The individual must redefine for the self a new identity and program for action that implements this identity.

In this chapter, I conceptualize the loss of a relationship as an uncoupling process whereby identity transformation is necessary. Given this conceptualization, I discuss how specific concepts within the perspective of social structural symbolic interactionism can shed light on the experience of a relationship loss. To illustrate these concepts, I present findings from a study examining responses to and coping with non marital relationship loss.

Social Structural Symbolic Interactionism

Symbolic interactionism and role theory are theoretical approaches prominent in sociological social psychology. According to Stryker and Statham (1985), these two frameworks share several elements in common. First, both theoretical frameworks emphasize the subjective experiences and performances of individuals from the perspectives of participants in social processes. Individuals behave toward objects, events, and other persons on the basis of meanings or subjective experiences with those phenomena. Second, both role theory and symbolic interactionism depict society and the individual as reciprocally influenced by each other; neither can be understood fully without the other. Finally, both theoretical frameworks take "the theater as a major metaphor of social life, making central use of the concept of 'role' in their analyses (although some symbolic interactionists may not use the term)" (Stryker & Statham, 1985, p. 312).

In addition, role theory and symbolic interactionism complement each other. For example, critics often attack symbolic interactionism on the grounds that as a sociological theory it lacks a more adequate sense of social structure. This structured sense of society is evident in role theory, with its fixed notion of roles and role expectations. On the other side, role theory is often criticized for the lack of a more adequate sense of how aspects of social life are constructed and developed extemporaneously and through interaction. Symbolic interactionism offers solutions for this constructed process (for more discussion on strengths and weakness of both, see Stryker & Statham, 1985).

In sum, both theoretical frameworks address the criticisms of the other, and they share many common principles. Thus, Stryker and Statham (1985) present a provocative social psychological theoretical framework resulting from the integration of ideas from both symbolic interactionism and role theory. They label this integrated framework *a social structural symbolic interactionist perspective*. They state that this integration of perspectives addresses the lack of social structural constraints in symbolic interactionism and the lack of focus to how social behavior may be constructed in role theory, while retaining the viewpoints that meaning emerges and is constructed through social interaction, that meanings people assign to objects and events organize behavior, and that interaction proceeds on the basis of shared systems of meaning.

By combining both role theory and symbolic interactionism, we allow both social structure and constructed meaning through interpersonal interaction to be prominent themes. In other words, if meaning emerges through interaction and interaction is constructed by social structure, then by studying social interaction, we also study the impact of social structure on the construction of meaning for individuals.

Roles, Identities, and Role Identities

Identities are the descriptive statements individuals assign to the self. In other words, identities are the categories people use to specify who they are, to locate themselves relative to other people (Michener, DeLamater, & Schwartz, 1990). In this view, the union or combination of all one's identities formulates the self.

Roles are positions people occupy in groups that contain expectations regarding behaviors and attitudes while in that position. Role expectations are shared understandings or norms that tell us as occupants of a role what actions we can anticipate from one another as we go about activities in that role.

According to McCall (1977), for each social position that a person occupies, or aspires to occupy in society (e.g., wife, father, daughter, partner, student), he or she tries to sustain a role identity. McCall and Simmons (1978) further state that a role identity is defined as "the character and the role that an individual devises for him/herself as an occupant of a particular position. Such a role identity is his/her view of him/herself as he/she likes to think of him/herself being and acting as an occupant of that position" (p. 65). Once individuals accept a social position, they begin to imagine or view themselves as performing in that position. Individuals learn the behaviors and attitudes expected of specific social positions (social roles) within society through interacting with groups, systems, and institutions in society. The contents of the role identity provide the individual with expectations and norms that specify how to interpret incoming information as well as how to behave in certain situations.

Individuals acquire several role identities depending on the number of social positions that they occupy in society. These role identities are organized within the individual according to a prominence hierarchy. This hierarchy of identities is influenced by a person's performance in a role identity, the support from others given to an identity, the degree of self-commitment to a specific identity, and the extrinsic and intrinsic gratifications achieved from a role identity (McCall & Simmons, 1978).

Role Identities and Close Relationships

When individuals form a romantic dyad with another person, they occupy a socially defined position (role) as partner, lover, or spouse. Where individuals place this identity in their prominence hierarchy of identities depends on the gratification they achieve from the identity connected to the relationship; the degree of their self-commitment to that identity; the support others give to that identity; and the number of opportunities they have to engage in the role of partner. The higher the identity of partner is located on the hierarchy of identities, the more central and significant the identity is to the person's total self.

When a relationship terminates, the role identity of partner no longer obtains support from others. Further, because the "other" no longer exists as a partner, the opportunities to engage in that role identity diminish. The higher the partner identity was located on the prominence hierarchy, the harder it may be for the individual to disassociate from the identity, because the identity was more salient to the individual's social self. Consequently, if a relationship ends, it may be costly and distressing, depending on the degree to which the identity of partner was significant to the individual.

Study of Relationship Loss

To examine the degree to which identity variables influence reactions and coping to relationship loss, I conducted a study (Orbuch, 1988). The specific relationship loss examined was nonmarital relationship loss. The subjects were 80 men and 70 women who were randomly drawn from the Madison, Wisconsin, telephone book and the University of Wisconsin registrar's list. I obtained a random sample to ensure that every individual (and thus every kind of nonmarital relationship) had an equal chance of being selected for the study. A total of 2,337 names were generated from these two sources. Each name was then called on the telephone for a screening interview.

The telephone screening interview was used to identify individuals who (a) were never married, (b) were between the ages of 20 and 39 years old, and (c) had experienced a romantic relationship loss in the last 16 months. One hundred and eighty individuals met these criteria and became respondents in the study. I then asked these individuals to complete a questionnaire that would be mailed to them. The questionnaire asked about their experiences with the loss, including questions aimed at assessing the importance or significance of the relationship and partner identity. Out of 180 individuals to whom I sent questionnaires, 150 individuals completed and returned the questionnaire (83% response rate).

All 150 subjects fit the screening interview criteria. Of the 150 respondents who participated, 59% were students at the University of Wisconsin-Madison and 41% were nonstudents. Of those respondents who were in school, the majority of the respondents were seniors and graduate students (78%). The mean age of the respondents was 26 years old.

The average length of the relationship before the loss was 1.6 years. In addition, the majority of the respondents rated the status of their terminated relationship as exclusively dating or living together. Respondents had experienced the relationship loss between 1 week and 16 months ago, with a mean of 5.9 months. (For a more complete description of the study and sample see Orbuch, 1988.)

Results

A confirmatory factor analysis on the emotional, cognitive, behavioral, and physical reaction items revealed the existence of two distinct but related factors. The first factor measured a reaction that consists of anger. This factor explained 15% of the variance in the factor analysis, and considered as a scale, the five items produced a coefficient-α of .71. Multiple-regression analyses indicated that after controlling for student status and age of the respondent, the degree to which an individual feels anger was positively and significantly affected by the variables representing salience of the partner identity (e.g., anger was greater if the respondent did not initiate the termination, was positively affected by the length of the relationship, was positively affected by the degree to which the respondent felt that the relationship would last a lifetime, and was positively affected by the amount of emotional effort the respondent put in the relationship). These identity variables were more significant in predicting the degree of anger than investment-oriented variables (e.g., degree of self-disclosure, amount of time spent together, number of friends in common, etc.)

The second factor measured a reaction consisting of sadness and withdrawal. This factor explained 18.8% of the variance in the factor analysis, and considered as a scale, the 10 items yielded an α of .89. Multiple-regression analyses indicated that after controlling for student status and age of the respondent, the degree to which an individual feels withdrawal also was positively and significantly affected by the variables representing salience of the partner identity (e.g., withdrawal was greater if the respondent did not initiate the termination, was positively affected by the degree to which the respondent thought the relationship would last a lifetime, was positively affected by the length of the relationship, and was positively affected by the amount of emotional effort the respondent put in the relationship). Again, these identity variables were more significant in predicting the degree of withdrawal than investment-oriented variables (e.g., the degree of self-disclosure, the amount of time spent together, the number of friends in common, etc.).

I also measured the degree to which individuals sought advice from their friends, family, clergy, and professionals in the 1 to 2 months after the termination. The results indicate that although gender was not a significant predictor of the degree of experienced anger or experienced withdrawal, gender did explain a significant amount of the variance in the advice-seeking coping measure. Women were more likely than men to turn to family, friends, and professionals for advice and/or help after the termination. In general, however, although individuals do a great deal of advice seeking after the termination of a marital relationship (Weiss, 1975), the present sample of individuals did not seek a great deal of advice or help from others after their relationship loss. On the average, individuals sought advice and/or help from only 1.17 sources, out of a possible 4 sources.

Discussion of Results

Reactions

Researchers have characterized the aftermath of divorce in a variety of ways (for review, see Spanier & Thompson, 1984). According to Spanier and Thompson (1984), the time frame varies across studies, but in general, researchers find that responses to divorce are characterized by an overall reduction in behavioral and emotional well-being—a situation labeled as distressing to the individuals involved.

More specifically, Spanier and Thompson (1984) characterize four responses to divorce: acceptance, anger, guilt, and loneliness. A comparison of the two reactions found in my study of nonmarital relationship loss (Orbuch, 1988), anger and withdrawal, to the reactions experienced by divorcing individuals (as implied by the literature) suggests that the responses to nonmarital loss are similar *in content* to two of the responses to marital loss—that of acceptance and anger. In addition, the majority of respondents reported that in the 1 to 2 months after the loss of their relationship they felt somewhat lonely (44%) or very lonely (38%). (Guilt was not a response reported by individuals in this study.) Whether the responses of individuals in this study are the same in terms of *intensity* to those of divorcing individuals, however, is a question that this study obviously cannot address because both populations were not sampled.

The results from this study also indicate that variables representing how important the relationship and the identity of partner was to the respondent were more significant in predicting degree of distress than investment-oriented variables.

Advice-Seeking Coping Behaviors

There are three possible explanations for why individuals who experience nonmarital loss do not seek substantial advice or support. The first explanation proposes that the individual experiencing a nonmarital loss does not feel comfortable in seeking support for the loss because of the presumed negative reactions, lack of recognition for the loss, and lack of support by others. This explanation assumes that the individual feels distress and despair following a nonmarital loss, yet he or she does not seek social support, aid, or advice to cope with the situation. Unfortunately, this explanation cannot be confirmed or refuted using the present data. Both relationship losses were not examined in the same study. However, this explanation will be discussed further.

The second explanation for these results posits that individuals experiencing a non-marital loss do not encounter a high level of distress and therefore they do not *need* to seek advice or support for the termination. Again, unfortunately, this second explanation cannot be confirmed or refuted using the present data. Future research must (a) use control samples with which to measure relative individual levels of distress in individuals aged 20 to 39 or (b) empirically compare distress levels of individuals experiencing nonmarital loss with those experiencing marital relationship loss or other types of relationship losses.

The third explanation for these results posits that individuals' advice-seeking responses were influenced by their first confiding attempts. Again, respondents in my study (Orbuch, 1988) sought advice from 1.17 sources, out of a possible 4 sources. These individuals may have confided in another person after the relationship loss and received satisfactory responses and empathy from this confiding attempt. Thus, further confiding attempts were not necessary. On the other hand, they may have received a nonempathic or unhelpful response from this primary confidant and, because of this response, decided not to confide or seek advice again about the loss. Recent research on the confiding attempts of sexual assault survivors suggests that the response (nonempathic–empathic) of confidants can influence psychological well-being as well as future attempts to seek advice (Harvey, Orbuch, Chwalisz, & Garwood; 1991). My study (Orbuch, 1988) did not assess the quality or content of the responses in the advice-seeking attempts.

Impact of Social Structure

Assume that the first preceding explanation is valid: An individual experiencing a nonmarital loss feels distress after the loss but does not feel comfortable in seeking advice or support from others. What might cause this uncomfortable feeling? How did the individual arrive at this meaning structure?

The loss of a marital relationship and the loss of a nonmarital relationship are similar in that they both involve a consequential shift from being a member of a couple to being a single person. Although the two types of relationship losses are similar in that they both involve a transition from being a member of a couple to being a single person, I propose that the two relationships differ substantially in other respects. I posit that the termination of a marital relationship and the termination of a nonmarital relationship differ in two basic respects. Frist, the intact dyads and their members are differentially supported and acknowledged by individuals and institutions in American society. Individuals and institutions in American society recognize and acknowledge the marital dyad to a greater degree than the nonmarital dyad. Second, because of the differential acknowledgment of the two intact dyads, when the dyads dissolve or terminate, individuals in American society provide differential recognition and support to the terminations and to the individuals involved in the losses. I propose that the lack of recognition of intact nonmarital relationships and consequently of the termination of nonmarital relationships affects the degree to which individuals seek help or support for these terminations from others.

Structural Support or Validation

Individuals and institutions can give several dimensions of recognition to relationship losses. These dimensions can be classified into two general categories. First, for some relationship losses, roles, along with identified behaviors and attitudes expected (role expectations) in these roles, are socially provided or designated. Role identities are established in part through the institutional validation and recognition of a role or social position. For example, when an individual experiences a divorce, he or she acquires a role identity ("divorced person"), which provides the individual with expectations and norms that specify to some degree how to behave during the termination. On the other hand, when an individual experiences a nonmarital relationship termination, there appears to be no recognized social position (role) such as a "nonmarital separated person," containing expectations and norms for how to behave that an individual could acquire to guide him or her through the experience of a nonmarital termination. Without the establishment of a social position (role), no role identity is developed, and individuals may have difficulty giving meaning to the situation.

The second category of recognition is associated with the degree of aid and/or support that individuals receive from others when they experience the loss of a relationship. When a person acquires the role identity of a "divorced person," provisions may be made to aid the individual through the stressful transition. For example, the legal system within American society confers and recognizes the status of the divorced. A system of rules has been set up by the law to confront and aid the divorced person. Specific documents must be signed, child custody and alimony agreements must be made, and specific courts exist to handle only divorce. The occupation of a divorce mediator, an arbitrator for divorce situations only, even exists to help couples through the divorce process. Further, specific counselors and support groups have been designated to teach, support, and confirm individuals experiencing divorce. In addition, rituals or norms of behavior have been reasonably accepted for divorced individuals (e.g., regular grieving is acceptable, dating others is not pushed on individuals immediately after the divorce, etc.).

On the other hand, for the individual experiencing a nonmarital loss, the same kinds of provisions are not made to help this individual through the stressful transition. The legal system has not yet played a major role in these losses (except under special circumstances whereby legal agreements regarding property etc. are signed between the individuals before the loss). There also appears to be a lack of available support groups for individuals experiencing nonmarital relationship losses, where individuals might be able to place their loss in perspective and gain support from others in the same situation.

Finally, the individuals themselves may not feel that their nonmarital relationship loss is recognized and supported by others. Several of the respondents in the previously described study on nonmarital relationship loss (Orbuch, 1988) reported that they did not seek advice or support from others (especially family), because they felt others would not acknowledge the seriousness of their relationship loss. Some respondents stated that they were leery of reporting their experiences to others because they feared sentiments such as "Well, at least you didn't get married," "The best divorce is before you get married," or "Don't worry, there are more fish in the sea."

In sum, individuals in American society validate and provide support for those individuals experiencing a marital relationship loss whereas this degree of validation and support appears lacking for those individuals experiencing the loss of a nonmarital relationship. By validating a marital termination, society acknowledges the existence of a social position (divorced person), containing expectations and norms regarding behavior in that position. Thus, when an individual experiences the loss of a marital relationship, he or she acquires a role identity ("divorced person") that can help the individual learn and guide his or her behaviors through the loss. When a person acquires the role identity of a divorced person, provisions are also made to aid the individual through the stressful transition from being a member of a couple to being a single person.

I propose that the degree to which institutions and groups in society recognize a relationship loss by providing a role identity and support or aid for those involved in the loss influences the meaning individuals assign to the loss, the experience of the loss, and the degree to which individuals seek advice or help from professionals, family, and friends. A further examination of how society differentially "institutionalizes" relationship losses is needed. In addition, further research is required to address more specifically how the process of the "institutionalization of a relationship loss" affects an individual's meaning structure and experiences of the relationship loss.

Conclusion

People have an intense desire to search for meaning after a relationship loss (Harvey, Orbuch, & Weber, 1990). How society can impact on that meaning structure has been the focus of this chapter. If relationship loss is conceptualized as an uncoupling process whereby identity transformation is necessary, then the tenets and concepts of social structural symbolic interactionism can provide a framework in which to examine how social structure can impact on this identity transformation and thus give meaning to the individual experiencing the event. To elucidate this process, this chapter focused on the loss of two relationships, the nonmarital relationship and the marital relationship.

Social structural symbolic interactionism focuses on how the meanings that individuals assign to objects and events can be influenced by social structure via interpersonal interaction. I have proposed that the systems, institutions, and groups within society influence the meaning structures individuals assign to relationship loss through differential support and recognition of these relationship losses. This framework and these propositions are worth pursuing in future research.

Further, if the social systems in our society begin to recognize or give support to certain relationships and, thus, to the losses of these relationships (e.g., nonmarital relationship losses, gay and lesbian relationship losses), then different meaning structures might emerge for individuals experiencing these relationship losses. For example, if social policy changes so that our social institutions begin to recognize gay and lesbian marriages and/or the rights of individuals who cohabit (e.g., Domestic Partnership Ordinances), these social policy changes also may impact on the meaning structures that individuals give to these relationships and to the losses of these relationships. These meaning structures may change for those experiencing the relationship losses as well as for those others in whom they confide. Finally, as our society begins to experience varying relationship losses, perhaps individuals will also influence the systems who recognize, acknowledge, and support the relationship losses.

References

Berkman, L. S., & Syme, S. L. (1979). Social networks, host resistance, and mortality: A nine-year follow-up study of Alameda County residents. *American Journal of Epidemiology, 109*, 186–204.

Campbell, A., Converse, P. E., & Rodgers, W. L. (1976). *The quality of American life*. New York: Russell Sage Foundation.

Duck, S. W., & Lea, M. (1983). Breakdown of relationships as a threat to personal identity. In G. M. Breakwell (Ed.), *Threatened identities* (pp. 53–73). New York: Wiley.

Freedman, J. (1978). *Happy people: What happiness is, who has it, and why*. New York: Harcourt Brace Jovanovich.

Harvey, J. H., Orbuch, T. L., Chwalisz, K. D., & Garwood, G. (1991). Coping with sexual assault: The roles of account-making and confiding. *Journal of Traumatic Stress, 4*(4), 515–531.

Harvey, J. H., Orbuch, T. L., & Fink, K. (1990). The social psychology of account-making: Meaning, hope, and generativity. *New Zealand Journal of Psychology, 19*, 46–57.

Harvey, J. H., Orbuch, T. L., & Weber, A. L. (1990). A social psychological model of account-making in response to severe stress. *Journal of Language and Social Psychology, 9*, 191–207.

Harvey, J. H., Weber, A. L., & Orbuch, T. L. (1990). *Interpersonal accounts: A social psychological perspective*. Oxford: Basil Blackwell Press.

Holmes, T. H., & Rahe, R. (1967). The social readjustment scale. *Journal of Psychosomatic Research, 11*, 213–218.

House, J. S. (1977). The three faces of social psychology. *Sociometry, 40*, 161–177.

House, J. S., & Mortimer, J. (1990). Social structure and the individual: Emerging themes and new directions. *Social Psychology Quarterly, 53*, 71–80.

Johnson, M. P. (1982). Social and cognitive features of dissolution of commitment to relationships. In S. W. Duck (Ed.), *Personal relationships 4: Dissolving personal relationships* (pp. 51–74). London & New York: Academic Press.

Lynch, J. J. (1977). *The broken heart: The medical consequences of loneliness*. New York: Basic Books.

McCall, G. J. (1977). The social looking-glass: A sociological perspective on self-development. In T. Mischel (Ed.), *The self: Psychological and philosophical issues* (pp. 274–287). Oxford: Blackwell.

McCall, G. J., & Simmons, J. L. (1978). *Identities and interactions*. New York: Free Press.

Michener, H. A., DeLamater J. D., & Schwartz, S. H. (1990). *Social psychology* (2nd ed.). New York: Harcourt Brace Jovanovich.

Milardo, R. M. (1987). Changes in social networks of women and men following divorce. *Journal of Family Issues, 8*(1), 78–96.

Orbuch, T. L. (1988). *Reactions to and coping with non-marital relationship termination*. Unpublished doctoral dissertation, University of Wisconsin-Madison.

Peplau, L. A., & Perlman, D. (1982). *Loneliness: A sourcebook of current theory, research and therapy*. New York: Wiley-Interscience.

Rusbult, C. E. (1983). A longitudinal test of the investment model: The development (and deterioration) of satisfaction and commitment in heterosexual involvement. *Journal of Personality and Social Psychology*, *45*, 101–117.

Spanier, G. B., & Thompson. L. (1984). *Parting: The aftermath of separation and divorce*. Beverly Hills; Sage.

Stryker, S., & Statham, A. (1985). Symbolic interaction and role theory. In G. Lindzey & E. Aronson (Eds.), *The handbook of social psychology* (3rd ed., pp. 311–378). New York: Random House.

Vaughan, D. (1986). *Uncoupling: How relationships come apart*. Oxford: Oxford University Press.

Weiss, R. S. (1975). *Marital separation*. New York: Basic Books.

Part V
Concluding Comments

12
Divorce: A Comment About the Future

GRAHAM B. SPANIER

During the mid-1970s, the United States experienced, but did not notice, a demographic milestone: For the first time in any given year, more marriages were ended by divorce than by the death of a spouse. The numerical dominance of divorce over death has occurred every year since 1974 and will likely continue well into the future. In this brief chapter, I address some of the larger social and demographic issues suggested by the growing imbalance in the path to marital disruption as well as present some thoughts about future research needs.

I focus primarily on divorce in this commentary, rather than on other types of relationship loss, and use a social demographic perspective. Demographic analysis can be powerful, because nothing is more persuasive than hard facts, and the demography of marital disruption forces us to examine, first and foremost, what national data reveal about the number of divorces granted, divorce rates, and divorce trends. Once confronted with the reality of these data, we are led to consider how the institutions of marriage and family are affected by current divorce experience, how this may change in the future, and what issues must be addressed by future social science research.

A Powerful Demographic Reality

First some facts. Since 1974, there have been more than 1 million divorces each year in the United States (National Center for Health Statistics, 1990). After a dramatic climb in divorce rates that began in the early 1960s, we reached a peak in 1981, with 1.2 million divorces. The number of divorces and the divorce rate have both leveled off since then but remain at a high level compared to American divorce experience from all earlier eras, with the exception of the brief period following World War II when divorce rates climbed temporarily to a level now seen on a sustained basis.

Most family demographers estimate that between one half and three fifths of all first marriages contracted in the 1980s are likely to end in divorce. When one considers the approximately 1 million children involved in their parents' divorce each year, we reach a total of about 3.4 million adults and children who are directly affected by a divorce each year.

Divorce is clearly a profound form of relationship loss, both for the adults and children involved. It should also be noted that the impact of divorce carries over to other relatives in the extended family network, friends and work associates, and others. In our society's highly romanticized view of family life in America, we are socialized to anticipate marriages lasting well into adulthood, perhaps into old age, with the death of a spouse marking the conclusion of a long relationship. Under such circumstances, the death of a spouse, although a profound loss, nevertheless represents a conclusion of sorts. With divorce, a legal bond has been broken; but the relationship may often continue. Couples divorce; children and parents do not. Consequently, when children are involved, the mother and father will likely be forced by circumstances to maintain some form of tie. Even when no children are involved, couples may find that their pasts, their geographic locale, their networks of friends and relatives, their financial circumstances, and other factors may inadvertently conspire to maintain a relationship.

The data highlighted here should leave little doubt that divorce will continue to be a phenomenon found in the mainstream of American society well into the future. It is also clear that although age at marriage, marriage rates, divorce rates, and remarriage experience, will fluctuate, we can expect that a substantial majority of men and women will eventually marry. Perhaps half of those who ultimately divorce, and most of those who remain married, will have children. How then, does our society cope with such weighty social challenges, and how should social scientists channel their energies in the study of these topics?

Big and Small Questions

There are big questions and smaller ones. Among the big questions are whether the American family will persist, given the demographic and social changes that confront us (Spanier, 1989). Are the current changes confronting American families indeed indicators of pathology, deterioration, and instability? Are the changes seen in the 1970s and 1980s simply modern-day variations in marriage and family life that do not really threaten the basic foundation of the institution, or do such changes represent convincing evidence of fundamental redefinitions of traditional family bonds? Such big questions are generally untouchable through social science research, so we customarily focus on the smaller questions that can be reached. Smaller questions are not unimportant questions. Rather, they are those that are more readily within the grasp of the social or behavioral scientist. They are questions that can be addressed through experiments, surveys, analysis of existing data, or observation. If we are productive enough to answer enough small questions, and if we are clever enough to see how the smaller questions are related to the big questions, then we have the opportunity to understand more than any one study can investigate. We are guided substantially in such endeavors by theories or conceptual frameworks. This is where the contributions to this volume can begin to chart the course.

The chapters of this book highlight some of the current and emerging perspectives on relationship loss. There are some trends. One notable trend is the evolution of the life-course perspective (see Chapter 8 in this volume). Although this perspective should be considered an important approach in its own right, it is clear that sensitivity to the dynamics and variability of the life course are influencing other approaches as well. We are likely to see an increasing number of studies in the 1990s that take a life course, developmental approach.

The phenomenological approach (Chapter 10) was common in early social science investigations into topics such as divorce and death of a loved one, but the prominence of this approach was eroded during the 1960s and 1970s by the powerful emergence of empiricism in the social sciences. More recently, phenomenological approaches have begun to emerge again with credibility, and we are likely to see in the literature a healthy mix of empirical and phenomenological studies. Much of the best new social science combines techniques from both domains.

The social demographic approach summarized by Sweet and Bumpass (Chapter 4) provides a basis for understanding societal trends and inter-relationships between social phenomena. It allows us to make projections, and it often helps explain social forces that act on populations as well as individuals or families. I have found that this perspective is extremely helpful for viewing the big picture and then for setting the stage for other researchers whose contributions emanate from a social psychological approach.

Several contributions to the book guide us in exploring how various social psychological perspectives such as social exchange (Chapter 3), attribution (Chapter 9), attachment (Chapter 5), and symbolic interaction (Chapter 11) can be used to better understand relationship loss. Such approaches form the core of the accumulated research literature on the sociology and psychology of relationship loss, and this is likely to be the case through at least the coming decade.

Other approaches highlighted in this book, such as the dialectical (Chapter 7) and the linguistic (Chapter 6), have not been applied much to the study of relationship loss, but they nevertheless offer some valuable insights. It seems unlikely that we will see more than a few contributions in the near future that will rely on the approaches outlined in these presentations. This may say more about the history of social science training and the visibility of certain theories and conceptual frameworks than it does about what such approaches have to offer.

Reconciling the Imbalance

The raw demographic reality that the majority of marriages are ended by divorce, not death, will baffle many who are committed to the notion that the marriage and family are the fundamental social institutions—the building blocks—of our society. Most social scientists have reconciled their traditional notions of societal structure and function with the high incidence of societal disruption by looking beyond marriage and divorce rates.

One can argue that marriage was never intended to last 50 years or more; relatively early ages at marriage, combined with longer life expectancy, force a "lifelong" marriage into periods that span several decades. One might argue further that the demands of modern society on marriage are unprecedented in complexity and intensity; marriages that last, then, have done so in the face of very great pressures and threats that in the normal course of events could be expected to tear relationships apart. Others correctly argue that the majority of individuals who divorce—in fact about three fourths of such individuals—eventually remarry. More than half of divorced persons have remarried within 4 years of the final divorce decree. This might suggest that most individuals who divorce are not rejecting marriage as an institution but rather that they did not find their particular relationship to be workable.

Many philosophers, researchers, and clinicians have pondered an appropriate question: What is it about our social fabric, our societal demands on relationships, and the character of our family institution that promotes such disruption? We have plenty of answers, but not yet enough. Until the 1970s, Goode's (1956) classic study of divorce was the only comprehensive piece of research on divorce in the post-War era. Since the mid-1970s, there has been a rapid acceleration of research on the topic, with hundreds of published articles and dozens of books. These studies have focused by and large on the etiology and demography of divorce, the aftermath of divorce, remarriage and stepparenting, issues of coping across the transition to divorce, complexities of interrelationships surrounding divorce, and therapeutic techniques across these domains. I remain concerned, however, that after hundreds of such studies we still do not have sufficient insight into the big questions. Thus, we must consider appropriate courses of scholarship for the future that might better address such questions.

Future Research Directions

The essays in this volume help chart the course for further inquiry into both the big and small questions that lie ahead. Many of the studies conducted over the past 15 years could have profited from being rooted in one of the conceptual frameworks elaborated in this book. Research on the smaller questions unquestionably is needed, but it stands the best chance of advancing the study of divorce if it can be integrated better within the broader domain of studies. Such integration requires a fuller appreciation of the work drawn from similar conceptual frameworks as well as studies looking at similar questions drawn from different conceptual frameworks.

My principal argument, however, is that we must pursue more vigorously a line of research that addresses the big questions. Elsewhere (Spanier, 1989), I have argued that the contemporary American family is faltering, but we have also seen the basis for hope. The hope lies in our ability to transcend those circumstances and forces that disrupt families. Of course, it is clear than in countless marriages, divorce provides relief for a marriage that has failed, relief for a husband and wife that find the marriage unworkable, and sometimes relief for children of the marriage who find a peaceful home with one parent a healthier environment than a two-parent household full of turmoil. Nevertheless, marital stability is generally seen as desirable by society; childhood socialization tends to emphasize marital stability as normative, marital disruption as deviant.

If we accept for the moment the popular wisdom, we are led to consider what important questions the next generation of research must address to assist in our understanding of more stability in marriages and families. Or, if we do not know the questions, what then will lead us to them? I shall mention just a few examples, because my intent is to be illustrative rather than exhaustive.

I think first of the need for a broad cross-cultural analysis. Divorce experience differs significantly across societies. Even among modern Western societies, we find important differences in divorce attitudes, propensity, rates, and customs. What cultural characteristics are more or less conducive to marital stability? Numerous other questions should then follow. Such questions lead to many avenues of inquiry for anthropologists, sociologists, and demographers, for example. Murdock, Winch, Goode, and other pioneers made early attempts to examine cross-cultural variables, but little additional progress has been made.

Turning to a second example, we still have much to learn about the relationship between marital quality (how "good" a marriage is) and marital stability (whether or not a marriage remains intact). Understanding this connection better would, I believe, significantly enhance our understanding of the dynamics of divorce (Lewis & Spanier, 1979). Why do so many low-quality marriages remain intact? What are the forces, in the face of low marital quality, that move a couple across the threshold from marriage to divorce, or that encourage desperately unhappy men and women to remain together?

I am also intrigued by cross-disciplinary possibilities. Some research on divorce has coupled the talents of psychologists and sociologists. Collaborations, however, between economists and psychologists or between biologists and sociologists are very rare; it is plausible that some of the most important questions in the study of human relationships lie at the interchange between such disciplines. For example, economists have used the theories and methods of economic demography or the concepts of supply and demand to explain aspects of divorce. Such research could result in more powerful explanations if reconciled with experimental psychological studies or sociological survey studies. Similarly, there is a growing body of research on biological influences on a wide range of human behavior once thought by many social scientists to be solely within the domain of socialization and culture; yet, there has been negligible attention to the confluence of biology, socialization, and culture in relationship formation, relationship dynamics, or relationship loss. Profound, basic questions could be posed from such a perspective.

These are but a few examples of where we have bypassed some intriguing "big" questions. I have not intended to be very exhaustive in posing such questions but rather to be illustrative. The hope for tackling the bigger questions lies in more multidisciplinary cooperation, the ability to take a more global perspective, and the courage to depart from the safer "small" questions and to confront the risks of the larger questions.

References

Goode, W. J. (1956). *After divorce (women in divorce)*. New York: The Free Press.

Lewis, R. A., & Spanier, G. B. (1979). Theorizing about the quality and stability of marriage. In W. R. Burr, R. Hill, F. I. Nye, & I. L. Reiss (Eds.), *Contemporary theories about the family* (pp. 268–294). New York: The Free Press.

National Center for Health Statistics. (1990). Advance report of final divorce statistics, 1987. *Monthly Vital Statistics Report, 38* (12, Suppl. 2). Hyattsville, MD: Public Health Service.

Spanier, G. B. (1989). Bequeathing family continuity. *Journal of Marriage and the Family, 51*, 3–13.

13
Close Relationship Loss As a Set of Inkblots

Geᴏʀɢᴇ Lᴇᴠɪɴɢᴇʀ

In his book *Marital Separation*, Robert Weiss (1975) suggested that every person who separates from a long-standing marriage develops an *account* to explain what went wrong in the relationship, a story about the marital failure that focuses on significant events or themes in the marriage and allocates the blame for the breakup between self and spouse, and perhaps to third parties. Weiss wrote:

> The account is of major psychological importance to the separated, not only because it settles the issue of who was responsible for what, but also because it imposes on the confused marital events that preceded the separation a plot structure with a beginning, middle, and end and so organizes the events into a conceptually manageable unity. (p. 15)

So it is with the topic of this volume, which examines relationship losses in general—not only marital breakups. Many ambiguities must be ordered and conceptualized, as we project "structure" on the concepts of this broad area of discourse. I focus on five different projective stimuli, or inkblots, that need structure—much of which is provided by different chapters in this insightful collection. These five fuzzy concepts are (a) close relationship; (b) loss; (c) determinants of relationship loss; (d) processes of loss, or of breakdown and breakup; and (e) consequences of a loss. (The first two terms derive from this book's title, the others from its three main section heads.)

What Do Those Key Terms Mean?

Close Relationship?

Writings on relationship loss usually pertain to the destruction of an extremely close relationship, such as a marriage or a parent–child relationship, rather than to the ending of more casual relationships. Researchers have focused mainly on highly interdependent or nurturing relationships, which, if lost, are difficult or impossible to replace. It is the loss of a loved one, someone on whom we have centered our energy and devotion, that creates notable difficulties; not surprisingly, there is far less interest in the loss of casual relationships.

Nonetheless, seemingly close relationships differ greatly in their actual closeness. Some long-standing unions contain little interdependence, others much. Some marriage partners have drifted apart long before they decide on physical separation, others feel bound to each other inextricably. As some investigators (e.g., Berscheid, Snyder, & Omoto, 1989; Simpson, 1987) have recently confirmed, our distress at breakup is highly affected by how mutually influential our relationship was, or by how large a part of one's life is torn away.

Must the attachment necessarily be to another human? Or can it be equally significant to suffer the loss of a long-time pet, or a job, or one's home? We have hardly begun to define the range of distressing loss objects. As I see it, the significance of our loss depends on the extent of our involvement with the lost object: If a large part of one's life revolves around one's relationship with one's dog, or with one's job, its disappearance—especially if unexpected and involuntary—has great psychological significance. The stronger our emotional attachment, the more searing is its destruction (see Chapter 5 in this volume). Thus, it is more useful to appraise a person's dependence on a given tie than to assume, a priori, that particular categories of relationship lead to the greatest sense of loss.

Nevertheless, it does appear that certain relationships have the greatest *potential* for intimacy and emotional involvement. For instance, in this book, Ann L. Weber (Chapter 10) reports that, when a group of Elderhostel members wrote about the loss of one "important close rela-tionship," most of them described the loss of a spouse and far fewer wrote about losing a parent or a child. In this volume, therefore, most authors concern themselves with the breakup of heterosexual peer rela-tionships, which usually embody the highest intimacy. Two chapters limit their focus to marriage and cohabitation (Chapters 4 and 9), four others extend it to romantic liaisons in general (Chapters 1, 3, 6, and 7), while three chapters consider all forms of attachment between infancy and old age (Chapters 5, 8, and 10). Although most of these chapters are extremely insightful, they differ markedly in how they conceive the close relationship.

How Close Is *Close*?

Perhaps it is obvious that much close relationship loss pertains to ties that have become increasingly distant. What was once a strongly connected tie may have become a weak shadow of its former self. In the case of estrangement, the remaining ties experienced by leavers are generally weaker than those of the left. Even in bereavement, a relationship after a long terminal illness—such as a paralyzing stroke or Alzheimer's disease—has often declined markedly from an earlier time. One's feeling of deprivation depends markedly on one's own and the other's life stage as well as on the stage of the relationship. In other words, "close relationships" are not always how they appear; public impressions do not necessarily match private emotions (Berscheid, 1983). Seemingly serene pairs may, underneath, consist of two distanced individuals who are merely keeping up a pretense of congeniality, whereas two noisily conflictful partners may in fact be highly dependent on one another. It is well to remember that caution in drawing inferences about close relationship loss.

Loss?

Loss, too, has a variety of referents. Some losses are sharply defined, such as death or a final divorce decree. Other losses are less clear, such as one's gradually diminishing connections in the deterioration of a marriage or a good friendship, and even in a parent–child relationship. As Duck (Chapter 1), Blieszner and Mancini (Chapter 8), and others have pointed out, many losses occur gradually over time—such as the protracted, incapacitating illness of a loved one or the drifting apart of formerly close partners—so that, when the relationship actually ends, the event itself is an anticlimax. The experience of loss, then, depends on the nature of the process that precedes it. Some losses are felt to be catastrophic—like the tearing out of a large part of one's own life—and recovery requires much healing. Others, especially those of long-suffering sick people or of dragging, unhappy relationships, may be encountered with relief— although not every survivor is willing to admit such feelings.

There are important differences, furthermore, between the death of a loved one—the topic for analyses of grief or bereavement—and more voluntary forms of estrangement or separation. Death is irreversible, whereas other forms of loss are potentially retrievable. Death may be attributable entirely to physiological or chance events. In contrast, the reasons for intentional forms of separation or breakup must, at least partly, be explained in terms of psychological causes. The grieving process, therefore, tends to differ from one form of loss to another—as do the antecedent processes that lead to such a loss.

Hazan and Shaver (Chapter 5) link an adult's experience of losing an attachment relationship to a child's feeling of abandonment by a care giver. Citing Bowlby (1953, 1973), they note a process that begins with protest, anxiety, and anger and is followed by despair and depression and eventually by detachment and increasing independence. Although people differ greatly in the intensity of their reactions to attachment loss, Hazan and Shaver (Chapter 5) emphasize the cross-age and cross-cultural universals. Although there are major differences between loss through death and through separation, they highlight the parallels among the underlying emotional reactions.

Most of this book's chapters pertain to social or psychological separation rather than to death. Several authors (e.g., Duck, Chapter 1; Metts, Chapter 6; Cupach, Chapter 7; and Blieszner and Mancini, Chapter 8) concern themselves with the temporal processes by which once-close relationships deteriorate, emphasizing that separation does not happen all at once. Disengagement, especially if it extends over a long time and allows an exploration of alternatives, seems to cushion a loss; in psychological separations where one member has a greater desire to leave than does the other, the initiator is likely to experience the loss far sooner and more gradually and to be less distressed by the eventual termination, than is the abandoned member (e.g., Hagestad & Smyer, 1982; Hill, Rubin, & Peplau, 1976; Vaughan, 1986). Nonetheless, even when a separation is preceded by years of unhappiness, it is hard to predict the amount or the length of one's emotional distress when at last it becomes final (e.g., Spanier & Casto, 1979; Weiss, 1975).

Construing Loss

The meaning of a person's loss, then, is intimately tied to the meaning of the destroyed relationship and to one's own role in its destruction. In cases of one's former attachment eroding over time and of one preparing oneself for new alternatives, as occurs in many cases of bereavement and estrangement, a person may have largely worked through the loss. In other cases, the loss is psychologically profound; then it requires time, patience, and new social involvements to renew one's self-assurance and feeling of personal integrity.

Determinants of Loss?

Death

Does a death follow a lengthy, incurable illness or a sudden accident? Was it expected or unexpected? How old, and at what life stage, was the deceased? How well prepared for the death were the departing individual and the bereaved? Each of these questions is touched on to some extent in this book, but the important psychological question is how well the bereaved persons were able to ready themselves for the postloss readjustments.

Separation and Divorce

The causes of couple breakup can be attributed to either individual partner, to the relationship between them, and to the external environment or events. Divorcing partners often have quite different views of when, why, and how their breakup began and what were its most significant determinants (e.g., Vaughan, 1986). At the most general level, though, it is likely (a) that the factors that attracted them initially to one another have suffered a decline; (b) that, at some point, alternative attractions began to exceed the internal attractions; and (c) that the restraints against leaving the relationship have become weaker than the forces that push one or both partners toward breakup (see Levinger, 1965, 1976; Rusbult, 1980; see also Chapter 3 in this volume). The specific determinants of couple breakup in particular cases or populations, and the temporal processes associated with relationship deterioration, remain to be further investigated.

Sweet and Bumpass (Chapter 4) review recent findings on the demographic antecedents of marital disruption. They confirm earlier findings (e.g., reviews by Goode, 1961; Levinger, 1965) that low age at marriage, black race, and low education are significantly related to marital instability and disruption, and report that it continues to be most likely to occur during the early years of a marriage. Their data on the breakup of premarital cohabiting relationships suggest, furthermore, that the less conventional a couple is, the more likely it is to experience relationship disruption.

Further Thoughts About Determinants

Many losses are perceived as being primarily due to individual or physiological causes, whereas others are attributed to relational or psychological causes. One's perception of causality is, of course, strongly associated with one's feeling of personal responsibility; thus, regardless of the objective reality, it is important to understand people's subjective perceptions of the reasons for a given loss.

Process?

The fourth concept pertains to the processes that lead to a loss. This book does not address the processes leading to death, and it seems we know even less about its social or psychological causes than about the attendant physiological processes. As implied here, however, sudden death creates shock, incredulity, and impairment in the survivors, whereas gradual decline helps to prepare them for coping with their bereavement. And the deceased's readiness for passing on also influences how kin and friends respond to the loss. I hypothesize that when a dying person expresses a clear desire to stop living, it helps his or her loved ones too to accept the demise.

In the case of estrangement and separation, the processes are very different, but they have been far more carefully studied (e.g., Vaughan,

1986). They generally involve the partners' distancing themselves from each other and eventually engaging in acts of disloyalty toward one another, so as to produce anger and feelings of betrayal (e.g., Pittman, 1989). It would also be useful to know, more specifically, how and when the attractions to a partner decline. By what process do one or both partners come to contemplate alternatives to the existing relationship? Finally, if the boundaries containing the relationship are weakened, how and when does their weakness become apparent?

Various authors have written about processes of relationship decline (e.g., Duck, 1982; Levinger, 1979, 1983; Vaughan, 1986). From her extensive study of marital breakup, Vaughan (1986) has suggested that "uncoupling" usually involves a series of steps that include the following: (a) "secrets," or the breakdown of frank communication in one or more areas of a relationship; (b) "the display of discontent," whereby espec- ially the initiator begins to define negatively one or more aspects of the previously positive relationship; and (c) a transition from one's role as "partner" to a more ambiguous role of "independent person," while trying to cover up one's leave taking. Vaughan finds that eventually, in such an uncoupling process, the leave taker makes public his or her dissatisfaction; this then sets in motion new processes that involve the other partner.

Communication researchers attend especially carefully to the processes involved in the breakup of a relationship. In this volume, Metts (Chapter 6) sensitizes us to the "language of disengagement" and how it reflects both similarities and differences across couples. She believes that face management is critical, both to justify one's own position and to make separation easier for the partner. Her face-work model presents a way of conceiving people's tactics and strategies of disengaging from a close relationship, but I think it would be possible to conceive of dimensions other than "politeness" and "severity of the offense" for formulating the analysis.

In Chapter 7, Cupach writes persuasively about the dialectical opposit- ions involved in the disengagement process. He emphasizes that the very nature of relating to another human being implies contradictions and tensions—between autonomy and connection, openness and closedness, and novelty and predictability. Cupach suggests that the rigid display of any of these extremes tends to harm a relationship, as does a mismatch- ing of two partners' behavioral tendencies. His dialectical approach emphasizes the cyclic nature of relationship maintenance and change, and it implies that relationships break down when one or both members are unable to deal with its oppositional tendencies.

Blieszner and Mancini (Chapter 8) widen the definition of process to include both the life spans of individual partners and the life course of their changing statuses across the years. Their developmental perspective enables us to consider the varying meanings of loss within the contexts of both individual lives and of the families they belong to. This suggests a series of criteria—for example, "on-time" versus "off-time" role transitions or the spacing of losses within a particular family—that permit us to weigh the seriousness of losses.

Altogether, it appears that the process of loss must be considered along multiple dimensions, ranging from individual physical deterioration and illness to interpersonal distancing, malcommunication, and betrayal. One important question, only partly addressed by the chapters in this book and poorly understood in general, concerns the reversability of the decline: Under what condition is the deterioration process, once begun, amenable to reversal and repair? Until we can answer that question, our knowledge of these processes is rudimentary indeed.

Consequences?

It is possible to spotlight a vast variety of consequences when we regard the end of a formerly viable relationship. There are consequences to the surviving member of a pair relationship (i.e., the spouse or close partner), the dependent kin (especially young children or aged parents), the wider social network of friends or family, the community at large, and the wider society. Furthermore, people's feelings about the loss can range from deep distress to profound relief, depending on the warmth of the relationship and the extent to which one felt attached or oppressed by it. Such a broad range of consequences may be direct or indirect, immediate or long-term, and thus can hardly be summarized in this brief comment.

Death

The consequences of a death can range from extreme trauma and inconsolable grief to a sense of admiration and even fulfillment. The most important issue may be whether the demise occurs off time—through accident, premature illness, or impulsive suicide—or on time, at the end of a long, productive life (see Blieszner & Mancini, Chapter 8). In cases of the latter kind, families and friends may rally around those most strongly affected so that, in some instances, survivors may feel even more support and solidarity than before the bereavement.

Divorce or Separation

The psychological and social consequences are rather different in the case of marital separation. This experience has far less precedent in social tradition, and it is far harder for members of one's social network to offer help and support. Furthermore, the continued existence of the other member of the broken tie—and the continuing interdependence regarding unfinished business in the relationship—greatly complicates both one's feelings and one's practical demands (see Vaughan, 1986; Weiss,

1975). As Bohannan (1970) has pointed out, the central members of a marital separation face a series of experiences in six overlapping realms, which he labeled (a) emotional, (b) legal, (c) economic, (d) coparental, (e) community, and (f) psychic divorces. Each of those consequences has been considered elsewhere in some form (e.g., Bohannan, 1970; Levinger & Moles, 1979; Weiss, 1975).

The present volume emphasizes the psychological consequences. Grych and Fincham (Chapter 9) examine both adults' and children's attributions about the dissolution of a marriage; they suggest that developing a coherent account can help such survivors gain a better feeling of control over their social world and restore their self-image. In her discussion of the phenomenology of accounts (Chapter 10), Weber makes a similar point: that "account making is a strategy for coping . . . [as well as] an end in itself." Orbuch (Chapter 11) writes at length about other important aspects of personal identity that must be considered when we appraise the consequences of relationship loss. Nonetheless, the social and economic consequences of separation must also be considered if we wish to formulate a broadly relevant analysis of this phenomenon.

Conclusion

This collection of chapters emphasizes primarily the psychological and communicational aspects of relationship loss, and it addresses most of its attention to estrangement rather than bereavement. If we are ever to attain a comprehensive understanding of the phenomena under this rubric, I think we will need to build more explicit bridges between voluntary and involuntary ways of ending relationships, between psychological and physical losses. Perhaps we can learn better how to use ideas from attachment theory, family development theory, and more sociologically oriented theories to articulate more clearly the fuzzy concepts associated with the causes, processes, and consequences of close relationship loss.

References

Bohannan, P. (Ed.) (1970). *Divorce and after*. New York: Doubleday.

Berscheid, E. (1983). Emotion. In H. H. Kelley, E. Berscheid, A. Christensen, J. H. Harvey, T. L. Huston, G. Levinger, E. McClintock, L. A. Peplau, & D. R. Peterson, *Close relationships* (pp. 110–168). New York: W. H. Freeman.

Berscheid, E., Snyder, M., & Omoto, A. M. (1989). The Relationship Closeness Inventory: Assessing the closeness of interpersonal relationships. *Journal of Personality and Social Psychology, 57*, 792–807.

Bowlby, J. (1953). Some pathological processes set in train by early mother–child separation. *Journal of Mental Science, 99*, 265–272.

Bowlby, J. (1973). *Attachment and loss: Vol. 1. Attachment*. New York: Basic Books.

Duck, S. (1982). A topography of relationship disengagement and dissolution. In S. Duck (Ed.), *Personal relationships 4: Dissolving personal relationships* (pp. 1–29). New York: Academic Press.

Goode, W. J. (1961). Family disorganization. In R. K. Merton & R. A. Nisbet (Eds.), *Contemporary social problems* (pp. 390–458). New York: Harcourt, Brace.

Hagestad, G. O., & Smyer, M. A. (1982). Dissolving long-term relationships: Patterns of divorcing in middle age. In S. Duck (Ed.), *Personal relationships 4: Dissolving personal relationships* (pp. 155–188). New York: Academic Press.

Hill, C. T., Rubin, Z., & Peplau, L. A. (1976). Breakups before marriage: The end of 103 affairs. *Journal of Social Issues, 32*(1), 147–167.

Levinger, G. (1965). Marital cohesiveness and dissolution: An integrative review. *Journal of Marriage and the Family, 27*, 19–28.

Levinger, G. (1976). A social psychological perspective on marital dissolution. *Journal of Social Issues, 32*(1), 21–47.

Levinger, G. (1979). A social exchange view on the dissolution of pair relationships. In R. L. Burgess & T. L. Huston (Eds.), *Social exchange in developing relationships* (pp. 169–193). New York: Academic Press.

Levinger, G. (1983). Development and change. In H. H. Kelley, E. Berscheid, A. Christensen, J. H. Harvey, T. L. Huston, G. Levinger, E. McClintock, L. A. Peplau, & D. R. Peterson, *Close relationships* (pp. 315–359). New York: W. H. Freeman.

Levinger, G., & Moles, O. C. (1979). *Divorce and separation: Context, causes, and consequences*. New York: Basic Books.

Pittman, F. (1989). *Private lies: Infidelity and the betrayal of intimacy*. New York: Norton.

Rusbult, C. E. (1980). Commitment and satisfaction in romantic associations: A test of the investment model. *Journal of Experimental Social Psychology, 16*, 172–186.

Simpson, J. A. (1987). The dissolution of romantic relationships: Factors involved in relationship stability and emotional distress. *Journal of Personality and Social Psychology, 53*, 683–692.

Spanier, G. B., & Casto, R. F. (1979). Adjustment to separation and divorce: A qualitative analysis. In G. Levinger & O. C. Moles (Eds.), *Divorce and separation: Context, causes, and consequences* (pp. 211–227). New York: Basic Books.

Vaughan, D. (1986). *Uncoupling: How relationships come apart*. Oxford: Oxford University Press.

Weiss, R. S. (1975). *Marital separation*. New York: Basic Books.

Subject Index

Author Index